Ancient Apologetic Exegesis

Ancient Apologetic Exegesis

Introducing and Recovering Theophilus's World

STUART E. PARSONS

◆PICKWICK *Publications* • Eugene, Oregon

ANCIENT APOLOGETIC EXEGESIS
Introducing and Recovering Theophilus's World

Copyright © 2015 Stuart E. Parsons. All rights reserved. Except for brief quotations in critical publications or reviews, no part of this book may be reproduced in any manner, without prior written permission from the publisher. Write Permissions, Wipf and Stock Publishers, 199 W. 8th Ave., Suite 3, Eugene, OR 97401.

Pickwick Publications
An Imprint of Wipf and Stock Publishers
199 W. 8th Ave., Suite 3
Eugene, OR 97401

www.wipfandstock.com

ISBN 13: 978-1-62564-809-9

Cataloging-in-Publication data:

Parsons, Stuart E.

    Ancient apologetic exegesis : introducing and recovering Theophilus's world / Stuart E. Parsons.

    xvi + 238 p. ; 23 cm. —Includes bibliographical references and index(es).

    ISBN 13: 978-1-62564-809-9

    1. Theophilus, Saint, active 2nd century. 2. Apologetics—History—Early church, ca. 30–600. 4. Bible—Criticism, interpretation, etc.—History— Early church, ca. 30–600. I. Title.

BR1720 T47 P3 2015

Manufactured in the U.S.A.   01/26/2015

Parsons, Stuart E. "Coherence, Rhetoric, and Scripture in Theophilus of Antioch's *Ad Autolycum*." *Greek Orthodox Theological Review* 53, nos. 1–4 (2008) 155–222, reproduced by permission.

For Angela

Contents

Preface | ix
Acknowledgments | xv
Abbreviations | xvi

1. Theophilus and His Life with Scripture | 1
2. Scripture and a Forgotten Genre | 13
3. Scripture and a Forgotten Orality | 33
4. Scripture and a Forgotten Coherence | 65
5. Scriptural Anthologies and Testimonia (Excursus) | 125
   Epilogue | 156

Appendix 1: Methodological Notes | 167
Appendix 2: Scripture Usage Tables | 183

Bibliography | 211
Ancient Document Index | 225
Modern Authors Index | 237

Preface

ONLY A CENTURY AFTER the apostles, the growing Christian movement appeared similar in many ways to its present-day forms. It displayed great religious vitality. Many followers of the Nazarene maintained steadfast commitment to his lordship, this during a period of sudden, unexpected persecutions. Yet in other ways, it differed greatly. While there was a common commitment to certain core beliefs and associated worship traditions, as attested in Clement's "rule of our tradition," Irenaeus's "canon of truth," and Tertullian's "rule of faith," it engendered at the same time a wide spectrum of theological forces unique to that age.[1] Truly, a distinctive type of Christianity flourished in the age of the early Christian apologists. Not surprisingly, distinctive strains of exegesis pervaded that period. But today, these distinctive habits of exegesis of that distant apologetic age lie forgotten and hidden behind our own anachronistic assumptions. Along with introducing the general shape of one of these strains of ancient apologetic exegesis, its recovery is the aim of this study. Much of our literature discounts the exegesis of Theophilus and other early Christian apologists as a mysterious disgrace. But by probing their culture, we rediscover a forgotten form of exegesis.

We might assume that a forgotten form of exegesis is only a secondary matter for our understanding of early Christianity. But this assumption would lead us astray. In reality, Scripture and exegesis of it are tightly and inseparably tied to the Christian message. At the beginning of his best-selling volume, *The Spirit of Early Christian Thought*, Robert Louis Wilken discusses how extensively early Christianity transformed Western civilization. As one of his generation's foremost specialists on early Christianity who has invested a lifetime of scholarship on the intellectual world of the early church, Wilken would know. After considering aspects of early Christianity which powered its wide cultural impact, he writes, "But what has impressed

---

1. *1 Clem.* 8.2; Irenaeus, *Haer.* 1.10.1; 2.28.1; 3.12.6–7; Tertullian, *Apology* 47.

me most is the omnipresence of the Bible in early Christian writings."[2] The Bible profoundly shaped early Christian life and thought, and changed the intellectual flow of Western culture.

Unfortunately, while Scripture was central in the experience of the early church, its function in the age of the early Christian apologists who lived only a few generations after the days of Jesus himself remains either little understood or else, typically misunderstood. Modern critics tend to forget significant realities of that age. The extant writings of Theophilus of Antioch, bishop of the capitol city of the eastern province of the Roman Empire a century after the apostles, can serve as vehicles for exposing these forgotten realities. Expose them we must, for current literature often misunderstands or dismisses second-century exegesis. My thesis is that when we look behind anachronistic views of ancient genre, literacy, and rhetoric, we discover a hidden Theophilus and a forgotten form of second-century exegesis.

Notice that I do not claim that the distinctive mode of exegesis practiced by Theophilus and other second-century apologists who dialogued with Greco-Roman pagan religionists was employed by every single early Christian apologist in a monolithic sense. As my argument unfolds, it will become clear, particularly in chapter 4, that the intended audience of the apology makes all the difference in the world. But Theophilus's audience was unavoidable and addressed by numerous other Christians. We shall see that while his exegesis was only one of several pervading the early apologetic age, it was nonetheless important, even essential, in the face of Greco-Roman religious pressures.

Second-century Christians responded to challenges from their pagan neighbors by defending their faith through protreptic writings. The ancient protreptic genre consisted of exhortation to abandon an inferior philosophy or manner of living in order to adopt a superior one. The protreptic genre is foreign to our modern age, but it was common in late antiquity. While specialists may acknowledge the protreptic genre of various early Christian writings, they often fail to consider seriously ancient expectations about protreptic writings. As a result, they import historically-dubious theological criticisms that misunderstand the actual purposes of ancient protreptic writings. They also fail to discover the biblical justifications that early Christians constructed for their protreptic efforts. So in chapter 2, I examine functional dynamics of Scripture in this now largely-forgotten genre. To this end, I demonstrate that Theophilus intentionally withheld soteriology from *Ad Autolycum*, which is presently a disputed point in scholarly

---

2. Wilken, *Spirit of Early Christian Thought*, xvii.

literature. Present-day confusion on this point owes to modern blindness to an ancient genre that may be unfamiliar to modern eyes but was most prominent in the apologetic age. Concerning this point, it may seem that I perform theological renovation of *Ad Autolycum*, but that impression is false. Rather, I merely call scholarship to give up rash and anachronistic theological judgments of Theophilus and other early apologists, and take a more historically appropriate "agnostic" view of soteriology in their protreptic writings in light of their genre. I also will show Theophilus's own carefully-constructed exegetical and theological justifications for his protreptic writings. There was a very specific intent that shaped the ways that the early Christian apologists used Scripture, but it is one that is only seen when we take seriously a now-forgotten literary genre.

In Gospel studies, James D. G. Dunn and others have broken through an impasse produced by the blindness of our own highly-literate, modern world to the pervasiveness of illiteracy in late antiquity and to the great memory abilities of oral cultures. But unfortunately, this sensitivity has not penetrated much into studies about patristic exegesis. In chapter 3, I show what such a sensitivity reveals about the function of Scripture in the apologetic age, the age of the early Christian apologists beginning in the late first century but whose heyday was the second century. In this regard, we shall see several insights about how Scripture functioned amid the high illiteracy of that apologetic age. For one thing, we will find that even though Theophilus himself likely could read and write, he used Scripture in ways that resonated powerfully for those many illiterate members of his flock. We will also find that much of the time, he retrieved biblical passages by memory. Thus, he modeled a life fixated on Scripture even for those who could not read. We will also discover subtle indications that his biblical arguments rested *mainly* on portions of Scripture that he did *not* quote, portions that only those who habitually carried their Bibles not between the covers of a book, but rather in their memories, would recognize. In short, we will find that the majority of his uses of Scripture remain hidden from readers who must rely on written texts. In Theophilus's writings, quoted biblical phrases are only the "tip of the iceberg." The great mass lies beneath. We shall see some examples of what lies below the surface. By these examples of powerful biblical arguments based on passages that are not quoted at all, but which come automatically to the minds of those who retrieve Scripture by memory, I will expose biblical dynamics in the largely-oral culture of the apologetic age, dynamics powered not by biblical quotations, but rather, by allusions and reminiscences. Like a "mouse that roared," these seemingly insignificant uses of Scripture, largely ignored in much of the literature about patristic exegesis, often resound more loudly than the more prominent quotations.

In so doing, I will also provide a call for further research in a new direction, even if space does not allow a complete survey all of the plenteous allusions and reminiscences in Theophilus's writings. The culmination of these examples of "what lies below the surface" will be a comprehensive treatment of the Book of Job in Theophilus's extant works. This comprehensive treatment of Job will serve as a capstone for this chapter, a programmatic example of taking orality and memory seriously in studies of the apologetic age.

Present-day scholars of patristic exegesis are starting to avoid anachronistic errors of prior research partly by remembering the rhetorical world of late antiquity. While this remembrance may seem quite familiar in the eyes of NT scholars, it is nonetheless fresh and exciting to present-day patrologists.[3] This approach is sorely needed for investigating early Christian apologists such as Theophilus. Like some of his fellow apologists, he has often been regarded as a disorganized writer who did not understand very much of Christian teaching. But this typical view of him is the very opposite of historical reality. I argue in chapter 4 that despite prior claims of scholarship, there was a masterful coherence running throughout every section of *Ad Autolycum*, built upon ancient judicial rhetoric in which Scripture played an absolutely essential and most central role. And his use of ancient rhetoric was inseparably intertwined with his use of Scripture in a way that may be unique to the apologetic age. Although his particular use of ancient rhetoric in essential concert with Scripture formed only one of several exegetical strains in that age, it may have been among the most prominent.

This study will unfold cultural features underlying the connections between Scripture and Theophilus's protreptic moves, his orality, and coherence. These cultural features obviously touched others besides Theophilus himself. They extended beyond his lifetime and beyond the city of Antioch. They were the coinage of late antiquity. It would be difficult to maintain that other apologists living in that age of high illiteracy did not also participate in the protreptic, largely-oral, and rhetorical world described herein.

I will also deal with media through which Theophilus accessed Scripture when I discuss his use of biblical anthologies and testimonia in a later chapter. To my knowledge, we have yet to see any published scholarship

---

3. However, this rhetorical-critical approach is nonetheless indeed healthy and alive in NT studies, and is by no means overworn. Fresh examples of this approach continually emerge even in fairly recent NT scholarship, as seen for example in Litfin's 1994 volume, *St. Paul's Theology of Proclamation*, and Long's 2008 contribution, *Ancient Rhetoric and Paul's Apology*.

Within patristic scholarship, the emergence of this new portrait of patristic exegesis is truly still ongoing, as evidenced for example by Greer and Mitchell's 2007 volume, *The "Belly-Myther" of Endor*, as well as by the focus on ancient epideictic rhetoric in Mitchell's 2002 book on Chrysostom's use of Pauline Scripture, *Heavenly Trumpet*.

focusing on Theophilus's use of biblical testimonia. We shall see that his fairly sparse use of these tools confirms insights in chapter 3 about Scripture's function in the highly-illiterate world where Theophilus served. While his elders often leaned on biblical anthologies and testimony sources, he was of a new generation that found little need for them.

In this regard, I will also describe a new electronic computational approach that overcomes the practical limitations of the manual methods which have been employed until now for comprehensively detecting use of testimonia and testimony sources in ancient writings. Manual methods are practically-speaking unable to discover many of the more obscure biblical testimonia collections. There are simply too many sections of the hundreds of ancient Jewish and Christian works that must be examined in order to find all of the patterns of Scripture usage that may indicate that writers used a testimonia collection. In connection with Theophilus of Antioch, over four hundred treatises must be examined.[4] There are dozens of thousands of treatise sections that must be examined, each one for over a thousand combinations of biblical passages used in combination. Besides exact matches of Scripture use, near-matches, plus or minus a few verses, are also important. In the end, hundreds of millions of Scripture use comparisons must be made for any investigation approaching comprehensiveness.[5] The sheer mass of these necessary comparisons overwhelm manual methods. As a result, truly comprehensive searches for all testimonia traditions influencing a writer are rarely, if ever, done. However, this new electronic approach, using custom software and a massive database of biblical references, can accurately perform the hundreds of millions of necessary comparisons in a reasonable amount of time. This electronic computational approach ushers in a new era in biblical testimonia studies.

---

4. For the specific treatises, see the appendix section, "List of Treatises Searched by the Application for Computerized Testimonia Searches (ACTS)."

5. These numbers are discussed in more detail prior to the discussion of this new electronic method.

Acknowledgments

I REMAIN IN DEBT to M. James Sawyer, my first theology professor, who sparked my interest in the field, and to my Doktorvater, D. Jeffrey Bingham, now serving Wheaton College, who fanned that initial spark and guided me towards the warm luminance of second-century studies. Professor Bingham not only directed my early explorations of *Ad Autolycum*, he also put Theophilus into my sights at the very start. I am also grateful to Christopher Spinks and the editorial team at Pickwick Publications for their careful labors.

I also extend grateful appreciation to the *Greek Orthodox Theological Review* for permission to republish an essay, with some minor corrections and refinements, as chapter 4 in this present work. It originally appeared as:

> Parsons, Stuart E. "Coherence, Rhetoric, and Scripture in Theophilus of Antioch's *Ad Autolycum*." *Greek Orthodox Theological Review* 53, no. 1–4 (2008) 155–222.

This analysis has also been enriched by assorted members of the North American Patristics Society, especially Everett Ferguson, a past president, who all kindly and skillfully offered feedback on earlier presentations of various portions over the last ten years or so. Similar to the sweeping transformation of a lowly caterpillar into a butterfly, this study has developed rather radically over the past decade in its structure and its details, I think for the better. I alone am responsible for its weaknesses.

Abbreviations

ACTS	Application for Computerized Testimonia Searches
Autol.	*Ad Autolycum*
BAGD	Bauer, Walter, et al. *A Greek-English Lexicon of the New Testament and Other Early Christian Literature: A Translation and Adaptation of the Fourth Revised and Augmented Edition of Walter Bauer's Griechisch-deutsches Wörterbuch zu den Schriften des Neuen Testaments und der übrigen urchristlichen Literatur.* 2nd ed. Chicago: University of Chicago Press, 1979.
BG	Berlin Gnostic codex
LXX	Septuagint Greek Old Testament
NHC	Nag Hammadi codex
NHMS	Nag Hammadi and Manichaean Studies (formerly Nag Hammadi Studies)
NS	New Series
NT	New Testament
OT	Old Testament
PGL	Lampe, Geoffrey W. H. *Patristic Greek Lexicon.* Oxford: Clarendon, 1961.

1

Theophilus and His Life with Scripture

THE GREAT BODY OF New Testament scholarship uncovers much about first-century Christian thinking and experience. Brilliant Christian writers such as Origen, the Cappadocians, and Augustine draw scholarly attention to the third, fourth, and fifth centuries. But oddly, despite this flood of attention to both the first century and to the third to fifth centuries, the second century often escapes notice, despite its almost living memory of Jesus and his apostles from only a generation or two prior. Yet we bypass the second century only to our own loss.

Theophilus was one of the foremost second-century Christian leaders, bishop of the church at Antioch, capital city of the eastern province of the Roman Empire. We know little of his life. In what little of his writings that survive, he mentioned that at one time he did not believe in the possibility of resurrection, but he later changed his mind and that by encountering the Jewish Scriptures, he came to believe in the God of whom they spoke.[1] Eusebius, the ancient church historian, mentions Theophilus's service as the sixth bishop of Antioch. He and Jerome thought well of Theophilus's writings against various heresies. Jerome mentions various writings by the bishop which he considered quite suitable for building up the church. Sadly, virtually all of Theophilus's writings named by Eusebius and Jerome are now lost.[2]

---

1. Theophilus of Antioch, *Autol.* 1.14.

2. Helpful introductory overviews of Theophilus are provided in Parsons, "Theophilus of Antioch"; Quasten, *Patrology*, 1:236–42; and Zeegers, "Theophilus von Antiochien."

The second century was a dangerous time to be a Christian. Local persecutions sometimes arose unexpectedly and with little warning. One infamous local persecution was in the year 177 C. E., close to when Theophilus wrote his third letter to Autolycus, when the Romans executed the elderly overseer of the church in Lyons and some of his flock.

Martyrdom was not sought, and Christians were to flee persecution if they could. But if they were taken, they were frequently given a choice of renouncing Christianity and worshipping the emperor in exchange for freedom, or else suffering public torture and death. Christians encouraged one another to remain steadfast, since they regarded it better to suffer the brief tortures of the Romans and receive the reward of eternal life, than to escape Roman torture only to face an eternity of suffering.

The most renowned of the martyrs of Lyons was not a member of the clergy or a prominent citizen, but a humble slave girl named Blandina. She was not expected to remain very steadfast because she was small and weak. The crowd in the amphitheater was therefore astounded to observe that Blandina lasted so long under successive tortures. Her endurance encouraged her companions, and ultimately encouraged Christians throughout Asia Minor who read of her sufferings when an eyewitness account came to them.[3]

When she would not recant her faith, Blandina was hung from a stake, in a rather fitting way given her religious identity, as if she were hanging from a cross. Dangerous beasts were released around her, but they did not attack. At the end of the day, she was taken back to prison. Again she was brought into the arena. There, before the crowds, she was successively whipped, exposed before dangerous animals, and baked on a large skillet (τήγανον) over a fire.[4] Rather than renounce her faith, she confessed her allegiance to Christ and her own innocence of wrong-doing. Finally, she was enclosed inside a net so that she could be repeatedly tossed and gored to death by a bull.

Not too long after the torture and execution of Blandina, Theophilus complained to his pagan Roman friend Autolycus that Christians were being persecuted unto death daily.[5] In light of the severity and recurrence of Roman persecution, it would not have been surprising if Theophilus had adopted a bitter or fearful tone toward Roman non-Christians, or if he had refused to correspond with any of them.

---

3. Extracts of the eyewitness account are preserved in Eusebius, *Historia ecclesiastica* 5.1.

4. While Eusebius spelled the term τήγανον, the alternate spelling τάγηνον appears in some other ancient writings.

5. Justin made a similar complaint only a few decades prior. See *Dialogue* 18.

It is therefore surprising to find Theophilus a decade or two before the end of the second century sending three treatise-length letters to his pagan friend Autolycus.[6] With these letters, he endeavored to persuade Autolycus to forsake worship of Greco-Roman gods and to embrace Christianity. These three letters are collectively entitled *Ad Autolycum*, or in English, "To Autolycus." As for Autolycus, none of his letters or other writings survive.

It is not unreasonable to think that this correspondence between Theophilus and Autolycus was genuine and more than a mere literary invention, although such invention was not impossible. At any rate, it is likely that the content of *Ad Autolycum* accurately reflects actual Christian/pagan dialogues. Neymeyr shows that Christian teachers in the second century were in fairly harmonious contact with churches, but also had frequent interaction with non-Christians as they answered questions during their public lectures. Therefore, Theophilus would likely have been well aware of specific challenges to Christian teaching from Greco-Roman religionists, not only those which he learned directly via friendships with non-Christians such as Autolycus, but also those he learned second-hand from Christian teachers and others in his community who also dialogued with non-Christians.[7]

In Theophilus's three letters to Autolycus, he exhibited neither anger, bitterness, nor fear towards Autolycus on account of Roman persecution

---

6. Scholarship has followed Harnack's view that the final letter of *Ad Autolycum* was composed sometime shortly prior to the death of Emperor Commodus, since its chronology records the deaths of Commodus's predecessors but not his own (*Autol.* 3.27). However, Erbes disputes Harnack's claim that Theophilus would not have omitted Commodus' death if it had already occurred. According to Erbes, Theophilus did not want to record up to the present. He only desired to explain major currents of history. Recent events were not relevant to his purposes. Erbes mentions that Eusebius similarly excluded recent entries from his bishop chronicle (Erbes, "Lebenszeit des Hippolytus," 630–31; Harnack, "Theophilus von Antiochien und das Neue Testament," 1–21). Accordingly, Erbes argues that *Ad Autolycum* was written relatively late, no earlier than 200 C.E., since Clement did not know it circa 200–202, and since Theophilus's statements about persecution appear to reference persecutions of 203 C.E. (Erbes, "Lebenszeit des Hippolytus," 630). However, this argument by Erbes has not been accepted by most scholars. One indication that Theophilus was concerned not merely with major historical events but also with recent details appears at the end of *Autol.* 3.27, where he meticulously recorded reigns of recent emperors such as Titus, Domitian, Trajan, Hadrian, Antoninus, and Verus. Since his chronology is not only quite comprehensive but also very detailed, even including many recent emperors, it is likely that he meant to treat the entire range of history. Also, a comprehensive history would well satisfy his explicit (*Autol.* 3.1) goal to demonstrate inadequacies of pagan chronologies.

7. Neymeyr, "Christliche Lehre im 2. Jahrhundert," 158–62.

against Christians.[8] While he sharply critiqued Greco-Roman religious ideas in the letters, he nonetheless maintained a friendly tone towards Autolycus.[9]

This is not the only surprise that we find in *Ad Autolycum*. In his entire defense of Christianity, he did not once mention Jesus by name in reference to the historical Christ.[10] Nor did he discourse on the earthly ministry of the historical Christ, the Incarnation, or the Cross. Neither did he emphasize the theme of divine grace. Not only so, the organization of *Ad Autolycum* sometimes appears curious, haphazard, and somehow less than adequate to the modern reader. For these reasons, Theophilus has been regarded by various scholars as being a disorganized writer who did not understand very much of Christian teaching.

However, this stereotypical picture of him is deceptive. Actually, he contended for his faith in a sophisticated and sure way according to the conventions of *his* age. If we truly grasp the protreptic form of his letters, we would be better able to comprehend his actual thought. And even if modern readers are sometimes unimpressed with the structure of *Ad Autolycum*, it would have made a second-century rhetor proud. And we shall see that Scripture played a central, fairly unique, and essential role in this truly brilliantly-conceived structure.[11] If we miss the ancient rhetorical role of Scripture in *Ad Autolycum*, we misunderstand Theophilus himself.

---

8. For critical editions, modern language translations of *Ad Autolycum*, and important studies of it, see Kannengiesser, *Handbook of Patristic Exegesis*, 1:472–73; Quasten, *Patrology*, 1:236–42; Zeegers, "Theophilus von Antiochien."

9. It was apparently typical in the second century for Christian apologists such as Theophilus to enjoy friendly interreligious dialogue with pagans and non-Christian Jews. For example, Justin and Trypho likewise enjoyed friendly intercourse even as they strongly disagreed with each other on multiple issues. See Justin, *Dialogue* 8–9.

10. His two uses of the name refer to Joshua the son of Nun, whose name in Greek ('Ἰησοῦς) is identical to Jesus.'

11. While Theophilus knew no formal New Testament canon, he knew most of the books that later compose such canons, and he regarded them to have authority very close or identical to that of the Old Testament. However, it is cumbersome to constantly use phrases like "books which later compose the New Testament." Therefore, "New Testament writings," "New Testament books," "Bible," "biblical," and the like are freely used in the present study, even though explicit references to a New Testament canon only begin to occur during Theophilus's lifetime, and even though unequivocal evidence for use of the term διαθήκη, "testament," as a book title only first appeared in Christian writings with Clement of Alexandria (Kinzig, "Καινὴ διαθήκη," 519–44, shows that διαθήκη occurred as early as Justin as a theological concept, but only later as a book title). It is likewise cumbersome to constantly use phases like "νόμος texts, by which Theophilus means writings which are later called the Old Testament." Therefore, phrases like "Old Testament" or "Hebrew Scriptures" are sometimes used in the present study, even though Theophilus often simply referred to these as the words of the prophets, or referred to Old Testament texts, even some outside the Pentateuch, as God's

Not only misunderstanding the force and content of his argument, modern readers sometimes denigrate the biblical exegesis of Theophilus and other early apologists. For example Dulles asserts, "When they insist on the perfect accord among the Biblical authors, they gloss over important differences between mutually opposed traditions."[12] He suggests that the reason for these excessive glosses is that "they wrote before the dawn of critical history."[13] However, his discussion does not fully consider ancient rhetorical and theological reasons motivating them to emphasize biblical unity. But by exploring ancient rhetorical and biblical motives for Theophilus's exegetical moves, we can gain a more nuanced appreciation of them, indeed a more historical view of them, and thus be less inclined to fall into anachronism.

We will see in what follows that Theophilus knew some prominent Jewish exegetical traditions. But did he study the Hebrew Scriptures in their original languages? This is not likely. We find several reasons to suspect that he did not know Hebrew. For one thing, so many of his quotations from the Hebrew Scriptures use either the identical or only slightly modified Greek wordings of ancient Septuagint translations, this indicating that he relied upon them. For another thing, in places we find ignorance on his part about Hebrew grammatical nuances which are obscured in Greek translations. For example, Hebrew texts of Gen 4:10 present the Hebrew word for "blood" in the construct plural Hebrew grammatical form. Ruzer shows that exegetes of the patristic period who knew Hebrew noticed this form of the word and commented upon its theological significance, but Greek-speaking exegetes ignorant of Hebrew did not.[14] Neither did Theophilus. He only dealt with Gen 4:10 when he discussed the blood of Abel in his account of humanity's early generations.[15] While he made much of the loca-

νόμος (for example, *Autol.* 1.11; 2.8; 2.33). While such phrases as "Old Testament" and "New Testament" are therefore used, these will refer to the texts considered inspired by Theophilus himself. Thus, these terms will not necessarily be restricted to texts contained in present-day canons. Most typically, the phrase "inspired texts" is used to refer to certain Old Testament and New Testament books, plus some others, simply because Theophilus stated throughout *Ad Autolycum* that such writings are produced by writers who were inspired by the Spirit of God. Sometimes the term "Scripture" is used, because Theophilus used the Greek equivalent of this term to refer to various Old Testament books.

12. Dulles, *History of Apologetics*, 30.

13. Ibid.

14. Ruzer, "Cave of Treasures," 263–64.

15. *Autol.* 2.29. Theophilus seems to have followed an exegetical tradition in his discussion of Abel's blood. He asserted that the land rejects the blood of murder victims starting after the murder of Abel. This is striking since a rejection of blood by the land is not explicitly mentioned in Genesis 4. However, a rejection of dead flesh by the land does appear in the Greek text of the *Life of Adam and Eve* 40.4–5, where the

tion from which Abel's blood cried to the Lord, Theophilus did not notice or comment upon the construct plural form of the word denoting Abel's blood, apparently because the Septuagint uses a singular word to denote Abel's blood. One might think that Theophilus knew Hebrew because he did discuss the etymology of some Hebrew words, asserting for example that the Hebrew word for "Eden" means "luxury" (τρυφή).[16] But beyond these few Hebrew etymologies, there are simply no other suggestions in *Ad Autolycum* that Theophilus knew Hebrew, and his few Hebrew etymologies were all traditional and already known among Greek-speaking Jews.[17] And so it is no surprise that his Hebrew etymology connected to the word "Eden" was already expressed by Philo.[18]

Scholarly dialog about Theophilus's use of Scripture has been advancing for some time. In 1859, Karl Otto recognized the importance of biblical allusions, not just quotations, for properly understanding Theophilus's use of NT texts.[19] His survey of the allusions is helpful partly because it references four quite plausible allusions not listed even in Marcovich's superb index of biblical quotations and allusions in *Ad Autolycum*. These four biblical allusions are considered in chapter 5, since they are included in the database used by my ACTS software that was used to comprehensively identify possible use of testimony sources.[20]

Adolf von Harnack argued in 1890 that Theophilus had no New Testament canon, and that although he knew some New Testament epistles, he

---

land declares after the murder of Abel that it will not receive any dead body until the death and burial of Adam. The writer mentioned this rejection by the land in order to explain why Cain was not able to hide the body of Abel in a grave. And an exact parallel is provided by Pseudo-Philo (*Liber antiquitatum biblicarum* 16.2). The writer explained that, after God drove out the murderous Cain, God commanded the land to no longer swallow blood, saying, "No more would you swallow blood" (*Non adicias ut deglutias sanguinem*). The treatise was likely composed in Palestine sometime between 135 BCE and CE 100. See Harrington, "Pseudo-Philo," in Charlesworth, *Old Testament Pseudepigrapha*, 2:298-300.

16. *Autol.* 2.24.

17. Bardy, *Théophile d'Antioche*, 10. As for Theophilus's etymology in *Autol.* 2.29 of the name "Eve," this could have been constructed using knowledge of Semitic words, as Zeegers argues. However, it is also not impossible that this etymology is based instead on Greek words, as Zeegers herself acknowledges. See Zeegers, "Satan, Eve et le serpent," 152-69.

18. Philo of Alexandria, *Legum allegoria* 1.45-46.

19. Otto, "Gebrauch neutestamentlicher Schriften bei Theophilus," 617-22.

20. These four allusions are Matt 5:8 in *Autol.* 1.2; Matt 7:12 in *Autol.* 2.34; Eph 4:18 in *Autol.* 1.7 and 2.35; and Titus 2:12 in *Autol.* 3.9. See chapter 5 regarding ACTS software and an innovative computational method for identifying ancient testimony sources.

did not regard them to be Scripture.[21] In Harnack's view, Theophilus nonetheless understood these books to be inspired by the Spirit, and specifically, paraphrases of God's Word.

Robert M. Grant in 1947 provided a helpful discussion of the biblical text-types of Theophilus, and also which books Theophilus considered to be Scripture.[22] He remarked that scholars have been unable to identify Theophilus's Septuagint text with any one text-type.[23] Grant's inability to identify Theophilus' biblical text-type is entirely understandable, since we now know that during the second century, the LXX was still in great flux, and there were a multitude of now-lost versions of it.[24] He also presented a point-by-point refutation of Harnack's argument that Theophilus did not consider New Testament epistles to be Scripture. He argued that Theophilus considered twelve and possibly fifteen of the New Testament books to be inspired, but not quite as authoritative as the Hebrew Scriptures. He also presented a detailed analysis of Theophilus's biblical chronology.[25] Grant provided helpful insights into Theophilus's use of biblical texts in his 1957 essay, "Scripture, Rhetoric and Theology in Theophilus."[26] He argued that although Theophilus placed a good deal of explicit biblical quotation with accompanying exegesis in his second letter, he elsewhere used Scripture quite differently, alluding rather than quoting explicitly. Grant explained that these frequent allusions to biblical texts functioned rhetorically for the bishop and allowed him to construct theological arguments. While Grant did not provide the detailed rhetorical analysis of *Ad Autolycum* that I provide in chapter 4, he did open the gate leading toward that productive avenue.

Grant's 1947 response to Harnack demands further attention here, because it establishes how Theophilus viewed what was later called the Old and New Testaments. Harnack's and Grant's viewpoints revolve around terminology that Theophilus used as he defended Christians from ominous charges of treason against Rome. And indeed, the need for his defense was quite urgent. As a provincial capital, Antioch hosted a temple to Rome and to the emperor where regular religious sacrifices were offered to him.[27] It

21. Harnack, "Theophilus von Antiochien und das Neue Testament."

22. Grant, "Bible of Theophilus," 173–96.

23. Ibid., 177. For a recent exploration of the text-type of Theophilus's Genesis 1–3 text, see Prostmeier, "Genesis 1–3 in Theophilos von Antiochia," 359–94.

24. See Law, *When God Spoke Greek*, 75–79.

25. Grant, "Bible of Theophilus," 183–84, discusses which books Theophilus considered inspired. The chronology is discussed on 189–95.

26. Grant, "Scripture, Rhetoric and Theology in Theophilus," 33–45.

27. Concerning temples to Rome and to the emperor in provincial cities, see

would have been strikingly obvious to city residents that their Antiochene Christian neighbors refused to bow the knee to the emperor. The civic loyalty of Theophilus and his flock would have been continually under suspicion. They could not simply capitulate to emperor worship, since doing so would sabotage their claim of worshipping the only true God. Nonetheless, Theophilus could not side-step responding to the charge that Christians are politically subversive on account of refusing to worship the emperor. His solution to this quandary was to compose a rich series of allusions, recollections, and short quotations mostly from Romans 13 and 1 Peter 2, plus one citation of an Old Testament text, Prov 24:21–22, all of which reinforced his point that Christians are good citizens, since they are commanded to obey, honor, and pray for kings and other governing authorities.[28] Regarding these uses of Christian inspired texts[29], Harnack claims that although Theophilus knew various NT epistles, he did not regard them to be Scripture.[30] Harnack does not deny that Theophilus considered such epistles inspired, but objected to the claim that Theophilus referred to them as Scripture.[31]

But the crucial point is not really whether Theophilus *referred* to the epistles as Scripture, but whether he indeed *considered* them such, notwithstanding his terminology. He implied in the opening line of *Autol.* 3.12 that the prophets and the gospels exist on the same level in regard to both inspiration and authority. He claimed that the prophets and the gospels are consistent precisely because every inspired one (πνευματοφόρος) spoke by the one and same Spirit of God. And he was not the first to understand OT writings and the gospels to be entirely consistent, for it is obvious to all

---

Ferguson, *Backgrounds of Early Christianity*, 211–12.

28. Book two of Josephus's *Contra Apionem* provided essentially the same answer that Theophilus did. While the Jews do not worship the emperors, they pray for them. Jews as well as Christians had to answer this charge of subversion.

29. Since ancient writers typically alluded to Scripture and other texts more often than they explicitly cited them, we necessarily rely on verbal parallels when identifying uses of Scripture in ancient texts. So as to draw from some degree of scholarly consensus regarding use of Scripture in *Ad Autolycum*, uses discussed in this study unless otherwise noted are those appearing in both Marcovich's and *Biblia patristica*'s biblical indexes. This approach is analogous to Bingham's method for reliably identifying distinctly Matthean uses of gospel texts by Irenaeus. See the discussion on verbal parallels in chapter 3 as well as Allenbach, *Des origines*; Bingham, *Irenaeus's Use of Matthew's Gospel*; Marcovich, *Theophili Antiocheni*. I do not attempt to confirm or critique Grant's discussion of what OT and NT books Theophilus knew, for which, see his "Bible of Theophilus."

30. Harnack, "Theophilus von Antiochien und das Neue Testament," 17–18.

31. Indeed, perhaps a few years after Theophilus corresponded with Autolycus; Irenaeus was the earliest Christian writer to clearly denote the four Gospels to be "Scripture" (Bingham, *Irenaeus's Use of Matthew's Gospel*, 5–6).

students of *1 Clement* that the author sees a seamless continuity between Judaism and Christianity.[32] Theophilus's stated theory of inspiration that one Spirit of God inspired both prophets and inspired Christian writers, with the result that all of the inspired texts are consistent with one another, was indeed a traditional early Christian theology of inspiration.[33]

Harnack himself traces outlines of a theology of inspiration in *Ad Autolycum*, arguing on the basis of *Autol.* 2.9, 22; 3.12-14 that Theophilus considered not only the NT writings, but also other works such as the christianized *Sibylline Oracles*, to have the same level of authority as the Old Testament.[34] Harnack demonstrates varying estimations of the Sibyl in second-century Christianity, and then uses this variety to argue against Zahn's contention that a stable NT canon had developed by CE 160. Harnack is appalled by Zahn's thesis, because he sees the use of inspired writings in the second century to have been profoundly buffeted by historical forces. Accordingly, Harnack maintains that there was greater diversity of opinion among second-century Christians concerning which works were inspired than Zahn admits.[35]

But even if Harnack admits that Theophilus considered NT writings to be inspired, he nonetheless insists that Theophilus did not consider them to be Scripture. Harnack bolstered this view by claiming that Theophilus's defense against treason did not depend essentially on such passages as Rom 13:1, but only on Prov 24:21-22. Texts from NT epistles such as Rom 13:1 only supported the argument by re-expressing through paraphrase the content of Prov 24:21-22.

However, Grant adequately answers Harnack here by showing that (1) Theophilus indeed called texts quoted from certain NT epistles the "the divine word" (ὁ θεῖος λόγος) in *Autol.* 3.14; (2) since he considered the prophets to include the gospel writers in *Autol.* 2.34, he might well have included Paul; (3) at roughly the same time as Theophilus, Clement of Alexandria numbered the apostles among the prophets; (4) the phrase introducing the use of the NT epistolary texts in *Autol.* 3.14, "and moreover" (ἔτι μὴν καί), put those texts for Theophilus at essentially the same level of authority as

---

32. For this consistency in *1 Clement* (not Clement of Alexandria), see Skarsaune, "Development of Scriptural Interpretation," 381-82.

33. *Autol.* 3.12. Similarly see Irenaeus of Lyons, *Adversus haereses* 2.28.3; and Pseudo-Justin, *Cohortatio ad gentiles* 16.

34. Harnack, *Neue Testament um das Jahr 200*, 39-40.

35. See especially the thesis statement in Harnack, *Neue Testament um das Jahr 200*, 4-7. Throughout the monograph, Harnack criticizes Zahn for undervaluing variations in second-century attitudes concerning canon.

OT texts and the gospels.[36] Thus, while Theophilus never called certain NT epistles "Scripture" (γραφή) in a technical sense, he essentially treated them as such on a functional level. Since he regarded them as inspired, this should not be surprising.

Massaux showed in his masterful 1950 dissertation on the use of Matthew up to the time of Irenaeus that Theophilus knew Matthew, Luke, John, Acts, and a number of Paul's letters. Massaux analyzes all of the distinctly Matthean texts and notes that Theophilus often reproduced nearly the exact text of Matthew in his quotations although sometimes with minor wording variations, this indicating a literary dependence on Matthew. Massaux sees in *Ad Autolycum* a predominant dependence on Matthew over the other canonical gospels.[37]

Simonetti presented a helpful analytical overview of Theophilus and the inspired texts in his 1972 "La sacra scrittura in Teofilo d'Antiochia." Contra Harnack, and agreeing with Grant, Simonetti held that Theophilus used the phrase "divine word" (θεῖος λόγος) in reference to New Testament texts themselves. He also observed that Theophilus's exegesis of Genesis highlights a principle of patristic exegesis in general: difficulties encountered in controversial passages are decided according to theological distinctives of various communities.[38] A major strength is Simonetti's judicious description and assessment of the use of the inspired texts in *Ad Autolycum*. One of the few weaknesses of this piece is that, being an older study, it relied on overly-simplified exegetical categories such as "letterale" ("literal") and "allegorica" ("allegorical"). Another weakness is simply that limitation imposed by the short length of his essay, so that although he produced a well-balanced and very helpful overview, a detailed treatment of the use of the inspired texts in *Ad Autolycum* is lacking.

Zeegers-Vander Vorst's 1975 essay, "Les citations du Nouveau Testament dans les Livres Autolycus de Théophile d'Antioche" is an important survey of Theophilus's general use and understanding of the NT.[39] While she did not deal with his use of the NT in connection with Greco-Roman rhetorical standards, she did supply a particularly helpful overview of Theophi-

---

36. Grant, "Bible of Theophilus," 183–84. Grant here cites Clement of Alexandria, *Stromata* 5.6.38. Grant does not think that Theophilus viewed the Pauline texts exactly as he viewed OT texts, since he asserted on pp. 188–89 that they were inspired and were probably "on the way to becoming scripture."

37. Massaux, *Influence of the Gospel of Saint Matthew*.

38. Simonetti, "La sacra scrittura in Teofilo," 197–207.

39. Zeegers, "Citations du Nouveau Testament," 371–82. Her *Citations des poètes grecs* has become the standard reference for those interested in how well Theophilus and other Christian apologists knew the Greek poets they so often cited.

lus's use of the NT. She concluded that while Theophilus used of most of the books typically included in various NT canons, and while he considered the gospels as authoritative equals of the Hebrew Scriptures, he mostly relied on the Hebrew Scriptures. She shows that Theophilus was profoundly informed by the Hebrew Scriptures whenever he interpreted NT writings. She argues that Theophilus's reticence to use gospel texts, and his use of Pauline literature in arguments which she characterizes as "antipauliniens," could not be explained by ignorance, but rather, by his apologetic purpose and his profound sense of the unity between the Hebrew Scriptures and the gospel message.[40] She provided a different sort of analysis in her 1976 "La création de l'homme (Gn 1, 26) chez Théophile d'Antioche."[41] While her former essay provided a general and comprehensive analysis of how Theophilus used NT texts, she gives in the latter a detailed analysis of exegetical traditions and Theophilus's innovation regarding a single verse, Gen 1:26. She shows that he was informed by a rich set of Jewish exegetical traditions, but also that he adopted them in a distinctly Christian direction.

Schoedel observed in 1993 that while Grant argued in his earlier writings that Theophilus's exegesis was rabbinic, he argued in his later writings that the bishop's exegesis fed both from early rabbinic exegesis and from Philo's Hellenistic Jewish exegesis.[42] Schoedel shows that the sixteen parallels in *Ad Autolycum* to rabbinic exegetical traditions that Grant identified are actually not as close as Grant thought. Schoedel thus persuasively argues that Theophilus appropriated Hellenistic Jewish exegetical techniques rather than rabbinic ones.

This conclusion by Schoedel that *Ad Autolycum* lies closer to Hellenistic Jewish exegetical traditions than to Palestinian ones is not surprising in light of the analogous case of Justin Martyr. Günter Stemberger observes that Justin indicates personal familiarity with Jewish thought.[43] Although Justin was born in Samaria and so might have known early rabbinic traditions, it has not been established that he himself debated with the rabbis. Confirming Skarsaune, Stemberger shows how the evidence indicates

---

40. Ibid., 374–77, 382.

41. Zeegers, "Création de l'homme," 258–67. The literature on early patristic use of Gen 1:26 is illuminating. Besides Zeegers's essay, see especially Nautin, "Genèse 1,1–2, de Justin à Origène," 61–94; and Winden, "Der Anfang," 3–48.

42. Schoedel, "Theophilus," 279–97. Schoedel responds to arguments of his mentor, Robert M. Grant, that Theophilus was a Jewish-Christian. He shows that Grant's claim that a form of Jewish Christianity had developed in Antioch is based on tenuous evidence.

43. Stemberger, "Exegetical Contacts," 569–86.

instead that Justin debated Scripture not with with rabbinic Jews, but with Diaspora Jews.[44]

None of the above-mentioned studies of Theophilus and Scripture provide a comprehensive, monograph-length treatment of how Scripture functions in his writings. To my knowledge, we have not yet seen a single monograph on Theophilus and Scripture. The stereotypical view of Theophilus as a disorganized writer with a tenuous grasp of Christianity does not square with historical reality. Rather, Theophilus cast Scripture in his profoundly protreptic letters to play a compelling, and very central and indispensible role in his classic and precise rhetoric of witness interrogation. When we judge by second-century standards rather than modern ones the intent, potency, and coherence of Theophilus's writings, the persisting stereotypical view of him must fall away. The approach we will take also engages dynamics of ancient orality and recollection as well as contributing to the new emerging portrait of patristic exegesis, one avoiding anachronisms of older scholarship, through renewed awareness of ancient literary practices. Scripture functioned in a particular and distinctive way in second-century apologies, a way that scholarship has not yet truly perceived.

Apart from offering in chapter 5 a comprehensive treatment of evidence of Theophilus's use of some biblical testimonia and other testimony sources, and supplying some footnotes about exegetical traditions connected to some key biblical passages, I probe no further into exegetical traditions. While there remains much more to be said about Theophilus and exegetical traditions, a full treatment would require a vast exploration extending far beyond the scope of this study.

---

44. Skarsaune, *Proof from Prophecy*, 429. There is a good amount of literature on the question of whether Justin was anti-Jewish. Recent representative views of both sides of the debate are given in Sanchez, *Justin apologiste*; and Wilson, *Related Strangers*.

2

Scripture and a Forgotten Genre

SCHOLARSHIP, EVEN IN RECENT years, typically pays lip-service to the ancient protreptic genre (consisting of exhortation to abandon an inferior philosophy or manner of living in order to adopt a superior one) of *Ad Autolycum* by acknowledging this reality in introductory discussions but then disregarding it while making bold and rash theological evaluations of Theophilus. It should be no surprise then, if the stereotypical view of *Ad Autolycum* is often anachronistic, for theological assessments are often distorted by modern assumptions that patristic specialists frequently read back into Theophilus's second-century world. But if we want to comprehend his ideas in their true historical sense, then we must do more than simply note the protreptic genre of *Ad Autolycum* up front, only to forget this reality as we delve deeper into its details.

The only writing by Theophilus of Antioch which survives is *Ad Autolycum*. No writing by his friend Autolycus survives. Indeed, we know virtually nothing about Autolycus. Despite these limitations in our knowledge of the specific occasions for the writing of each letter to Autolycus, much can be gained through analysis of *Ad Autolycum* in light of its second-century literary setting.

Before we can understand how Scripture functions in *Ad Autolycum*, we must truly and precisely establish what kind of writing it is, and what Theophilus hoped it would accomplish. Only after doing this will we accurately and historically perceive how he marshaled Scripture in his letters to Autolycus. In the course of this, I will discuss ancient protreptic literature and traditions in further detail. I mean to demonstrate in this present chapter that Theophilus intentionally withheld soteriology from *Ad Autolycum*, which is presently a disputed point in the literature. I also intend to present some reasons why he so withheld his soteriology, in light of both his culture and his reading of Scripture. Eventually, in chapter 4, we will see that Theophilus's ancient judicial rhetorical strategy was absolutely fitting, precisely because he wanted to place in *Ad Autolycum* protreptic appeals rather than his soteriology. Indeed, we will find that he and his fellow Christian apologists would have been as horrified at the notion of revealing his full soteriology to a hostile pagan such as Autolycus as a loving widower would feel about revealing graphic details about his dear wife's painful, bloody death in a violent road crash to his despondent little son. Thus, besides making an important argument of its own, this present chapter also lays a crucial foundation for the arguments that I will erect in later chapters.

THE PROBLEM OF THE THEOLOGICAL AND LITERARY NATURE OF AD AUTOLYCUM

Some scholars, though not all, argue that *Ad Autolycum* was intentionally written in order to convey a soteriology. László Perendy, James Tabor, and Rick Rogers present the most recent arguments for this, and they lay out similar logic. While Tabor's is the earlier of these arguments, Rogers's is quite similar to Tabor's and is the most detailed. Therefore, we will consider first Rogers's view of *Ad Autolycum*. He argues that *Ad Autolycum* presents a soteriology of "salvation through law," situated along the same trajectory as that of the Epistle of James.[1] Rogers considers the theology of *Ad Autolycum* to be a "protreptic theology," that is, a theology which would be presented to potential converts to awaken in them an awareness of the need for a Christian morality, but which is less complete than what would have been taught to the church. Rogers is not the first to characterize *Ad Autolycum* as protreptic. Aimé Puech voices a similar observation. Puech names the *Epistle to Diognetus* as a comparable early Christian protreptic work.[2] But Rogers's treatment of *Ad Autolycum* is distinctive. He argues that while *Ad Autolycum* is protreptic, it also presents soteriology, albeit one that later orthodoxy may have considered inadequate.[3] Rogers focuses much of his efforts on the theological exposition and analysis of *Ad Autolycum*, believing that *Ad Autolycum* contains a soteriology. He attempts to shield that soteriology from criticism by arguing that it lies on a Jamesian trajectory.

---

1. Rogers, *Theophilus*.
2. Puech, *Apologistes Grecs*, 208.
3. Rogers, *Theophilus*, 26.

The criticism is real. Schultze evaluates *Ad Autolycum* harshly: "But it appears out of the question, that an Antiochene bishop had written a text filled with so many follies and errors."[4] Likewise, Bauer forcibly rejects Theophilus's theological sense: "To me, there is no comparison between the superior theologian Irenaeus and the shallow babbler of the *Apology to Autolycus*."[5] Robert M. Grant declares concerning Theophilus, "He was unable to understand clearly either the Christian faith or the Hellenistic philosophies opposed to it."[6]

If Theophilus indeed intended *Ad Autolycum* to present a soteriology as Rogers argues, and if scholars such as Bauer and Grant take such a dim view of it, then one wonders why early Christian readers of *Ad Autolycum* did not spurn its soteriology just as various modern readers such as Bauer and Grant have. The answer, according to Rogers, lies in works of Theophilus to which the early church had access, but which are now lost. By way of support, he cites remarks about Theophilus by early Christians such as Jerome and Eusebius of Caesarea.[7] Jerome knew several works authored by Theophilus: "Against Marcion," three volumes "To Autolycus," "Against the Heresy of Hermogenes" as well as "other short and elegant treatises, well fitted for the edification of the church."[8] Jerome also mentioned other works attributed to Theophilus, "On the Gospel" and "On the Proverbs of Solomon," which he may have suspected that others wrote in Theophilus's name, since he noted that their style seemed deficient. Rogers claims that Jerome did not criticize the theology of Theophilus in *Ad Autolycum* but instead considered the work "well fitted for the edification of the church."[9] Eusebius noted that Theophilus joined with other orthodox writers in combating the Marcionite heresy.[10] Eusebius chose not to cast the theology of Theophilus

---

4. Schultze, *Altchristliche Städte*, 57.
5. Bauer, *Orthodoxy and Heresy*, 18n38.
6. Grant, *After the New Testament*, 157.
7. Rogers, *Theophilus*, 3–4.
8. Jerome, *De viris inlustribus* 25, ANF translation.
9. On this point though, it could be that Jerome was referring to Theophilus's "other short and elegant treatises" rather than to *Ad Autolycum*.
10. *Historia ecclesiastica* 4.24.1. Desjardins provides a very helpful overview of significant views in patristic scholarship of the concept of heresy in the second-century world, as well as a survey of studies which treat the various meanings of αἵρεσις in the first and second centuries. See Desjardins, "Bauer and Beyond." See also Osborn, "Defense of Truth," 119–44.

Perhaps the most influential study of orthodoxy and heresy in early Christianity is Walter Bauer's 1934 *Rechtgläubigkeit und Ketzerei im ältesten Christentum*, published in English translation in 1971 as *Orthodoxy and Heresy in Earliest Christianity*. Reaction to Bauer's thesis has been extensive. The most helpful surveys of this response appear

in any negative light. Rogers posits that Theophilus's reputation as a fighter of heresy may have saved him from being grouped with heretical adoptionists such as the late-third-century figure Paul of Samosata and the fourth-century writer Marcellus of Ancyra.[11]

Regarding Theophilus's specific soteriology, Rogers argues that Theophilus held a Jamesian soteriology whereby law (νόμος) sanctifies and obedience to it is essential.[12] He finds a nuanced treatment of νόμος in *Ad Autolycum*. He identifies four dispensations of νόμος. The first is that of creation where law functioned in the form of the creative command, διάταξις. The second dispensation is that of paradise where law appeared in the form of the command, ἐντολή, concerning the tree of knowledge. The third is the "fixed period of time" (τακτὸς χρόνος) where law leads the faithful through an education (παιδευθείς). The content of this education consists of a primary law, the Decalogue of Moses, and a secondary law, expressed in the Hebrew prophets, Solomon, Jesus, and Paul.[13] The final dispensation is that of the resurrection, experienced by those who have been faithful to law.

The function of law during Rogers's third dispensation, the "fixed period of time," relates most centrally to the controversy over whether *Ad Autolycum* was meant to express a soteriology. In this dispensation, the mercy of God operates but at the same time, law-keeping is demanded and is according to Rogers, "an effective means of salvation" in Theophilus's mind.[14] Here is "a salvation achieved through a life lived in accordance with God's nomos."[15] Rogers believes that law-keeping according to *Ad Autolycum* results in salvation but does not mean that grace has no role at all, only that "human righteousness and salvation are inseparably bound in the teach-

---

in Desjardins's above-mentioned essay; in an appendix of *Orthodoxy and Heresy*, in which Robert A. Kraft had in 1971 updated a 1964 survey of this response by George Strecker; and in Harrington, "Reception of Walter Bauer's *Orthodoxy and Heresy*." A survey of some more recent responses also appears in Yamauchi, "Gnosticism and Early Christianity."

Bauer contributes positively to scholarship by showing that earliest Christianity was no uniform monolith and was diverse its manifestations. However, Turner and several other critics argue that Bauer's monograph is flawed, because he only concerns himself with relations between the Roman party and heretics, but fails to understand the nature of orthodoxy as theological consensus rather than simply the viewpoint of a powerful and oppressive party. Bauer's argument is also criticized for exaggeration and for arguing from silence. The most extensive critique in English of Bauer's view of orthodoxy and heresy is Turner, *Pattern of Christian Truth*.

11. Rogers, *Theophilus*, 5–6.
12. Ibid., 173.
13. Ibid., 177.
14. Ibid.
15. Ibid., 143.

ings of *Ad Autolycum*."[16] Theophilus differed from James notably in that for James, law is essential but ultimately Λόγος is the source of salvation, while in *Ad Autolycum*, νόμος is its source.

Rogers does not think that Theophilus equated νόμος to the Mosaic law. He notes for example, that when Theophilus introduced the concept of νόμος in *Autol.* 1.11, he pointed not to Exodus 20 but rather to Prov 24:21–22a, and a New Testament concept.[17] In Rogers's view, νόμος for Theophilus was simply the expressed "voice of God."[18]

Rogers is unwilling to say, because of the acceptance of Theophilus within orthodoxy by the early church and because of the protreptic nature of *Ad Autolycum*, that Theophilus simply denied the incarnation and the passion of Christ and their value for salvation. To Rogers, Theophilus championed religious ideas similar to Hellenistic Judaism and a νόμος-based soteriology which, with James and Irenaeus both, "condemned empty Christianity and cheap Grace, a brand of Christianity that is best identified as nomistic Christianity."[19]

Tabor takes a similar approach to that of Rogers, and comes to similar conclusions.[20] For example, he notes that Justin had no qualms about expounding the atonement provided by Christ and on this basis, Tabor expects Theophilus to have also discussed this theme if he had considered it truly significant.[21] However, this comparison of Justin and Theophilus is problematic, since it does not take into account the differing audiences in view. Atonement themes indeed shine brightly in Justin's *Dialogue* but present nary a glimmer in Theophilus's *Ad Autolycum*. However, given that Justin debated in the *Dialogue* with the Jew Trypho concerning whether it is the Jews or the Christians who correctly understand the Hebrew prophets, while Theophilus dialogued with a Gentile pagan friend who very likely knew virtually nothing of the prophets, the comparison is worthless. That the themes of Justin's *First Apology* differ significantly from his *Dialogue* and yet harmonize nicely with Theophilus's *Ad Autolycum* only confirms the emptiness of Tabor's comparison.

Like Rogers, Tabor also concludes that Theophilus understood salvation to follow from obedience. Like Rogers, Tabor also views Theophilus's theology as being akin and almost indistinguishable from that of Hellenistic

---

16. Ibid., 183.
17. Ibid., 120.
18. Ibid.
19. Ibid., 183.
20. Tabor, "Theology of Redemption."
21. Ibid., 171.

Judaism. Tabor has no doubt that *Ad Autolycum* presents Theophilus's soteriology. Truly, Rogers follows and greatly extends the trail blazed by Tabor.

However, Rogers's claim that *Ad Autolycum* presents a soteriology has been challenged by Weinrich.[22] Weinrich's challenge weighs against Tabor's analysis also, given the similarity in their theological assessments of *Ad Autolycum*. Weinrich's critique is twofold. First, in light of his estimation that Rogers fails to overturn Bentivenga's claim that Theophilus did not provide a Christology in *Ad Autolycum*, Weinrich questions how a Christian soteriology is even possible if there is no Christology.[23] We should remark here that Perendy does not overturn Bentivenga's claim either, since he references it but does not really engage with it. Second, since Rogers argues that Theophilus must have had an ecclesial theology which was wider than the narrow protreptic theology of *Ad Autolycum*; but also that the supposed νόμος-based soteriology of *Ad Autolycum* was considered by Theophilus sufficient for achieving salvation; then the ecclesial theology loses its purpose. These are weighty critiques, and ones which I believe are fatal for both Rogers's and Tabor's analysis. But if Theophilus did not use νόμος as a foundation for soteriology, then how did he use it?

I claim that Theophilus used νόμος as an epistemic device rather than as a soteriological motif. He tipped his hand when he explained at the end of *Autol.* 1.5 that even if an earthly king is not seen, nevertheless his laws and commands, as well as other signs of his activity and authority, make it clear that he indeed exists. Theophilus only explicitly claimed here that God's works and powers serve as indications of divine activity by which Autolycus ought to be convinced. However, he had just immediately prior mentioned kingly powers, *laws* and *commands* by which human kings *make themselves known*. This suggests an implied purpose for the pervasive occurrence of references to divine law in *Ad Autolycum*. Divine law, given through God's prophets, is given not so much to save non-Christians like Autolycus, but rather, simply to open their eyes to the reality of the one true God. Rather than offering salvation per se, divine law in *Ad Autolycum* merely opens the door to its possibility at a later time. Theophilus desired that Autolycus would come to perceive the reality of the true God by perceiving the excellence of his law.

Similarly, after the extended discussion in *Autol.* 3.9–15 of God's law and of its expression in the prophets and the gospels, he concluded *Autol.* 3.15 by expressing the aim of *Autol.* 3.9–15. His aim here is *not* that Autolycus might receive salvation as a result of reading this portion of the letter. It

---

22. Weinrich, Review of *Theophilus of Antioch*.
23. Bentivegna, "A Christianity without Christ."

is rather that Autolycus might *know* (ἐπιστῆσαι) about Christian praxis and ordinances, and thus *become a philosopher indeed*. In Theophilus's mind, his friend was not yet ready to receive salvation per se. This is why Theophilus never intended to present his soteriology in his letters to Autolycus. We shall see shortly that this move of withholding of soteriology in apologetic writings was quite common in his age, even if it is not in our own. Faulty modern assumptions have created the present confusion in the literature concerning whether or not *Ad Autolycum* contains a soteriology.

The most recent attempt to derive a soteriology from *Ad Autolycum* is Perendy's.[24] He essentially follows Rogers's argument. But there are two main differences which distinguish Perendy's treatment from Rogers.' First and most obviously, Perendy's is far shorter, since he intends to provide only an outline of Theophilus's theology in his essay rather than a monograph-length analysis. Second and more to the point, while Perendy essentially agrees with Rogers, he does characterize *Ad Autolycum* differently, not as a νόμος-based soteriology but as a catechesis. Specifically, Perendy understands *Ad Autolycum* to be a work intended as an apology when Theophilus sent his first letter, but a work which had turned into a catechesis by the time he sent the third letter. Accordingly, Perendy considers *Ad Autolycum* to be a catechesis which offered initiates a very introductory systematic theology. But his claim that *Ad Autolycum* had turned into a catecheses is unsatisfactory, for he does not try to provide external evidence for a catechumenate in late-second-century Antioch. As for internal evidence of it, he merely claims that Theophilus moved beyond mere apology into catecheses since he included statements in the letters which began to touch upon what we would today call theology proper, and doctrines of revelation, creation, anthropology, and Christology.

But this is simply too flimsy a support for Perendy's claim, especially since there is no real evidence of a catechumenate in late-second-century Antioch. Admittedly there have been attempts to establish a catechumenate even in the first century. Selwyn and others argue that certain NT letters contain pre-baptismal catechesis. But other scholars point out that these attempts only rely on vague thematic similarities between the NT and later formal catechesis. As for the second century, we find a catechumenate in some places but not in others. Clement of Alexandria mentioned a catechumenate.[25] But while Justin mentioned that initiates who received baptism also agreed with Christian teaching, he gave no specific evidence that a

---

24. Perendy, "Outlines of Systematic Theology."
25. *Stromata* 2.18.

catechumenate existed in Rome at the time.[26] Recent liturgical scholarship recognizes that earlier scholars too easily read later catechetical developments back into earlier times and that they too easily assumed that catechetical development was uniform across the early Christian world.[27] And recent NT scholarship recognizes that vague thematic similarities between NT teaching and later catechesis cannot establish a first-century catechumenate. Given that Perendy's internal evidence is akin to that of the unpersuasive NT arguments and that he does not provide external evidence of a late-second-century catechumenate in Antioch, we must question whether Theophilus wanted to provide any catechesis whatsoever in his letters to Autolycus.

I will argue later in this present chapter that Theophilus's theological and biblical convictions about Adam's transgression absolutely prevented him from disclosing both soteriology and catechesis in the letters to Autolycus. I believe that Theophilus would have been horrified at the very thought of such a disclosure. Speaking more broadly, I want this present chapter to establish that *Ad Autolycum* is *nothing* other than a masterful example of ancient protreptic. Then later in chapter 4 we will see still further evidence that the letters to Autolycus are truly protreptic and that Theophilus knew that his friend was not yet ready for a soteriology.

ANCIENT PROTREPTIC LITERATURE

I want to show that Theophilus's use of νόμος as an epistemic device and not as a soteriological one was entirely appropriate for his addressee, a pagan friend. Moreover, in order to paint a truly historical picture of the matter, I also want to show that Theophilus was pre-conditioned by the protreptic traditions of his age to use νόμος for epistemological ends and not at all for soteriological ones.

The Greeks and Romans, including Hellenistic Jews, used protreptic approaches. Their methods for composing protreptic speeches, λόγοι προτρεπτικοί, are not described in any surviving ancient rhetorical handbook. Therefore, the typical structure of protreptic appeals can only be discerned by inductive examinations of surviving speeches. Aune's survey of these studies notes that a protreptic appeal was typically twofold or threefold, consisting of a attack on a competing philosophy or way of life, a promotion of the preferred one, and sometimes a concluding appeal to

---

26. *Apol.* 1.61, 65.

27. On recent turns in early Christian catechetical studies, see Bradshaw, *Origins of Christian Worship*, 30–55, 161–84.

embrace the preferred philosophy or way of life.[28] This is exactly what we find in *Ad Autolycum*.[29]

Protreptic approaches appear even in the New Testament. The Lord himself made one, recounted in Matt 19:16–30. While Jesus taught that sinners may gain salvation through faith in himself according to gospel narratives such as Luke 23:39–43, he mentioned none of this when he dealt with the rich young man of Matthew 19. Rather, he told the young man that eternal life is gained by keeping God's commandments. When the young man was then confronted concerning his materialism and his resulting failure to heed a commandment of generosity, he became sorrowful and left. But Jesus did not stop him. He seemed to want to induce nothing more than repentance from materialistic obsessions and religious over-confidence. Jesus gave the young man something less than the fullness of that soteriological teaching that he could have given. He knew that before the man could be ready for soteriology, he needed to be willing to embrace an alternate way of life. Matthew's account contains the typical components of ancient protreptic, for there is an attack on an inferior way of life (one of materialistic rebellion), promotion of a superior one (a life of generous piety), and a personal exhortation to embrace that new way of life.

Consider in greater detail the verbal and conceptual parallels between Matthew 19 and *Autol.* 2.27.[30] Theophilus's claim that anyone obeying God's commandments "can be saved" (δύναται σωθῆναι) recalls the cry of the disciples after they heard Jesus' remarks about how hard it is for a rich man to enter the kingdom of heaven, "who then can be saved?" (τίς ἄρα δύναται σωθῆναι;). Theophilus's claim that all those who obey God's commandments can be saved recalls similar assertions in Matt 19:25 and 19:17. Where Jesus judged the rich young man of Matthew 19 to ready for very basic instruction but not ready for a full soteriological message, so Theophilus judged Autolycus.

Paul provided a similar protreptic approach in his famous sermon before the Areopagus of Athens, where he did not preach the Cross and divine forgiveness to the Epicurean and Stoic philosophers standing around him that day in the great marketplace, but only judgment, resurrection and

---

28. Aune, "Protreptic literature," in *Early Christian Literature*, 383–86.

29. See the discussion of Theophilus's "meta-logic" at the end of chapter 4.

30. While neither *Biblia Patristica* nor Marcovich's scripture indexes specify that Theophilus used Matt 19:25, Grant notes in his edition of *Ad Autolycum* that Matt 19:25 should be compared with this statement by Theophilus.

especially, the folly of idolatry.³¹ Indeed, these very same themes compose Paul's summary of his own introductory sermons intended for Gentiles.³²

These Christian protreptic predecessors could have easily inspired Theophilus. But his motivations for a protreptic approach penetrate even deeper still, much as the roots of an ancient oak grow nearly as far underneath the ground as its branches reach into the sky. Indeed, he constructed a sophisticated theological justification for his own protreptic strategy. To this we now turn.

BIBLICAL AND THEOLOGICAL FOUNDATIONS OF THEOPHILUS'S PROTREPTIC APPROACH

To understand just how important was the protreptic approach for Theophilus, we can consider some parallels between *Ad Autolycum* and Hebrews 5–6. Modern commentaries on the New Testament Letter to the Hebrews tend to provide a great deal of discussion about Heb 6:4–12 and the problem of exactly what is meant by the claim that those who have fallen into a certain apostasy can never be restored. But these modern commentaries also tend not to say much about Heb 6:1–2. Surprisingly, Theophilus of Antioch ignored Heb 6:4–12, but as I will argue below, built a substantival theological defense of Christian protreptic on the basis of Heb 6:1–2.

Theophilus did not either quote or allude to Heb 6:1–2. However, I contend that his apologetic strategy was nevertheless shaped by that passage. Theophilus was aware of the over-all context of Heb 6:1–2. In that connection, he alluded to Heb 5:12.³³ Most indexes of biblical citations and allusions for *Ad Autolycum* list an allusion to 5:12, including the indexes of Miroslav Marcovich, Biblia patristica, and the *Sources Chrétiennes* edition of *Ad Autolycum*.³⁴ Furthermore, Friedrich Loofs is also aware of this allusion

---

31. Acts 17:17–34.

32. See 1 Thess 1:9–10, which Polhill identifies as the only place in his writings where Paul summarizes his basic sermons for Gentiles, for which see Polhill, *Paul and His Letters*, 212. On the kinds of apologetic themes that early Christians brought before Gentile audiences in the first few centuries of the faith, see Daniélou, *Gospel Message and Hellenistic Culture*, 15–30; and Osborn, "Pattern of Apologetic," 1–22.

33. Hebrews lies among those biblical books sparsely represented in *Ad Autolycum*. The only other use of Hebrews besides the allusion to Heb 5:12 is an allusion to Heb 12:9 eight lines later. However, both Hebrews allusions stand on a scholarly consensus, for which see the "Verbal Parallels with Scripture" section in chapter 3. The allusion to Heb 12:9 is noted in *Biblia Patristica*, in Marcovich's index, and even in Otto's study of biblical allusions by Theophilus. See Otto, "Gebrauch neutestamentlicher Schriften bei Theophilus," 622.

34. Allenbach, *Des origines*; Bardy, *Théophile d'Antioche*; Marcovich, *Theophili*

to Heb 5:12, and actually uses a quotation from that verse, "Anfangsgründe der Sprüche Gottes" (elementary principles of the Word of God), to characterize the entire content of *Ad Autolycum*.[35]

Thematic Parallels

Spiritual progression was a prominent theological concept for Theophilus. His insight into it likely benefitted from Philo's Hellenistic Jewish tradition, even if Theophilus did not have direct access to Philo himself.[36] Philo depicted spiritual progression as a process whereby the initiated have their eyes anointed through exposure to the inspired writings of Moses. They then awake, as from a dream, wave off the fog before their eyes so that they might rush forward in their spiritual progression.[37]

Theophilus considered repentance to be a prerequisite for spiritual progression. Right at the start, he voiced Autolycus' challenge, "Show me your God" (Δεῖξόν μοι τὸν θεόν σου).[38] However, he did *not* then show God to Autolycus. Rather, he asserted that it is impossible to see God unless the eyes of the soul are able to see and the ears of the heart are able to hear. Because of sin, people cannot perceive God. Repentance removes the iniquity which obscures the eyes of the soul.

Antiocheni. Massaux also notes a possible reference to the verse. See Massaux, *Influence of the Gospel of Saint Matthew*, 3:141. Challenging this consensus, Grant, "Bible of Theophilus," 184–85, questions whether Theophilus actually knew Hebrews. He argues that the discussion in *Autol.* 2.25 about infants needing milk before solid food could have been based on observation.

35. Loofs, *Theophilus von Antiochen Adversus Marcionem*, 63.

36. Did Theophilus have direct access to Philo's treatises? The majority scholarly view is that he reflected themes and exegetical traditions held in common with Hellenistic Jews but did not seem to use Philo directly. For example, see Grant, "Studies in Theophilus," 108–10; and Meeks and Wilken, *Jews and Christians in Antioch*, 21. J. P. Martín makes a detailed case for direct literary dependence of Theophilus on Philo, supported by a striking series of thematic parallels, but Runia is not persuaded by the literary parallels. See the survey of scholarship and his reaction to Martín in Runia, *Philo in Early Christian Literature*, 110–16.

37. Philo of Alexandria, *De Somniis* 1.164, presented Moses as the revealer who leads the initiate and anoints his eyes so that the initiate perceives the beauty of the holy *logoi*. Runia, "Philo of Alexandria and the Greek *Hairesis*-Model," 134, following Nikiprowetzky, explains that it was common for contemporary philosohical treatises to use metaphor, and based on this, Philo intended this image of Moses only to signify the importance of the Pentateuch as a gateway to spiritual progress, and not to signify that the spirit of Moses actually encounters the initiate in an existential sense. See a similar concept in Philo of Alexandria, *De mutatione nominum* 2.

38. *Autol.* 1.2.

Furthermore, he believed that faith also is a prerequisite for spiritual progress. He re-introduced the figure of the eyes of the soul in *Autol.* 1.7–8 and considered the heart (referring to its hardness and its blinded eyes, rather than to its stopped ears, as in *Autol.* 1.2). Those who do not know God have blind souls and hard hearts. However, those who trust God, who is the Physician, will be healed and made alive. Just as physical healing requires a person to trust medical physicians, so also spiritual healing requires a person to trust God. He argued the primacy of faith with statements such as, "But let faith and the fear of God take the lead [("let . . . take the lead"): προηγείσθω] before everything in your heart,"[39] and "Or do you not know that with all undertakings, faith takes the lead (προηγεῖται)?"[40] The requirements of repentance and faith were the two essential prerequisites of spiritual progression according to Theophilus. These are exactly the two elements in Heb 6:1 of "a foundation" (θεμέλιος) and what is "elementary" (τῆς ἀρχῆς) of the message of Christ.[41]

The central eschatological themes in *Ad Autolycum* are resurrection, and the final judgment. These two themes are identical to those in Heb 6:2. Theophilus thus quite faithfully followed the eschatological content of that verse.

Theophilus did not say much about the initiation rites mentioned in Heb 6:2. However, this is understandable considering his audience. Since Autolycus was a skeptical pagan, Theophilus could not provide instruction about initiation rites. The explanation for this is seen in his argument in *Autol.* 2.25 against Marcionism concerning the Tree of Knowledge. Death did not enter into the world because the Tree was improperly created as an evil creation. Rather, Adam and Eve consumed the advanced knowledge of the Tree before they were ready. Since they were like infants, God intended them to partake of simple teaching, of the milk of the Word. Adam died because he violated proper spiritual progression by seizing advanced knowledge prematurely. Thus, Theophilus obeyed his own theological axiom when he withheld from Autolycus instruction concerning initiation rites. The only references to them are brief and apologetic in nature.

He may have referred to baptismal anointing when he explained the name "Christian," although this is not certain, since he may not have referred to a literal anointing but rather to a figurative anointing by the Spirit.

---

39. Ibid., 1.7.

40. Ibid., 1.8.

41. To be sure, Heb 6:1 refers to a particular type of repentance, namely repentance from dead works, which is arguably a call to a specific sort of faith appropriate to the argument of Hebrews as a whole. Nonetheless the theme of repentance is indeed present at least lexically.

Theophilus believed that the names of things correspond to their nature. We are called "Christians," χριστιᾶνοι, he argued, because "we are anointed," χριόμεθα, with the oil of God.[42] Since the name refers to a useful and holy anointing by the "oil of God," it should not be mocked.[43]

While the writer of Hebrews included instruction about baptism and about the laying on of hands, a rite also inapplicable to a skeptical pagan, Theophilus wisely and quite consistently withheld such instruction. To provide it before Autolycus embraces Christianity would be to make the same mistake Eve made, offering advanced knowledge to a recipient to whom that advanced knowledge was forbidden, because the recipient was not yet mature enough to properly digest it. This was a serious matter for Theophilus because he believed that the partaking of advanced knowledge by the immature Adam and Eve is what brought death to humanity instead of life eternal.

He then was quite faithful to Heb 6:1–2. Even if the passage did not *directly* inform him, he reflected at least a traditional Christian concern based on its content.[44] Theophilus had to give Autolycus elementary teaching about Christianity. He then followed the content of elementary teaching according to that passage. He regarded the prerequisites of spiritual progression to be repentance and faith. These are the same two prerequisites found in Heb 6:1–2. Repentance and faith are indeed prerequisites in Heb 6:1–2, since the writer called them "a foundation" (θεμέλιος). Furthermore, the order of these two prerequisites in *Ad Autolycum*, repentance before faith, matches their order in Heb 6:1. Since Autolycus was still a skeptical pagan, Theophilus withheld instruction about those initiation rites mentioned in Heb 6:1–2. He discussed two eschatological realities, which are identical to those of Heb 6:2. Other second-century writers certainly included such themes, but they also included others. However, Theophilus wrote apology and withheld his disclosure of soteriology.[45] Still, he remained faithful to the "elementary teaching of Christ" in Hebrew 6:1–2.

---

42. Grant, *After the New Testament*, 132, associates the "oil of God" in *Autol.* 1.12 with baptismal anointing.

43. *Autol.* 1.12.

44. It is relevant here that Paul likewise used an apologetic emphasizing ethics, faith, and eschatology when he spoke with a skeptical pagan, as recorded in Acts 24:24–25.

45. Cf. above discussion of *Autol.* 2.27 and the protreptic approach modeled in Matthew 19.

Theological Justification

If the concept of elementary teaching in *Ad Autolycum* harmonizes with Heb 6:1–2, *Autol.* 2.24–27 furnishes a theological justification for such harmony. Against Marcion and Apelles, Theophilus asserted that the Tree of Knowledge did not bring death because an evil Tree had been created, but rather because the first couple ate of it before they were ready, thus violating that starting point of advancement mentioned in 2.24.[46]

---

46. Cf. Apelles's interpretation of the Tree of Knowledge as poisonous, this preserved in Ambrose, *De paradiso* 7.35. Apelles had also complained that the injunction not to eat of the Tree was inferior, and given by an inferior god, since knowledge is not bad but good. Likewise, he had complained that this god improperly disciplined Adam, who being like an infant should not have been so treated as if he had moral maturity or already had knowledge of good and evil. Theophilus created a masterful reply to Apelles by seizing his own argument about the infancy of Adam and turning it against him. This was a standard rhetorical move. For this, see the discussion of challenging τόποι in *Autol.* 1.1 in chapter 4.

Apelles was not the only one to claim death came because the Tree was poisonous. In the *Apocryphon of John*, the Archons placed Adam in paradise and commanded him to eat, but the trees of their paradise were poisonous. The writer claimed that the fruit of the Tree of Life is death (NHC II/1, 21.34). Additional gnostic interpretations of Genesis likely motivated counter-interpretation by Theophilus. He explicitly asserted that God's injunction to Adam not to eat from the Tree was not motivated by jealousy "as some are supposing" (ὡς οἴονταί τινες). This was an explicit repudiation of the gnostic teaching represented in the *Hypostasis of the Archons*. The writer depicts the serpent in Genesis 3 as a helpful instructor rather than as a deceptive creature as in *Ad Autolycum*. Specifically, the serpent tells the woman that the Archon gave the prohibition against eating from the Tree because he is jealous (NHC II/4, 90.9).

The *Epistle to Diognetus*, perhaps written in the early second century although it may have been composed later, offered an interpretation of Gen 2:9 identical to that which Theophilus provided (*Epistula ad Diognetum* 12.2). The writer of the Epistle explains that "but [the tree] of knowledge does not destroy, rather disobedience destroys" (ἀλλ' οὐ τὸ τῆς γνώσεως ἀναιρεῖ, ἀλλ' ἡ παρακοὴ ἀναιρεῖ). Similarly, Theophilus explained "for it is not, as some are supposing, that the Tree possessed death, but rather disobedience" (οὐ γάρ, ὡς οἴονταί τινες, θάνατον εἶχεν τὸ ξύλον, ἀλλ' ἡ παρακοή). Theophilus here drew from what was perhaps a stock answer to Apelles based on Gen 2:9.

The idea of the infancy of Adam was uncommon in Palestinian Judaism. The rabbis typically understood the creation account of Adam to mean that Adam was created in a fully mature state (Schoedel, "Theophilus," 285). Yet as noted above, Philo wrote of the ability of Adam to progress and mature even though his discussion of the maturation process was not exactly similar to Theophilus's. This indicates that there likely was a notion in some Hellenistic Jewish circles of Adam being created in an immature state.

The concept of the infantile nature of Adam would persist in some Christian circles. Probably through the influence of Theophilus, Irenaeus of Lyons expressed a similar idea (Irenaeus of Lyons, *Demonstratio apostolicae praedicationis* 12). Irenaeus however, differed from Theophilus by focusing on the physical immaturity of Adam rather than on his spiritual and moral immaturity.

His specific language here is revealing. He asserted in *Autol.* 2.25 that Adam was not ready for the Tree of Knowledge because he was only an infant in respect to maturity. Adam was unable to receive knowledge in a worthy way just as a helpless, newborn baby is unable to feed on solid food and therefore must feed on milk. Healthy, succulent food that itself is in no way poisonous brings death when a toothless and disobedient child foolishly subverts a loving, parental command in order to partake. Theophilus's phrase "a child is born" (γενηθῇ παιδίον) alludes in the Greek to Matt 18:3 "you should become as children" (γένησθε ὡς τὰ παιδία), thus supporting the idea that he had new Christians in mind. When he mentioned "milk" and "solid food," he used the same Greek words which the writer of Hebrews used in Heb 5:12-13, alluding to those verses.[47] He thus linked God's intent regarding spiritual progression in Genesis 2 to spiritual progression in Hebrews 5. He stated that God tested Adam for two reasons. Firstly, "He desired to test him, whether he was obedient to his commandment" (ἐβούλετο δοκιμάσαι αὐτόν, εἰ ὑπήκοος γίνεται τῇ ἐντολῇ αὐτοῦ).[48] Adam was to exercise faith by being submissive despite the appeal of the forbidden fruit. Secondly, Adam was "to remain simple and innocent" (ἁπλοῦν καὶ ἀκέραιον διαμεῖναι) for a time, at the beginning of his movement towards spiritual maturity.[49] The same ideals appear also in Hebrews. The writer of Hebrews asserted in Heb 6:2 that the elementary doctrine of Christ includes faith and repentance, which entail submission to the commandments. The writer of Hebrews furthermore claimed that new Christians are to respond as infants in their movement towards spiritual maturity in the sense that they must master elementary things before they can be ready for advanced teaching. This theological parallel between *Autol.* 2.25 and Heb 5:12—6:2 justified Theophilus's allusion to 5:12. He did not at all tear the verse out of its context.[50]

He understood immortality as a state that is made attainable by the mercy of God. To seek it is to "move on to maturity" as Heb 6:2 urges,

---

47. As mentioned above, Loofs and also the indexes of biblical citations and allusions in the edition of *Ad Autolycum* of Marcovich, *Biblia patristica*, and the *Sources chrétiennes* edition of *Ad Autolycum* support this finding of an allusion to Heb 5:12.

48. *Autol.* 2.25.

49. "Simple and innocent" is preferred over the rendering in Grant's translation, "simple and sincere." Lampe (*PGL*) allows for rendering ἀκέραιος as either "sincere" or "innocent." However, it seems incongruous that Theophilus would assert that God desired Adam to be sincere only for a time. Furthermore, "innocent" harmonizes better with the immediately previous description of Adam as an infant.

50. 1 Cor 3:1-3 and 1 Pet 2:1-2 use similar imagery as Heb 5:12. It may be that these texts also influenced Theophilus, perhaps even subconsciously, even if his outlook conforms more closely to Heb 5:12—6:2.

out of that infancy which Adam had in the Garden. God could have left all of humanity in corruption and mortality. Yet in his compassion, God once more provided an opportunity to attain eternal life. In *Autol.* 2.27, the bishop described the choice that Adam had: either immortality after obedience or mortality after disobedience. Theophilus then wrote, "Therefore, what he [Adam] acquired for himself through negligence and disobedience, this God now presents to him through his own benevolence and pity, when people obey him." In other words, while Adam received mortality through his disobedience, humanity may by the benevolence of God receive immortality. Theophilus described humanity's second chance this way: "obeying the will of God, the one who desires can lay up for himself life everlasting."[51] Humanity justly experienced death and corruption as a result of disobedience. God graciously provides a second chance to advance *through elementary knowledge* onward toward immortality.

This concept of a second chance appears in first-century Christian thought. Clement of Rome held that the blood of Christ poured out for salvation wins the "grace of repentance" (μετανοίας χάρις). Thus, any who desire God find "opportunity for repentance" (μετανοίας τόπος).[52] Theophilus similarly saw an "opportunity for repentance" (ἀφορμή . . . μετανοίας) which is truly a gift, since it is given only because God is forbearing and merciful.[53] While Clement explicitly stated that opportunity for repentance comes thanks to the death of Christ, Theophilus, constrained by apologetic concerns, did not mention the Roman cross to his fellow Roman Autolycus, but spoke more vaguely of the mercy of God.[54]

Humanity, formerly doomed to mortality, may once again advance. God in his compassion has re-introduced the same opportunity that Adam and Eve once had. Theophilus explicitly equated these opportunities by asserting, "What he [Adam] acquired for himself through negligence and

---

51. *Autol.* 2.27. Theophilus's language about laying up eternal life for oneself recalls Matt 6:19, 20; and 1 Tim 6:19. This recollection involves a conceptual parallel, rather than a verbal one, since Theophilus used the verb περιποιέω, while the apostles used the verb θησαυρίζω. Such a conceptual parallel, as opposed to a mere verbal parallel, is characteristic of accessing a text by way of partial memory recall.

52. Lit. "place of repentance," an allusion to Heb 12:17. Clement provided this teaching on the "grace of repentance" in *1 Clem.* 7.4–5.

53. *Autol.* 2.26, 29.

54. Clement's allusion to Heb 12:17 is closer to the verse in a lexical sense. Theophilus used αφορμή instead of τόπος. This substitution of terms indicates that Theophilus recalled the content of Heb 12:17 on a deep conceptual level rather than on a surface, verbal level.

disobedience, this God now presents to him through his own benevolence and pity...."⁵⁵

What is significant in this statement is that Theophilus did not mention two opportunities which are similar. Rather, he mentioned only one, but it appears in two differing contexts. There is further support that these opportunities were identical for Theophilus. In *Autol.* 2.26, he explained the double creation account of humanity in Genesis. He saw it as a promise in figurative language that the opportunity by which Adam fell into mortality will appear again, so that Christians may rise through resurrection into immortality. He wrote, "it is *mystically* [μυστηριωδῶς] *written in Genesis, as twice being placed in Paradise*, on the one hand, the first being fulfilled when he was placed there, but on the other hand, the second will be fulfilled by means of the resurrection and judgment."⁵⁶ Because the literal account depicts humanity twice in the *same* garden, so humanity twice encounters the *same* opportunity. This is also why he used ἀφορμή ironically in the sense of both "opportunity" and "starting point," so as to create a double parallel between Eden and Christianity.

Theophilus referred to the beginning of progression with the word ἀφορμή which could denote either a "starting point" or an "opportunity." He used the term in an ironic way. Both before and after Adam's disobedience in Eden, people are confronted by an opportunity for either mortality or immortality, depending on what whether they incline themselves toward earthly things or heavenly things. Ironically, they are also confronted by a starting point. "Starting point" language is significant because it implies that maturity comes via a process rather than by an instantaneous event. Indeed both meanings of ἀφορμή are significant, because concepts of both opportunity and progression are prominent in *Ad Autolycum*.

Theophilus mentioned ἀφορμή three times. When he mentioned ἀφορμή in *Autol.* 2.24, the context is the period before Adam disobeyed. Theophilus calls this starting point the "starting point for advancement." However, when he mentioned ἀφορμή in *Autol.* 2.26 and 2.29, the context is the period after Adam disobeyed. Accordingly, he changed terminology and called this starting point the "starting point of repentance and confession."

55. *Autol.* 2.27.

56. Ibid., 2.26; italics added. Here is the only place in *Ad Autolycum* where Theophilus used a cognate of μυστήριον in reference to a non-literal sense of Scripture. He used it here to signify mimetic prophecy. But in *Autol.* 2.15, he used a cognate to refer to divine revelation appearing in the creation when he called the sun and the moon "the pattern [δεῖγμα] and type [τύπον] of a great mystery [μεγάλου μυστηρίου]." This also is mimetic prophecy, since Theophilus argued that Genesis 1:16 is a veiled prophecy of the Christian hope of the resurrection. He also used τύπος in *Autol.* 2.17 to refer to a non-literal sense of Scripture.

He knew that because disobedience and mortality are indeed tragic realities, repentance and confession are required before people may re-embark in spiritual progression. These starting points are identical in effect, since they all introduce the same progression towards immortality whereby one progressively matures by inclining toward heavenly things rather than earthly things. However, while the nature of this progression had not changed, the nature of humanity has. Humanity is no longer neutral. Therefore, repentance is now required before disciples can progress.

It is important to recognize the ironic way that ἀφορμή was used. Otherwise, the essential similarity of progression before and after Adam's disobedience is obscured. The *Ante-Nicene Fathers* translation of *Ad Autolycum* renders the phrase in *Autol.* 2.24 as "means of advancement" and the phrases in *Autol.* 2.26 and 2.29 as "opportunity for repentance and confession." But note the irony. Before Adam's disobedience there is *both* an "opportunity, ἀφορμή, for advancement (προκοπῆς)," *and* a "starting point, ἀφορμή, for advancement" according to *Autol.* 2.24. Likewise after Adam's disobedience, there is also *both* an "opportunity, ἀφορμή, for repentance and confession (τῆς μετανοίας)," *and* a "starting point, ἀφορμή, of repentance and confession" in 2.26 and 2.29. The genitive of both προκοπῆς and τῆς μετανοίας is directional when ἀφορμή is taken to mean "starting point," and attributive when it is taken to mean "opportunity." Yet these renderings of the genitive do not violate Greek syntax. In either context, before or after Adam's disobedience, opportunity for advancement and a starting point for advancement are both present. Theophilus intentionally used ἀφορμή ambiguously, utilizing both senses of the word to emphasize a double parallel between the economies of (pre-death) Eden and Christianity.

There are mixed opinions as to whether Theophilus considered the economy of advancement before Adam's disobedience equivalent to the economy after Adam disobeyed. For example, Bentivegna, who provides an extremely helpful assessment of the thought of Theophilus in his "A Christianity without Christ by Theophilus of Antioch," considers these two economies to be distinctly different.[57] He does not mention an ironic use of ἀφορμή, and translates ἀφορμὴ προκοπῆς in *Autol.* 2.24 as "principle of progress," and ἡ ἀφορμὴ τῆς μετανοίας in *Autol.* 2.26 as "the principle of conversion." By contrast, Zeegers-Vander Vorst understands Theophilus to have found a single economy, one also seen as identical in both the Old and New Testaments. Zeegers-Vander Vorst does not mention an ironic use of ἀφορμή either, but argues on the basis of statements by Theophilus about

---

57. Bentivegna, "A Christianity without Christ," 120–24.

New Testament fulfillment of Old Testament promises.[58] However, the above-mentioned ironic use of ἀφορμή creates a double parallel between the economies, which lends additional weight to the view that Theophilus indeed saw a single economy of salvation in both Testaments and indeed throughout time. Both before and after Adam's disobedience, it works essentially the same way.

Since Theophilus understood that the starting point that God provides to potential Christians is essentially a reintroduction of the same one he had originally provided to Adam, potential Christians can but must not make Adam's mistake. God did not intend Adam to eat prematurely from the Tree of Knowledge; likewise he does not intend people to learn advanced teaching before they learn elementary lessons. This is why Theophilus alluded to Heb 5:12 in his exposition of Genesis, and why the apologetic strategy of *Ad Autolycum* reflected the components of the elementary teaching of Christ in Heb 6:1-2. Shaped either directly or indirectly by Hebrews 5-6, Theophilus emphasized repentance, faith, resurrection, and final judgment. He believed that such Christian elementary teaching could enable his pagan friend to begin advancing toward immortality.

CONCLUSION

Scholarship has not yet sufficiently recognized that *Ad Autolycum* and other early Christian protreptic writings were meant to provide merely elementary teachings, and that they deliberately withheld soteriology. Modern writers have difficulty imagining how greatly protreptic writings pervaded the second century. As a result, current scholarship sometimes pronounces rash and anachronistic theological assessments of *Ad Autolycum*. Therefore, until some of the currently-lost treatises by Theophilus are discovered, scholarship must refrain from assessing the soteriology of Theophilus. This is not a call for a theological renovation of *Ad Autolycum*, but rather, a recognition that ancient protreptic literature was written for purposes other than that of disclosing soteriology. Truly historical studies of *Ad Autolycum* keep this reality foremost. Thus, I have argued, against an anachronistic tendency in scholarship, that *Ad Autolycum* is intentionally non-soteriological, albeit for profound theological reasons. *Ad Autolycum* functioned not as a soteriological work but as a proactive protreptic appeal and a defensive apology.

I will show in chapter 4 that instead of following modern literary standards, Theophilus followed the literary and rhetorical conventions used in ancient Roman apologies. I will also demonstrate there, in a very detailed

58. Zeegers, "Citations du Nouveau Testament," 371-82.

and historically-sensitive way, that the "meta-logic" of *Ad Autolycum* exactly matches that of typical Greco-Roman protreptic literature. In the process, we will discover that Scripture played a leading role on Theophilus's rhetorical stage. We will also see how well Scripture and classic judicial rhetoric allowed him to accomplish his protreptic objective. All of this builds support for the thesis of this volume, that when we look behind anachronistic views of genre, literacy, and rhetoric, we discover a hidden Theophilus and a forgotten form of second-century exegesis. For this, scholarship must pay more than lip-service to ancient protreptic.

But to truly perceive how central and essential was Scripture's role on Theophilus's rhetorical stage, we must also grasp how easily he could access Scripture by memory rather than through reading, and how artfully he could marshal it without reference to written documents. The following chapter will show, by means of objective criteria, just how true this was.

3

Scripture and a Forgotten Orality

THE PROBLEMS OF ORALITY, RECOLLECTION AND ΜΙΜΗΣΙΣ

What does it matter if we misunderstand how Theophilus handled Scripture? For one thing, this misunderstanding ultimately changes how we assess his comprehension of the message of Christianity. And indeed, Theophilus and the other second-century Christian apologists have long suffered suspicions concerning their understanding of the gospel. For instance, Schultze exclaims concerning *Ad Autolycum*, "But it appears out of the question, that an Antiochene bishop had written a text filled with so many follies and errors."[1] Grant, one of the most prolific scholars of Theophilus in recent memory, summarized Theophilus's thought by writing, "He was unable to understand clearly either the Christian faith or the Hellenistic philosophies opposed to it."[2] Theophilus's fellow apologists are often similarly dismissed.[3]

But if such dismissals of these early Christian thinkers are rash, then it is to our loss, since rash dismissals obscure our view of the past. Certainly it is beyond the scope of this present study to explore the basic shape of Theophilus's theology. But it is within our purposes here to examine what

---

1. Schultze, *Altchristliche Städte*, 57.
2. Grant, *After the New Testament*, 157.
3. Edwards et al., *Apologetics in the Roman Empire*, 10, 12, remark that the early apologists continually suffer from such lack of respect. They cite Gibbon, *Decline and Fall of the Roman Empire*, 1:457, 493, 498, by way of representative example.

may be a contributing factor behind such dismissals, which is that we can sometimes find ourselves at a loss to understand his handling of Scripture. Trained in historical-critical methods in which biblical passages are to be read strictly in light of their meaning for their original audiences, modern students of early Christianity may be amazed to discover Theophilus seeing his pagan friend Autolycus described in 2 Cor 11:19,[4] for example, when Paul had in mind the false, "super-apostles" of Corinth who would have torn their clothes in frustration had they heard Autolycus' ideas; or to find Theophilus using 2 Cor 7:1 to describe *moral* defilement such as shameless adultery, steamy fornication, and malevolent thieving,[5] when Paul had in mind the *religious* defilement of idolatry.[6] However, to dismiss Theophilus's handling of Scripture in this way would be to read him anachronistically. Rather, his use of the Bible can only be accurately and truly historically assessed in light of the literary standards of the second century, not those of our own.

Therefore in this present chapter, I aim to expose some intellectual blinders of our own highly-literate, written document-rich, modern culture with its expectations of exact quotation and assumption that texts are typically experienced only through reading, so that we may perceive now-forgotten but rich ways that Scripture actually functioned in Theophilus's largely-oral culture.[7] Even if these ways appear strange to us moderns, they made perfect sense in the second century. And after we perceive them, we will no longer stand for that all too common way of studying early Christian exegesis that only sees use of Scripture when there is a full- or partial-biblical quotation. Full and partial quotations are merely the "tip of the iceberg." The great mass of biblical usage lies beneath the surface, hidden from easy view.

In this chapter, I make much of oral culture in early Christianity. And indeed, second-century Antioch was highly-illiterate. Its literacy rate was surely under 10%, and may have been under 5%.[8] Furthermore, most of those able to read could do so only slowly and with great effort. Many who could read were unable to write.[9]

---

4. *Autol.* 3.4.

5. Ibid., 1.2.

6. Cf. 2 Cor 6:15–18.

7. Media research uses the term "oral" in a wide variety of ways. In this study, I use this term only to specify the characteristic of being oral as opposed to textual.

8. Dunn, *New Perspective on Jesus*, 90.

9. Botha, *Orality and Literacy in Early Christianity*, 44. To glimpse how deeply Scripture can nonetheless penetrate a highly-illiterate culture, we may consider the somewhat analogous experience of the fourth-century desert ascetics. For helpful overviews of the function of Scripture in that world, see Bamberger, *Praktikos*, xlv–vi; and

Of course, this does not necessarily imply that Theophilus himself was illiterate. While an illiterate man in the second century could indeed hold a high place in society, the good number of truly lengthy biblical quotations in Theophilus's surviving letters, which would been less likely to have been memorized than shorter quotations and which would have been somewhat difficult for him to include if he could not readily read them himself, suggests that he himself indeed could read.[10] And if so, there is every reason to suppose also that he was highly-literate, for he dealt not with the simple lists of a tradesman, but with the complicated and rich writings of the Greco-Roman poets and philosophers.[11] And even if he did not know them extensively, he was indeed quite familiar with many of their complex claims.[12]

Whatever the degree of Theophilus's own literacy, it would be hard to show that the church of Antioch, over which he presided, solely or even mainly included highly-literate sheep. This suggests that he could seemlessly shift back and forth between the worlds of his illiterate and his highly-literate flock. Given his culture, there is every reason to suppose that his media mix included healthy portions of biblical scripts for oral performance, deep wells of memorized Scripture, and as we will see in chapter 5, perhaps even some scriptural anthologies.

In view of this, we must consider oral techniques and memory-based mental dynamics which may seem unfamiliar in our highly-literate age, but which were wide-spread in antiquity. We then can view Theophilus's handling of Scripture through more historically-informed eyes, catching a deeper view of life in his mainly-illiterate world. As a result, we will be less likely to repeat errors of prior scholarship by denigrating his biblical exegesis simply because of our own cultural blinders.

Indeed, Theophilus research in general fails to take adequate account of how much Theophilus and his audience accessed Scripture via memory

---

Driscoll, *Ad Monachos*, 174–84.

10. For the lengths of his biblical quotations, see the scripture usage tables in the appendix. We shall see more about the relationship between quotation length and ease of memorization later in this chapter. For the surprisingly high social status of many illiterate people in late antiquity, see Botha, *Orality and Literacy in Early Christianity*, 26–28.

11. Media critics distinguish between "craftsman literacy," through which ancient craftsmen could read texts necessary for their work but could not comprehend complex abstract writings, and "scribal literacy," through which highly-educated people could read and understand complex, abstract texts such as the works of the Greek philosophers.

12. Zeegers shows in her seminal monograph that Theophilus knew the poets and philosophers largely through anthologies rather than through extensive study of their many treatises. See Zeegers, *Citations des poètes grecs*.

rather than reading, and is silent concerning the potent mental dynamics of that oral culture. It would be very difficult for any modern scholar who has only known her own highly-literate culture to have any truly accurate conception of the extensive memory feats possible in cultures where most thinkers were illiterate.[13]

But a truly historical study of how Scripture functions in early apologetic writings such as *Ad Autolycum* must always hold these historical concerns foremost. We shall see that powerful mental dynamics often activated in Theophilus's world when memorized Hebrew Scriptures echoed in Christian speech. Consequently, Theophilus was able to offer his apologetic for Christianity with a scriptural richness and sophisticated rhetorical power that seems foreign in highly-literate cultures. Even illiterate Christians, equipped with highly-developed memories, could appreciate it.

The study of literacy and orality in early Christianity is a burgeoning and welcome development.[14] However in this chapter, I in no way claim to deal comprehensively with all of the connections between this sub-field and ancient Antioch. Rather, my aim here is strictly limited.

I will first lay out a survey of Theophilus's use of Scripture expressed in terms of modern literary categories. While modern categories are not adequate for truly historical studies, despite their continued wide use in scholarship, this survey of Scripture usage provides a helpful initial overview, given that the modern categories continue to appear frequently in the literature. This survey will also alert us to the prominence of biblical allusion in Theophilus's writings, and help us to perceive that in the ancient world, Scripture could be used in rich ways even if it was not quoted. In other words, in this initial survey, we shall see how important allusions and reminiscences of Scripture were, how comparatively unimportant biblical quotations were, and how deeply Scripture could resonate in a world where people alluded to it more than they quoted it, partially because they generally could not read it. So this initial survey will function as a helpful foundational step towards removing our literate-culture fixation on quotations of written texts. This fixation blinds us moderns to the ways that largely-illiterate cultures experienced Scripture.

After this initial survey, I will build upon the work of McIver and Carroll to show, by use of objective criteria, that a sizable number of Theophilus's uses of Scripture sprung from memory recollection rather than reading.

---

13. For the impressive memory feats common to largely-illiterate cultures, see Dunn, *New Perspective on Jesus*, 35–56.

14. For recent perspectives, see Botha, *Orality and Literacy in Early Christianity*; McIver, *Memory, Jesus, and the Synoptic Gospels*; and Rodríguez, *Oral Tradition*.

Then, I intend to show, by the use of objective criteria based on the work of Skarsaune, that Theophilus had a deeper knowledge of the Old Testament than Christian writers earlier in the second century.

But if we should find that he accommodated his illiterate listeners by so frequently accessing Scripture in the way that they did—by memory, then how did that that method affect how he used Scripture? Was his use of Scripture in largely-illiterate Antioch very different from our own use of Scripture in our highly-literate environment? These are crucial questions for understanding how Scripture functioned in the ancient apologetic age. Therefore, I will next explore the operation in *Ad Autolycum* of certain sophisticated, memory-based dynamics typical of highly-illiterate cultures. We shall see that these provided great potency to Theophilus's uses of Scripture, a potency that appears very foreign to us moderns.

This chapter will conclude with example studies of patristic exegesis which are sensitive to illiteracy, oral culture, and memory-access of Scripture. The final example will serve as a capstone of this chapter. It lays out a comprehensive treatment of the Book of Job in Theophilus's surviving writings. It is meant to be a programmatic example of considering illiteracy and memory in studies of Scripture in the apologetic age.

VERBAL PARALLELS WITH SCRIPTURE

As I indicated, a helpful initial step towards removing our literate-culture fixation on quotations of written texts is that of discovering the great importance of biblical allusions and the relative unimportance of quotations in Theophilus's world. But how can we reliably distinguish between biblical allusions, biblical quotations, and mere reminiscences of a biblical passage? And even before we try to distinguish a use of Scripture into one of these categories, how can we reliably determine when a writer used a passage of Scripture in the first place? The answer is that scholars identify uses of Scripture in ancient texts by way of verbal parallels. I define uses of inspired texts in *Ad Autolycum* as those which appear in *both* Marcovich's and Biblia patristica's biblical indexes for *Ad Autolycum*, so as to find support in something of a scholarly consensus.[15] Direct examination in *Ad Autolycum*

---

15. In seeking this scholarly consensus in this way, I account for the numeration differences between the LXX numeration of Marcovich's biblical index and the Masoretic numeration of *Biblia Patristica*. As noted in the methodological section of appendix 2, OT citations in this present study accord with the numeration of the LXX, the same numeration used with both Grant's and Marcovich's Greek texts of *Ad Autolycum*.

4 Maccabees appears in Marcovich's index, but not in *Biblia Patristica*. So as not to exclude a work that Theophilus may have considered to be inspired, the single use of

of supposed uses of certain biblical passages, about which some dubious claims appear in some of the literature, validates the value of this kind of scholarly consensus.[16]

In addition, I employ a computational method which I call "usage database analysis" in order to categorize, consistently and comprehensively, all uses of Scripture in *Ad Autolycum*, on the basis of verbal parallels between *Ad Autolycum* and biblical texts. This method involves populating a computer database with Scripture word counts and *Ad Autolycum* word counts and subjecting this data to numerical analysis in order to consistently sort Theophilus's uses of Scripture into various modern categories such as "allusion," "citation," and "quotation," and in order to analyze distributions of his uses of Scripture. Reports are generated to show very precisely, consistently, and comprehensively how the types of Scripture usage and biblical books used differ in each portion of *Ad Autolycum*.[17] This method is analogous although not identical to that used by Ernest in his study of Athanasius and Scripture.[18] This usage database analysis produces a consistent and comprehensive overview using familiar modern categories of Theophilus's uses of Scripture. The results of this overview now appear.

SURVEY IN MODERN CATEGORIES OF THEOPHILUS'S USES OF SCRIPTURE

While it is most helpful to understand how Theophilus used Scripture by considering ancient categories which he himself would have recognized, nonetheless modern readers may also gain benefit from an initial "birds-eye" view of overall patterns using modern categories.[19] As promised, this "birds-eye" view of how he used Scripture will also alert us to the importance of biblical allusion in his world and the relative unimportance of quotations

---

4 Maccabees listed by Marcovich is also included in the present study, even though it appears in only one of these biblical indexes. On the OT and NT books Theophilus used, see Grant, "Bible of Theophilus," 173–96.

16. This consensus-based approach is analogous to Bingham's method for reliably identifying uses by Irenaeus of distinctly Matthean texts. See Bingham, *Irenaeus's Use of Matthew's Gospel*, 10–11.

17. For specific details of this method, see "Quotation and Allusion Terminology" in the appendices. While it is a computational approach, it should not be confused with the ACTS computational approach described in chapter 5.

18. Ernest, *The Bible in Athanasius*.

19. Those ancient judicial rhetorical categories that we shall investigate in chapter 4 are especially helpful for probing *Ad Autolycum* in a historically-legitimate manner.

in that world. Thus, this survey will challenge our modern fixation on written texts and on quotations from them.

In his first letter, Theophilus used only a few portions from the Hebrew Scriptures.[20] Just over half of them are from the Psalms. A little over 20 percent are from Job. The rest consist only of one or two uses each from Genesis, Exodus, Proverbs, Jeremiah, or 4 Maccabees.

His use of the gospels in his first letter is striking. He knew more than one, since he used Matthew, Luke, and John at various places in the three letters of *Ad Autolycum*. However, in *Ad Autoycum* 1, his only uses of the gospels are two quotations and one allusion, all of which come from John. As for his use of other Christian inspired texts besides the gospels, nearly 60 percent come from either Romans or 1 Corinthians. Just over 15 percent come from 1 Peter. The remainder consist only of one or two uses each from 2 Corinthians, Ephesians, and 1 Timothy.

In the very conclusion of the first letter, *Autol.* 1.14, his use of biblical allusions and reminiscences, heretofore minimal in this letter, dramatically and unexpectedly surges. The words in his biblical allusions and reminiscences per 1000 words of text, averaging about twenty throughout all of *Ad Autolycum* 1, up through *Autol.* 1.13, suddenly rises *tenfold* in the concluding appeal in *Autol.* 1.14–106, for *both* reminiscences and allusions.[21] But this dramatic surge is entirely understandable, for once he reached his conclusion, Theophilus has just finished his judicial rhetorical argument with all of its witness interrogation τόποι, a type of argument that simply demanded use of biblical citations and quotations but not allusions and reminiscences. So for his concluding appeal, he simply reverted to the same rich compositional use of Scripture by means of allusions and reminiscences in which he could so easily engage and which we also see in *Autol.* 3.24. Most of this compositional use of biblical allusions and reminiscences pile up in the final dozen lines of the letter. Here we find that most of his words are knit from biblical allusions and reminiscences. Theophilus introduced his final appeal with a veritable ecstasy of compositional use of Scripture, mostly in allusions and reminiscences:

> But if you resolve, you also must eagerly read the prophetic writings, and they will lead you more clearly in the way of escaping from eternal punishments and of gaining eternal benefits

---

20. For more detail concerning information in this present section, see the tables in appendix 2 of distributions of uses of Scripture and inspired writings in *Ad Autolycum*. The three categories in these tables, "prophetic books," "gospels," and "inspired writings," are translations of the ancient categories that Theophilus himself used. Early Christians considered all of the OT to be prophetic, rather than a mere portion of it.

21. See the scripture usage tables in the appendices for details.

from God. For *the one who gave the mouth for speaking and who formed the ear for hearing and made eyes for seeing* [Exod 4:11; Ps 93:9] will scrutinize all things and will judge justly, *rendering to each rewards for what is due* [Rom 2:6]. *To those who by patient endurance of good works seek imperishability, he will present eternal life* [Rom 2:7], joy, peace, rest and myriads of good things, *which neither the eye sees nor the ear hears nor comes to the heart of a person* [1 Cor 2:9]. *But to the unbelieving and despisers and those disobeying the truth, being won over by unrighteousness* [Rom 2:8], when they would be hauled about in adulteries and fornications and homosexual intercourses and greediness and lawless idolatries, there will be *wrath and anger, affliction and distress* [Rom 2:8-9], and *the consummation is: eternal fire will possess* such men [4 Macc 12:12].

Theophilus used the prophets in his second letter to Autolycus in a manner noticeably different than how he used them in his first letter. He used virtually no inspired texts in the early portions of the *Ad Autoycum* 2. This is not surprising, since here he focused on those who spoke for pagan gods, arguing that they gave inconsistent and therefore untrustworthy history.[22] However, he abruptly changed focus in *Autol.* 2.9–33, where he provided the oldest extant "commentary" of the early chapters of Genesis. So while most of his uses of the prophets in *Ad Autoycum* 1 are uses of Job or the Psalms, most uses in *Ad Autoycum* 2 are from Genesis. This is not surprising since much of *Ad Autoycum* 2 consists of his argument that Moses supplies the true history of the cosmos. The "commentary" on Genesis in *Ad Autoycum* 2 consists of a variety of uses of passages from Genesis, including ten citations, seventeen quotations, thirteen reminiscences, and twenty five allusions. They remind us that for Theophilus, allusions and reminiscences played at least as significant a role as did citations and quotations, even in what is essentially a biblical commentary.

In terms of ancient reading strategies, most of the uses of Genesis take the form of explanatory comment, but these are explained more precisely in terms of the judicial rhetoric by which Theophilus argued that the prophets provide the true history of origins, but pagan poets and philosophers do not.[23] We shall see in chapter 4 the full genius and power of this judicial rhetoric in *Ad Autolycum*. Since Genesis played such a key role in the judi-

---

22. Based on verbal similarity, *Autol.* 2.1–8 contains only a mere reminiscence of a single inspired text, 1 Cor 1:18 in *Autol.* 2.1. Theophilus also used this same verse in an early portion of his third letter to similar ends as his use of it here in an early portion of his second letter.

23. For ancient reading strategies, see Young, *Formation of Christian Culture*, 213.

cial rhetoric of *Ad Autoycum* 2, Theophilus provided a sort of commentary on its early chapters. He discussed the main features of the biblical narrative in Genesis 1–10. However, unlike many modern commentators, he did not provide an intentionally impassive, verse-by-verse exposition. Rather, he commented on the Genesis text specifically to support his own apologetic polemic. This is why some portions of the early chapters of Genesis, such as Genesis 8, received relatively little discussion, while others, such as Genesis 1 or the account of Cain and Abel, received far more extensive comment.

As far as prophetic writings outside of Genesis, Theophilus used these almost exclusively in citation form. There is one reminiscence from Deuteronomy, and two allusions from the Proverbs. But every other use of the prophetic writings beyond Genesis in *Ad Autoycum* 2 takes the form of a citation. This indicates that these texts were significant for Theophilus because they come from a special group: the prophets. Here he took special care to ensure that Autolycus would realize that a prophet was speaking. He therefore typically named or otherwise referred to the particular prophet with each use of a prophetic passage. We will see in chapter 4 that this was crucial for his judicial rhetoric in which he made the case that the prophets are trustworthy while the pagan poets and philosophers are not.

At least one other late-second-century Christian writer also placed special significance on the practice of citing or quoting the words of authoritative figures in the biblical text. Irenaeus of Lyons showed the authority of *spoken* words in the Genesis narrative by his tendency of citing or quoting *these* words rather than the non-spoken words of Genesis.[24] This practice by Irenaeus especially applied to those words from Genesis spoken by God. Kannengiesser posits that Irenaeus preferred to quote God's spoken words rather than quoting the spoken words of other figures, and rather than quoting non-spoken words from the text of Genesis, because the words of God himself were dramatic and effective for confirming Irenaeus's theology.[25]

However, Theophilus did not prefer to cite divinely spoken words. But this is entirely understandable in view of his own argument. It was a judicial-rhetorical one in which the prophets testify in support of Christianity, while the pagan poets and philosophers testify in support of Greco-Roman

---

24. Kannengiesser, "The 'Speaking God.'"

25. Kannengiesser, "The 'Speaking God,'" 342. For Irenaeus's use of Scripture, see also Balás, "Paul in Irenaeus's Five Books"; Bingham, *Irenaeus's Use of Matthew's Gospel*; Brox, "Biblische Hermeneutik des Irenäus"; Andia, "L'unité des testaments selon Irénée"; Margerie, "Irenaeus, Ecclesial Exegete"; Farkasfalvy, "Scripture in St. Irenaeus"; Ferlay, "Irénée de Lyon exegete"; Jourjoun, "Irenaeus's Reading of the Bible"; Noormann, *Irenäus als Paulusinterpret*; Norris, "Irenaeus's Use of Paul"; Reventlow, "Harmonie der Testamente"; and Vogt, "Geltung des Alten Testaments bei Irenäus."

religion. Theophilus did not need to highlight words spoken by God in the Genesis narrative, as Irenaeus did as he argued that the God of the NT and of the OT are one and the same. By contrast, Theophilus merely needed to show the trustworthiness of *his* witnesses, the prophets and apostles, and the untrustworthiness of pagan witnesses. This was "courtroom warfare." Like any good courtroom advocate, he needed to allow his audience to hear the actual words of his witnesses rather than mere allusions of these words. Therefore, he was especially careful to cite and quote the words of the prophets, rather than merely allude to them. He took special care to defend the trustworthiness of this group of friendly witnesses. Therefore, he emphasized that this group could be trusted in light of their virtuous lives and their consistent testimony in support of his argument. Therefore, whenever he used their words, he always identified the speakers as prophets. It is therefore not surprising that he only recalled or alluded to the words of the prophets when those words were from Genesis, a text which was his main witness in *Ad Autoycum* 2, and which he clearly identified up front as the testimony of the prophet Moses.

Theophilus cited not only the prophets in *Ad Autoycum* 2, but also the gospels, three times from John and once from Luke. In *Ad Autoycum* 1, Theophilus used only the Gospel of John but no other book from among the gospels. By contrast, he used both John and Luke in *Ad Autoycum* 2. He did not cite from any other Christian inspired texts in *Ad Autoycum* 2 except for these four citations from Luke and John. He cited John 1:1, 3 so as to support his Logos doctrine.[26] If his use of inspired texts in the form of citation

---

26. While Justin and Athenagoras merely recalled John 1:1–3 when they wrote of the eternal existence and creative activity of God's Logos, Theophilus explicitly cited the verses (Justin Martyr, *Apologiae* 2.6; Athenagoras of Athens, *Leg.* 10).

Jews such as Philo of Alexandria understood God as being assisted by his powers when he created humanity. This Jewish soil ultimately nurtured Theophilus's exegesis. When Theophilus used Gen 1:26 in *Autol.* 2.18, he explained that God conversed with his Logos and his Sophia, but he did not explicitly call them God's "powers." But in *Autol.* 2.22, he called the Logos God's "Power . . . and Sophia" (δύναμις . . . καὶ σοφία; I capitalize both titles in this translation for consistency). He found rationale for these titles in the assertions of 1 Cor 1:24 that Christ is the "Power of God and Sophia of God" (θεοῦ δύναμιν καὶ θεοῦ σοφίαν). Other Christian writings equated the Logos with the Power of God, such as *Acts of John* 109. Tatian called God's Ἀρχή the "Power of the Logos" (Λόγου δύναμιν, Tatian, *Oratio ad Graecos* 5).

On this point, perhaps Theophilus learned from Tatian. Where Tatian, *Oratio ad Graecos* 5, contains only an allusion to Col 1:15, *Autol.* 2.22 contains an exact quotation of Col 1:15b. Both writers, however, applied the verse to the Logos as the creative assistant of God, and linked it with John 1:1–3. According to Epiphanius, the teachings of Tatian were influential in Antioch around 170 C.E., so Theophilus might well have heard Tatian's use of Col 1:15 (Epiphanius, *Haeres.* 46.1). However, these observations do not necessarily overturn Grant's assertion that Theophilus did not know Tatian (Grant,

signifies a high degree of authority, as argued above, then his citing of the prophets and of gospels and his lack of citations of other inspired Christian texts confirms Grant's and Zeeger's observations that Theophilus attributed roughly the same degree of authority to the prophets and to the gospels. While he did not cite any Christian inspired texts in *Ad Autoycum* 2 except for these gospel citations, he did quote some passages from the NT epistles although without also citing the authors of these passages.

In *Ad Autoycum* 3, even more than in *Ad Autoycum* 1 and *Ad Autoycum* 2, Theophilus recalled or alluded to the prophetic writings, almost exclusively. Except for reminiscences of Matt 5:46, 1 Cor 1:18, 2 Cor 11:19, and an allusion to 1 Pet 3:20, every reminiscence or allusion in *Ad Autoycum* 3 was to a prophetic text.[27] None of these allusions and only two of the reminiscences were used in *Autol.* 3.1–8, dealing with philosophy, or in *Autol.* 3.9–15, dealing with ethics. They are found rather in *Autol.* 3.16–30, the final portion of the letter, dealing with chronology. Theophilus based this chronology on the biblical chronologies of Genesis 5 and 11, and on chronological data from the book of Judges. Reminiscences of inspired texts in *Ad Autoycum* 3, like the allusions, are oriented towards chronology. A little over 80 percent of them come from the historical narratives of 1 and 2 Kings and 2 Chronicles.

Just over 70 percent of allusions to inspired texts in *Ad Autoycum* 3 are found in a single small portion, *Autol.* 3.24, which consists of a summary of the biblical chronology extending from Adam to the prophet Samuel. Why are the allusions so restricted to this one small portion? The answer lies in Theophilus's rich compositional use of biblical allusion. He was able to produce a tight summary of biblical accounts of the earliest human generations that despite its compactness is nonetheless detailed and rich as a result of his compositional use of masses of biblical allusions and reminiscences.[28]

"Studies in Theophilus," 117–18). It may be that both Tatian and Theophilus drew from the same exegetical traditions. The literature on the Logos relating to second-century use of John chapter 1 is rich. See particularly Dörrie, "Der Prolog zur Evangelium nach Johannes"; Edwards, "Justin's Logos"; Goodenough, *Justin*, in which his Logos discussion runs throughout; Loofs, *Theophilus von Antiochen Adversus Marcionem*, 46–72; Zeegers, "Création de l'homme," 258–67; and Zeegers, "Logos chez Théophile" for her discussion of Theophilus's treatment of Logos. Important corrections of Loofs appear in Hitchcock, "Loof's Theory of Theophilus of Antioch as a Source of Irenaeus"; Noormann, *Irenäus als Paulusinterpret*, 34; and Rousseau, "Plan du livre v."

27. 1 Cor 1:18 and 2 Cor 11:19 appear as allusive echoes in *Autol.* 3.4. I will discuss the dynamics of allusive recollection connected to these echoes later in this chapter.

28. We saw a similar high concentration of biblical allusions and reminiscences in *Autol.* 1.14.

There are relatively few quotations in *Ad Autoycum* 3. There are only four, of texts in Genesis, Exodus, and Deuteronomy. However, there are a number of citations, taken from a wide range of the inspired books. None of them are found in *Autol.* 3.1–8, dealing with philosophy. Except for a citation of Moses concerning the forty-day length of the great deluge, none are found in *Autol.* 3.16–30, dealing with chronology. Almost all citations of inspired texts are found in *Autol.* 3.9–15, dealing with ethics. This is significant. Theophilus argued in *Autol.* 3.9–15 that the inspired texts, including the gospels and NT epistles, teach a more superior ethic than do the writings of the poets and philosophers. He had to reinforce to Autolycus the Christian identity of this superior ethic as well as its basis in the writings of the prophets. This is why almost every use of an inspired text in the ethical argument of *Autol.* 3.9–15 consists of a citation. Theophilus could not let Autolycus forget that only the prophets taught this superior ethic.

His gospel usage is curious. He used only the Gospel of John in *Ad Autoycum* 1, and used only Luke and John in *Ad Autoycum* 2. But he used only Matthew's Gospel in *Ad Autoycum* 3. He did not attribute these uses of Matthean texts to Matthew by name. Rather, he attributed them to the "gospel voice" (εὐαγγελίου φωνὴ) and to the "gospel" (εὐαγγέλιον).[29] And the only place where we find gospel citations in all of *Ad Autolycum* in which he named the human writer are his citations of John 1:1, 3 in *Autol.* 2.22. Theophilus was not terribly concerned in his ethical discussion in *Autol.* 3.9–15 about the identities of the human gospel writers. He did not fixate on the personalities of individual human gospel writers, or on the social concerns of individual early Christian communities. Rather, his fixation was on a unified teaching from the Spirit of God emerging through these writers.

ORALITY AND ALLUSIONS

Theophilus's Ability to Recall Scripture from Memory

Our survey in modern categories with its frequent mention of biblical allusions suggests that Theophilus could recall Scripture easily from memory. But could he really? We shall see. Scholarship has discovered some objective criteria for determining fairly reliably when a writer has recalled biblical texts out of memory as opposed to copying them from manuscripts. We can apply these objective criteria to the Scripture usage tables in the appendices, in order to measure the degree that Theophilus accessed Scripture from memory as opposed to reading. We shall see that he accessed a large

---

29. *Autol.* 3.13–14.

number of his uses of OT Scripture from memory. Then in the following section we will examine some of the distinctive and powerful dynamics which add rhetorical impact when people access Scripture from memory. This shift to the topic of rhetorical impact will set the stage for the following chapter, which deals with the role of Scripture in Theophilus's ancient rhetoric. But first, we must consider criteria which can indicate memory recollection of Scripture.

Some of these criteria surface in Skarsaune's account of the pattern of Scripture usage in first- and second-century Christianity.[30] He observes that short lengths of uses of the OT books in late-second-century Christian writings are typical of the uses of OT passages in the NT. Indeed most of these uses of Scripture are allusions rather than formal quotations. Thus, late-second-century Christians were like the NT writers, who alluded to OT passages three times as often as they formally quoted them. By contrast, mid-second-century Christians used OT Scripture mostly in the form of formal quotations of select passages. These select OT passages composed the early- and mid-second-century Christian OT proof-text tradition. These Christian proof-text-tradition uses of OT Scripture were fairly long as compared with first-century and late-second-century Christian uses of the OT, frequently more than five verses in length. Skarsaune explains these patterns by considering the media through which the Scriptures were transmitted to Justin Martyr. It may be that Justin relied on Septuagint manuscripts of each OT book that he quoted. However, Skarsaune shows that Justin actually relied on Septuagint scrolls only for *certain* biblical books. In addition to these book-length biblical manuscripts, Skarsaune shows that Justin also used quotations of OT passages found in the writings of other Christian authors, either in apologetic ones, or in testimonia collections (typically, anthologies of certain biblical quotations), or most likely, in a collection of small exegetical tracts. Each exegetical tract would have been composed of a single Scripture quotation followed by a brief exposition.[31]

What could be the reason for these patterns? Skarsaune explains that first-century Christian writers tended to be Jewish Christians who were equipped with a comprehensive understanding of the Hebrew Scriptures, and thus supported their arguments with a wide and rich variety of OT citations and allusions. However, early- and mid-second-century Gentile converts to Christianity possessed a relatively shallow grasp of the Hebrew Scriptures. Accordingly, their biblical citations and allusions tended to

---

30. Skarsaune, "From Books to Testimonies." This essay is based largely on his ground-breaking monograph about Justin Martyr's use of OT Scripture. See Skarsaune, *Proof from Prophecy*.

31. Skarsaune, "From Books to Testimonies," 207, 217.

include extensive use of a select number of Christian proof-texts, but only light use of biblical passages outside of traditional proof-texts. They copied those few non-proof-text uses of Scripture from whatever few biblical manuscripts they possessed. Moreover, they typically used relatively long quotations from these complete manuscripts. Skarsaune labels this period, when Gentile Christians were forced to rely on a Christian proof-text tradition mostly preserved in biblical anthologies or in written testimony sources for their access to OT Scripture, the "period of testimonies." However by the late second century and beyond, Irenaeus, Origen and Christian writers who followed attained extensive knowledge of the Hebrew Scriptures. They were similar to the first-century Jewish Christian writers who made masterful use of the entirety of the OT with abundant use of short biblical quotations, allusions, and reminiscences freely produced from memory.

This principle, that a wide variety of uses of Scripture, all of fairly short length, indicates their free recollection from memory, finds confirmation in a 2002 study by McIver and Carroll.[32] They use methodology borrowed from experimental psychology to construct memory experiments in order to determine textual clues that indicate whether a text has been reconstructed from memory, or whether the source text was copied. They argue that transmission via memory without recourse to copying indeed accurately reproduces the macro-meaning, although usually not the micro-meaning, that is, the words.[33] And they find that if sixteen or more words are accurately reproduced, then copying rather than memory transmission is indicated.[34]

Theophilus, by his own admission, converted to Christianity after encountering the writings of the prophets.[35] Moreover, he came to this faith and then became the head of one of the most important churches of the world at a time when Gentile Christians were beginning to attain the kind of extensive, deep, and memory-rich knowledge of the OT also seen in first-century Jewish Christians.

We can verify this by subjecting his uses of the OT to criteria that Skarsaune, McIver, and Carroll used in their penetrating studies.[36] The statistics

---

32. McIver and Carroll, "Existence of Written Sources," 667–87.

33. Ibid., 687.

34. However, if certain genres such as poetry, music, or aphorisms are transmitted orally, longer strings of words can typically be accurately transmitted via memory without recourse to copying.

35. *Autol.* 1.14.

36. My argument in this chapter implies that Theophilus easily straddled the worlds of the highly-literate and illiterate in Antioch, ministering biblical insights to both groups. He was extremely proficient both textually and orally. Accordingly, I reject the

and terminology for Theophilus's uses of the OT in what follows come from the Scripture usage tables in the appendices. As I noted earlier in this chapter, these tables were generated using the same type of comprehensive and objective word-count measures used by Ernest.[37] Now we turn to criteria used by Skarsuane, McIver and Carroll for assessing memory recollection of Scripture.

Percentage of Allusions and Reminiscences

While first-century Jewish Christians and late-second-century Gentile Christians knew the OT extensively enough by memory that the majority of their uses of it were by way of allusion and reminiscence, Justin and other Gentile Christians in the "period of testimonies" relied predominately on citations and formal quotations that they copied from manuscripts. When this generation used the OT, allusions and reminiscences were in the minority. But by contrast, the majority of Theophilus's uses of the OT are allusions and reminiscences, 149, or 63% of the total OT uses. This is a nearly two-to-one (2/1) ratio of using the OT by way of allusions and reminiscences over quotations and citations. Furthermore, this two-to-one ratio could be even higher since many of his citations may very well be allusive in nature given the short lengths of many of them. As I argue quite extensively in chapter 4, his use of Scripture was central to his ancient judicial rhetorical strategy. That strategy simply demanded extensive use of OT citations. Indeed, direct examination of all of Theophilus's OT citations reveals that only two out of his sixty six OT citations were not citations demanded by the specific judicial rhetoric which I demonstrate in chapter 4 that he used throughout virtually every portion of his three letters to Autolycus. Where he copied these from biblical manuscripts, it does not seem any way necessary that he did so out of lacking memory awareness of the given passages. Rather, it is quite plausible that like any good courtroom advocate, he strove to represent the words of his friendly witnesses as accurately as he could. This was simply a judicial rhetorical requirement. But even if not, his two to one preference for alluding or reminiscing over citing or quoting is impressive enough. By all of these measures, Theophilus is closer to Irenaeus and Origen with their rich stores of memorized OT Scripture than to Justin who relied strictly on

---

"Great Divide" theory that assumes that oral and written media are absolutely distinct and disconnected at a fundamental level. My use of McIver and Carroll's criteria for detecting memorized texts should not be taken to imply otherwise, not only since memorizing is distinct from communicating, but also since both literate and illiterate memorized.

37. See the "Verbal Parallels with Scripture" section earlier in this chapter.

written biblical manuscripts when he ventured beyond the narrow set of passages of the proof-text tradition described by Skarsuane.

Furthermore, even where Theophilus quoted the OT, most of his OT quotations were quite short, typical of memorized phrases. If we recall McIver and Carroll's finding based partly on methodologies borrowed from experimental psychology that that if sixteen or more words are accurately reproduced, then copying rather than memory transmission is indicated, it would not be implausible to think that even most of Theophilus's OT quotations were from memory.[38] If so, his memory recollection of OT Scripture would be much higher than the two-to-one ratio indicated by my usage database analysis akin to Ernest's analysis of Athanasius. But even though this is plausible, in reality Theophilus's memory recollection of OT Scripture is probably not greater than that ratio, given that twenty seven of his 149 OT allusions and reminiscences are from Genesis and occur within his "commentary" on the early chapters of Genesis in his second letter. If on the one hand, the great majority of his OT quotations were short enough to be nearly allusions, well under the sixteen word measure discovered by McIver and Carroll that delimits when one can be reasonably sure that a text has been copied from a manuscript, then on the other hand, we must acknowledge that twenty seven out of his 149 OT allusions and reminiscences could have been copied from his Genesis manuscript. He likely needed it to copy his three long, paragraph-length quotations from Genesis in his "commentary."[39]

Lengths of Uses of OT Scripture

Only five of Theophilus's OT quotations, a mere 19% of his total OT quotations are sixteen words or longer. We recall that McIver and Carroll discovered that accurate and precise quotations sixteen words or longer in length are copied from manuscripts rather than recalled from memory, so long as the quotations are not poetry, music, or aphorisms.

By these objective criteria, it is not hard to see that most of Theophilus's uses of the OT were typical of first- or late-second-century Christian use of the OT, typical of those who knew the OT well, and recalled it easily, and not the formal, lengthy quotations of early and mid-second-century Gentile Christians who were relatively unfamiliar with the OT.

---

38. After inspecting the scripture usage tables in the appendices, it is easy to see that the great majority of Theophilus's quotations are quite short.

39. For details of the three long Genesis quotations and the surrounding OT uses, see the tables in the appendices.

This tendency is well illustrated in *Autol.* 1.11–13. This portion was not devoted to formal exegesis. Rather, Theophilus occupied himself with answering objections concerning emperor-worship, the name "Christian," and the concept of resurrection. The two quotations in this portion of his letter are arguably unintentional quotations, since he wove them smoothly and almost unnoticeably into his discourse. The only certain intentional use of an inspired text is the one citation of Prov 24:21–22. The other ten uses of inspired texts were not explicitly referenced by Theophilus. They are mere patches of language which quietly slipped into his discussion. Most uses of inspired texts in *Autol.* 1.11–13 are compositional, and half of these compositional uses of inspired texts are allusions.

One might object that *Autol.* 1.11–13 may so illustrate his easy and almost unconscious use of allusions, but a portion devoted to formal exegesis, such as *Autol.* 2.9–33, would not display allusions so abundantly. Indeed, they are not as abundant in *Autol.* 2.9–33, but neither are they insignificant. Almost 40% of all uses of the inspired texts in *Autol.* 2.9–33 are allusions. So even in this portion devoted to formal exegesis, where we would not be surprised if there were no biblical allusions at all but only quotations and citations, *even here* we find that nearly half of Theophilus's uses of Scripture are allusions. These allusions are compositional, woven into the discussion in many cases probably unintentionally. Here it is good to note Gianbiagio Conte's argument that allusions transmit a "poetic memory" which may not even be noticed by the writer.[40] Accordingly, it is quite reasonable to see Theophilus as being like the late-second-century Christian writers whom Skarsuane describes who were so familiar with the words and phrases of the Scriptures that these became part of their very language. As a result, he and his Christian audience enjoyed the sophisticated and rhetorically striking mental dynamics connected to use of allusions and ancient mimetic recollection.[41]

What of the NT? I have focused on the OT above in order to draw a contrast between Theophilus and a mid-second-century Christian such as Justin so as to show that Theophilus came upon the scene when the age of testimonies was beginning to fade and abundant memory recollection of the OT was beginning to rise. But let us consider now whether these fairly

---

40. For details of Conte's concept of "poetic memory," see the following section, "Dynamics of Allusions and Allusive Echoes."

41. There surely was a Christian audience, since the letters to Autolycus were preserved by Christians from ancient times. There would have been good reason for Theophilus's Christian audience to appreciate the letters. As Aune notes, ancient protreptic works were useful to groups associated with those works in defining their self-identity. See Aune, "Apologetic literature," in *Early Christian Literature*, 52.

objective criteria from the studies of Skarsuane, McIver, and Carroll can show us any difference between the degree that Theophilus recalled the Hebrew Scriptures from memory and the degree that he recalled from memory what was later called NT Scripture.

Percentage of Allusions and Reminiscences

There is an intriguing difference in how Theophilus used NT passages as compared with OT ones. Whereas for the OT, the majority of Theophilus's uses of the OT are allusions and reminiscences, 149, or 63% of his total OT uses, a nearly two-to-one ratio; for the NT his uses of allusions and reminiscences are slightly in the minority. He used only twenty two, or 46% of his total NT uses by way of allusion and reminiscence. This is so partly because he quoted NT texts more than OT ones. Whereas only 12% of his OT uses of Scripture are in the form of quotations, fully 30% of his NT uses of Scripture are quotations. Might this suggest use of a Q document for some of them? It may be so. But the following discussion of the lengths of his quotations of NT Scripture will show that even most of his NT quotations may well have been memorized.

Lengths of Uses of NT Scripture

The average length of Theophilus's uses of OT passages outside of his "Genesis commentary" in *Autol.* 2.2–31 is eight words in length. By comparison, the average length of his uses of NT passages is five words in length. Only five of his OT quotations (19% of his total OT quotations) are sixteen words or longer. But no NT quotation anywhere is sixteen words or longer. We recall that McIver and Carroll discovered that accurate and precise quotations sixteen words or longer in length are likely to be copied from manuscripts rather than recalled from memory, so long as the quotations are not poetry, music, or aphorisms. Theophilus appears to have largely recalled his NT quotations from memory based on these indications, and probably recalled his allusions and reminiscences from memory to an even greater degree.

Since the evidence we have seen gives good reason to understand that Theophilus recalled many of biblical passages easily from memory, especially in the case of NT texts, it is not inappropriate to consider the unique and potent intellectual dynamics which activate when people recall Scripture by memory. Therefore, in the remainder of this chapter, I will discuss these dynamics by reference to some specific examples of them in *Ad Autolycum*. But to better understand these examples, we must first remind ourselves of some new scholarly perspectives on the nature and power of memory recollection of Scripture.

New Perspectives on Allusions

Elizabeth A. Clark and other scholars have noted that scholarly consensus has now swung away from an older tendency to categorize patristic interpretations of Scripture into simple categories such as "literal," "typological," and "allegorical."[42] A generation ago, Protestant scholars, such as G. W. H. Lampe, and Roman Catholic scholars, such as Jean Daniélou, characterized typology as historical and allegory as non-historical. Typology was understood to have originated from Palestinian Jewish exegesis, while allegory was thought to have developed in Alexandria with its Hellenistic influences. However, Henri de Lubac criticized the use of labels such as "typology" or "allegory" in this older research, since the church fathers themselves did not use them, and because he argued that interpretations by Origen traditionally categorized as allegory can be shown to fit Daniélou's definition of typology.[43] R. P. C. Hanson similarly argued that allegorical interpretation in the church fathers actually derived from Palestine rather than from Alexandria, as previously thought. Like Lubac, Hanson also argued that the division between typology and allegory is not as clean as older students of patristic exegesis had believed. Similarly, Jean Pépin showed that various biblical interpretations traditionally categorized as typological are instead allegorical. Henri Crouzel and Andrew Louth also contributed to a new conviction that the distinction between typological exegesis and allegorical exegesis would be foreign to the church fathers themselves, being rather a result of modern assumptions.[44] Additional light comes from Wilken, who

42. Clark, *Reading Renunciation*, 73–76.

43. Potterie enumerates the contributions by Lubac in helping scholars better understand the "spiritual exegesis" exemplified by Origen and his followers, and its implications for current exegetical practices. See Potterie, "Le sens spirituel de l'Écriture." This new view of spiritual exegesis transcends earlier and cruder understandings of exegesis performed by Origen and his followers. See also Martens, "Origen on the Reading of Scripture"; Martens, "Revisiting the Allegory/Typology Distinction"; Martens, *Origen and Scripture*.

44. Crouzel argues that while scholars have assumed that allegorism is foreign to authentic Christian revelation and that allegorical exegesis is an impurity contributed by Hellenism, in reality mere typology, as commonly conceived, is inadequate for describing biblical content dealing with heavenly eternal realities. Furthermore, symbolic representation, such as comes into play in allegorical exegesis, is essential for the religious perception of God. The infinite, eternal God cannot be entirely known, but is partially revealed by means of symbols. The modern distinction between typology and

shows that the older stereotype that Jews in late antiquity tended towards historical interpretation of the Hebrew Scriptures while the early Christians tended to allegorize them is indeed historically flawed. He argues that while Jewish exegetes often resorted to a historical rather than futurist interpretation of OT prophecies, this was typically a polemical maneuver against early Christian exegesis.[45] In truth, neither Jewish nor Christian exegesis in late antiquity was done in the solitude of the study, but was performed in an environment of religious contest. Jews also offered futurist interpretations, as reports from Justin and Jerome indicate. Wilken argues that the difference between early Jewish and early Christian exegesis of prophetic texts such as Isaiah 2 and Micah 4 is a difference in understanding of divine promises, and not a difference between whether one favored only the original historical sense of the text. He observes that early Christians did not reject a literal reading of prophetic texts because they favored the allegorical sense rather than the historical sense. Rather, *both* they *and* their Jewish contemporaries read the text in light of their own experience and historical position. Early Christians understood the Christ event as the fulfillment of texts like Isaiah 2 and Micah 4. They thus considered their own interpretations to be truly historical interpretations rather than non-historical allegories. As Wilken puts it, "Paradoxically, in the language of early Christian exegesis, the spiritual sense *was* the historical sense."[46] Because of these weaknesses of the older practices of simply distinguishing between typological and allegorical exegesis, scholars of patristic exegesis are now beginning to focus rather on how figurative readings of Scripture specifically function in patristic texts. Accordingly, this present study does not focus primarily on modern, artificial distinctions between literal, typological, and allegorical exegesis, or on modern categories such as "allusion" (although I will discuss allusions rather extensively as a preliminary step before moving away from modern categories and on to ancient ones) but rather on how Theophilus used the inspired texts according to reading strategies and rhetorical strategies which would have been recognized in his own day.

These ancient practices have received attention especially in a few recent scholarly perspectives concerning biblical allusions. Although "allusion" is a modern category of use of Scripture, these recent perspectives about allusions have nonetheless alerted scholars to the value of understanding use of Scripture in ways which the ancients themselves would have

---

allegory is artificial. It is too sharply drawn, and these categories are conceived too simplistically as compared with how figurative language actually functions in Scripture. See Crouzel, "Distinction de la 'typologie' et de l'allégorie.'"

45. Wilken, "*In novissimus diebus.*"
46. Ibid., 19.

recognized. So then these new perspectives on the modern category of allusion will prepare the stage in advance for our overviews of Scripture in *Ad Autolycum* which rely on ancient categories. And furthermore, these new perspectives also show the vital dynamics which play when biblical texts are accessed from memory rather than from consulting written biblical manuscripts. We will see that these dynamics associated with memory recollection of Scripture also activated in Theophilus's day, for ancient writers valued and championed even unconscious memory recollection of Scripture. So it is important to consider these new perspectives on the power of allusions, literary echoes, and memory recollection of Scripture. To these recent perspectives on allusion we now turn.

Importance of Allusions

There is sometimes a modern tendency to minimize the role of allusions of Scripture and to focus exclusively upon biblical quotations and citations. But refreshingly, this is not always the case. For example, Philippe Bacq argues for the importance of allusions in his study of the fourth book of Irenaeus's *Adversus haereses*.[47] By Irenaeus's own admission, the words of the Lord set the framework for the book. Accordingly, Bacq's analyzes Irenaeus's Jesus citations and other biblical passages that related to them.[48] Bacq notes in his analysis that most studies of patristic use of Scripture tend to distinguish between explicit citations, and simple allusions containing two or more words of a biblical text. He shows that while this distinction makes for easy categorization of how biblical texts are used, it ignores Irenaeus's actual polemical concerns.

Therefore, Bacq proposes a different distinction. "Key citations" are those biblical passages which exactly express a point Irenaeus wished to make, and serve to summarize a certain portion of his argument. "Supporting citations" are references to biblical texts which complement, support, and complete an argument built on key citations.[49] Approaches like Bacq's challenge the modern assumption that simple allusions are less important uses of Scripture than explicit quotations. This assumption sometimes obscures a patristic author's argument. Bacq provides an example: Irenaeus in his *Against Heresies* 4.1.1 made a simple allusion to Matt 23:9, a passage which Bacq, following Rousseau, identifies as the key giving thematic unity to the argument of 4.1.1–2 against Gnostic ideas that there are multiple

47. Bacq, *Alliance selon S. Irénée*.
48. Ibid., 18–19.
49. Ibid., 19.

heavenly fathers. Irenaeus alluded again to this biblical text in order to signal the conclusion of this argument.[50]

Bacq also observes that Irenaeus sometimes used "hook words" (also known as "link words") which link either biblical citations, or sub-points in a larger argument.[51] This practice of using link words to organize uses of Scripture was not unique to the second century. As suggested by later rabbinic tradition, early rabbis may have used it.[52] Paul of Tarsus used it in Rom 15:9–12, when he successively quoted Ps 17:49, Deut 32.43, Ps 116:1, and Isa 11:10. All these quotations are linked by cognates of "Gentile" (ἔθνος). The practice of joining texts by use of link words was even common in pagan Greco-Roman literature.[53]

Theophilus also used link words. It was one of the prominent ways that he wove together masses of biblical allusions into his discussion. Indeed, the link words served as spurs to his memory, helping him recall passage after passage which shared common link words. We find a prime example at the end of *Autol.* 1.5 where Theophilus reminded Autolycus that an earthly king is taken to exist even by people who do not personally see the king, because the laws and works of the king make his existence evident. This prepared the stage for Theophilus's application of this principle for the benefit of Autolycus, when he shifted the focus from earthly kings to the King of all.[54] Accordingly, *Autol.* 1.6–8 consists of rich networks of uses of inspired texts, taken mostly from texts in Job and Psalms which describe the power of God as Creator. Theophilus may have recalled Paul of Tarsus' similar discussion here. Paul engaged the same apologetic motif in his response to a crowd composed of worshippers of Zeus who wanted to offer sacrifices to Barnabas and himself as recorded in Acts 14. Paul declared to the crowd that there is only one true God. This one true God is he who created heaven and earth and seas and all creatures, and who kindly sends rain and crops and food. Theophilus likewise discussed the creative and providential work of the one true God in *Autol.* 1.6. Just as Paul discussed divine creation and providential care by means of the physical heavens, Theophilus did also. He tied together multiple biblical reminiscences by means of strings of link words related to the splendor of the physical heavens, such as "light" (φῶς),

50. Ibid., 19–20.

51. Ibid., 20.

52. In later rabbinic tradition, variety of midrash called *gezerah shewa* involved comparing passages containing a common link word in order to draw analogies. See Bacher and Lauterbach, "Talmud Hermeneutics," in *Jewish Encyclopedia*, 11:30–33.

53. Hays, *Echoes of Scripture*, 13.

54. *Autol.* 1.6–8. Theophilus offered Autolycus a second opportunity to perceive God by means of perceiving his laws, in *Autol.* 3.15.

and "treasuries" (θησαυροί) and by means of language referring to particular stars and various celestial phenomena.

This was not the only instance of his weaving multiple allusions together using link words. While the first two paragraphs of *Autol.* 1.7 in Grant's edition are separated on the basis of a topical difference, yet on closer examination we find a unity joining these paragraphs together. The first paragraph deals with God the Creator and providential ruler, while the second concerns Autolycus' blindness and its cure. Yet these two paragraphs are sewn together into one unit by lexical threads. These threads run through link words consisting of creation terms, such as "heaven" (οὐρανός), "heavens" (οὐρανοί), "earth" (γῆ), "sea" (θάλασσα), "waters" (ὕδατα), and "waves" (κῦμα). These link words lie only within inspired texts which he used rather than through any of his surrounding commentary.

Autol. 3.11 is also notable for its reliance on link words. All five passages cited, Isa 55:6–7; Ezek 18:21–23; Isa 31:6; 45:22 and Jer 6:9, contain a form of the verb, "to turn" or "to convert" (ἀποστρέφειν). This verb unites the citations, and also unites a conflation of two passages. And we will see that Theophilus used link words to join biblical text quotations and allusions elsewhere as well.

And in *Autol.* 3.13, Theophilus engaged in rich keyword liking of Prov 4:25–26 and 6:27–29. While Prov 6:27–29 clearly concerns adultery, as indicated by its local context in Proverbs 6, and by the mention of a neighbor's wife, Prov 4:25–26 itself does not. But the analogy in Prov 6:28 of walking on hot coals links that passage with Prov 4:26, through the key words of τροχιά, "paths," in Prov 4.26 and περιπατήσει, "would one walk," and πόδας, "feet," in Prov 6:28. And the parallels of imagery and verbal similarity create the kind of pleasing rhythms recommended to orators.[55]

Link words functioned as spurs to his memory. Through these, streams of recollected Scripture poured forth, when the link word in one allusion suggested to him another passage containing the same or a related link word. This process of suggesting biblical texts with the same or related link words then cascaded spontaneously, again and again. Once the initial link word squeezed forth, other instances of it followed, like floodwaters enlarging a crack in a dam, each wave easing the way for others following. After the initial use of a link word, floodwaters of biblical recollection gathered in his mind and burst through the initial crack. Biblical link words thus informed and unified his protreptic arguments. But there was even more in Theophilus's use of biblical allusions than use of link words. He also engaged in what has come to be called "literary echo."

---

55. Dionysius of Halicarnassus, *De compositione verborum* 7, 9.

Literary Echo: the Power of Scripture in a Highly-Illiterate Culture

Now we will peer even deeper into the orality of first- and second-century Christianity. In this world, allusions abounded. And allusions had great emotive and persuasive power, even ones containing few or no actual words from the biblical texts to which they refer, allusions that are more reminiscences than allusions per se. New Testament scholar Richard B. Hays sheds light for us in this regard. Hays emphasizes the power of literary allusions and reminiscences of Scripture through the concept of literary echo. He sees much of the NT guild at an impasse, seeking to explain Paul's use of Scripture in radically divergent ways, each shaped by differing theological pre-commitments, or else, simply ignoring the issue. With his background in English literature and literary theory, Hays notices that scholars of early modern poetry wrestling with analogous problems have been able to advance knowledge about literary allusions and reminiscences through inter-textuality theory. He harnesses their sensitivities in order to break the impasse. But his approach can also aid investigations of how Scripture functioned for early Christian apologists.

While he acknowledges that the term "inter-textuality" denotes differing dynamics and associated methodologies within literary criticism, Hays consciously adopts the narrow but quite fruitful approach to inter-textuality of John Hollander.[56] Hollander shows that the concept of literary echo can be traced not only in recent literature, but also in renaissance literature, and even ancient Greco-Roman literature.[57] What sets a literary echo apart from an allusion in Hollander's thinking is that an allusion requires authorial intent, while an echo of a source text in a later text can be unintended by an author.[58]

In the present study, I am not concerned about strictly distinguishing between allusions and echoes in every case, since Theophilus may sometimes have intentionally alluded to a passage secure in the knowledge that many in his Christian audience would recognize the allusion.[59] In other cases, as I will argue below, he was not conscious of echoing a biblical text, but was so shaped by Scripture that he did so nevertheless. Much of the time, we simply cannot know his mind. Of course, the multiple audiences of *Ad Autolycum*: Autolycus, other pagans like him, and the Christians of

---

56. Hollander, *Figure of Echo*.

57. See Hollander's lengthy appendix.

58. Ibid., 99.

59. I use the same criteria that Hays uses for identifying echoes. Various NT scholars agree with Hays that his satisfaction criteria is particularly helpful. See Hays, *Echoes of Scripture*, 29–33; Hicks, "Markan Discipleship," 183.

Antioch, complicate the issues of authorial intent and audience recognition of alluded texts. All the more reason to use the terms "allusion" and "echo" somewhat interchangeably.[60]

Hollander demonstrates in rich detail how a literary echo may but need not mimic the exact phrasing of a prior text. It could alternately mimic the mental imagery, aural effects, or even simply the mere verbal rhythm combined with only a slight hint of the imagery or language of a prior text.[61] Such echoes are often subtle and ghostly rather than garish and obvious. Hays brings Hollander's insights about literary echo to the letters of Paul, emphasizing especially their ironic, creative nature.[62] That is, an echo may quote only a short phrase from an older text, but the logic of the new text depends on remembering the unquoted portions of the older text. Furthermore, as Hollander shows, great writers do not merely and slavishly mimic prior works, and do not laboriously cite them. Rather, they delicately mimic portions of them, but also creatively transform the senses of what is mimicked, often in ironic ways, thus creating the echoes.[63] While literary echoes may ignore or violate the original senses of quoted portions, these moves are actually required for ironic and rhetorical effect when writers either drive readers to understand classic texts more deeply, or when they echo classic texts in the course of expressing original thoughts.

We see echoes in several places in Theophilus's letters to Autolycus. For example, there is only one biblical passage used in *Autol.* 1.2, in the form of a quotation of a mere five words from 2 Cor 7:1. Yet the argument in *Ad Autolycum* at this point draws support from nearby verses in 2 Corinthians which Theophilus did not see the need to quote explicitly, but which nonetheless resound through the spontaneous memory dynamic that literary echo entails. The "every defilement" (παντὸς μολυσμοῦ) of 2 Cor 7:1 was for Theophilus two things. First, it was the kind of ethical failing he had enumerated just before his use of 2 Cor 7:1, such as adultery, fornication, theft, swindling, and the like. And secondly, it was the taint of idolatry described in 2 Cor 6:15–18, which sounds by way of literary echo. This echo fits perfectly with his aim of awakening Autolycus to the true God, so that he might forsake the false gods of wood, stone, and metal, which Theophilus had just mentioned in *Autol.* 1.1.

---

60. For somewhat similar reasons, Hays also uses these terms interchangeably. See Hays, *Echoes of Scripture*, 29.

61. Hollander, *Figure of Echo*, 95–96.

62. Hays, *Echoes of Scripture*, 20.

63. Hollander helpfully provides technical terms for this creative and ironic violation of the original context, which he derives from Greco-Roman sources: *metalepsis* (Greek) or *transumption* (based on the Latin term). See Hollander, *Figure of Echo*, 114.

CAPSTONE EXAMPLE: A COMPREHENSIVE TREATMENT OF THE BOOK OF JOB IN THEOPHILUS'S EXTANT WRITINGS

To perceive how very richly Scripture functions in a largely-oral culture such as that of second-century Antioch (while acknowledging that Theophilus himself surely could read and write), consider for example his little two-page argument for the reality of God from the witness of creation in his first letter (not to be confused with his lengthy Genesis exposition in his second letter). Knowing that here he explicitly claimed to provide a proof from creation, we have good reason to wonder how the foundational creation account of Genesis plays in his proof.[64] Considering only references to biblical quotations and allusions which are so obvious that they are noticed in both Marcovich's critical edition and in Biblia patristica (which I do throughout), we are surprised to find *no* quotation or allusion to Genesis whatsoever, anywhere in the argument from creation![65] But if there are no quotations or allusions whatsoever to the Genesis creation account, nevertheless there seem to be reminiscences of it, beginning with the final phrase of the introductory opening lines. Theophilus described the orderly movement of the stars and "the orderly succession of days and nights and months and years."[66] Here we find remembrances of the fourth creation day when God created the stars and of first creation day of Genesis in which God created the day and the night which henceforth would proceed in orderly alternation. Then appear seven lines where Theophilus brought to mind the animals and fish created during the third and fifth creation days. Next appear two lines mentioning springs, rivers, and seasonal dews and rains. These words only faintly recall the seasons marked off by the lights of the fourth day and the gathering together of the waters during the third day of creation. Then in the following two lines, he described the complex motions of famous objects of the night sky including Venus, the Pleiades star cluster, Orion, and the star Arcturus. Here we might hear a faint echo of the stars and other lights in the expanse of the sky created during the fourth day. And yet, these faint reminiscences of Genesis leave us rather unsatisfied. For one thing, out of the 73 lines composing Theophilus's argument from creation in

---

64. He makes the claim in *Autol.* 1.6.1. For the location of the proof from creation argument within *Autol.* 1.6–8 based on those rhetorical expectations which would have been familiar to Theophilus and his audience, and for a rediscovery of the logical coherence of *Ad Autolycum* at both a high and detailed level, see the following chapter.

65. Marcovich, *Theophili Antiocheni*. Marcovich provides a notably rich biblical index. Biblical citations in this present study follow the numeration of the LXX.

66. Citation line numbers refer to those of Grant's Greek text.

Grant's Greek text, these faint echoes of Genesis compose only 11 of them. To their credit, they are compacted tightly together at the beginning of the argument, but then the majority of the argument seems to wander away from Genesis entirely into remembrances of other biblical books. Not only so, but the recollections of the creation days are jumbled, passing from day four, to day one, to day three, to day five, only to terminate back in day four again. And there is really no recollection of the second creation day anywhere. We might have expected Theophilus's argument from creation to draw heavily from Genesis one or perhaps from Romans one. But alas, it seems he had other texts in mind.

One of these was the account of Job. The faint reminiscences of Genesis which we have considered end with a mention of the star Arcturus. But this evidently brings to mind Job 9:9 where the star is mentioned also, for only five lines later, Theophilus alluded again to Job 9:9, this time by his phrase "storehouses of the south wind." Job nine seems to have lingered in the back of his mind, for a paragraph later he alluded to Job 9:8 by his phrase "spread out the heaven." But this was a compositional use of Scripture, for he combined this portion of Job 9:8 with an even longer portion from Job 38:18. But these four brief snippets from Job do not even begin to reveal how much this book of wisdom literature has influenced Theophilus's apology. Like the tip of an iceberg that gives only a hint of the enormous bulk hidden below the surface, these four snippets of biblical text signal to us that the real reception of Scripture in Theophilus's argument from creation is hidden just out of view.

Theophilus's conflation of Job 9:8 and 38:18 shimmers with biblical imagery but in a deceptively subtle way. Initially, we are tempted to assume that he selected these phrases of biblical creation language rather haphazardly. But closer examination reveals that by joining these two, he brought to mind Moses' distinctive idiom of God's creation (which John appropriated in his apocalypse to create what later came to be a canonical inclusio of the beginning and end of time and of the world). Theophilus conflated a phrase from an early Job chapter describing God creating the heaven with one from the end of Job describing divine creation of what is under heaven. Here then is the language of the first verse of Genesis, "In the beginning God created the heavens and the earth." And as Sailhamer shows, nearly every time the Pentateuch mentions the cosmos, it does so using the words of the Mosaic idiom "the heaven and the earth," which is to say, "the heaven and what lies beneath."[67] Theophilus echoed the imagery of the Mosaic idiom rather than

---

67. See Sailhamer, *Genesis Unbound*. While Sailhamer's exegesis of Genesis may seem novel and radical compared with typical modern interpretations, it is actually a modern analog of a prominent, long-enduring Medieval Jewish interpretation of the

the words themselves.[68] But literary echoes function so often on the basis of imagery rather than verbal correspondence, as Hollander has shown.[69] While the details of Genesis do not resonate in Theophulus' argument from creation, the foundational Mosaic creation idiom does.

Whereas the echoes of Genesis ring sparsely in a disorganized buzz, jumbling the chronology of the creation week, the echoes of the Lord's speech in Job 38 emerge in a rich, absolutely chronological, and very detailed sequence. This melody commences in the very introductory lines of Theophilus's argument from creation, where he expounded on the orderly variations of the winds, and of the paths of the stars.[70] Here there is a faint ring of Job 38:1–7 with its language about the great wind out of which the Lord spoke, and of the creation of the stars. But here is also a harmonic echo of Job 9:7–8a and its imagery of God commanding the stars and heavens. Theophilus's discussion turns to God's provision of the waters, using echoes of Job 9:8b and 38:8–11 with their imagery of God treading on the waves of the sea, shutting up the sea behind gates, and clothing it with clouds and mist. Job 9:8a rings again two lines later in the argument where Theophilus's speech about celestial objects in the starry sky recalls the Job language of God spreading out the heavens.[71] But here also reverberates Job 38:12's image of the Lord commanding the morning light, resonating in Theophilus's similar image. And when he mentioned the morning star, Orion, and the Pleiades star cluster in subsequent lines, we sense a reverberation of the subsequent phrases of both Job 9 and 38, for they address these very same starry objects. Behind the central ostensible issue of Theophilus's letter, why Autolyus could not see God, sound Job 9:11 describing Job's frustration at being unable to see God and Job 38:15 describing light withheld from the wicked. Theophilus then echoed the Job star passages again. Job 38 continues with images of light and darkness, the great depths of the sea, the storehouses of the snow, the hail, and the south wind, and the terrifying violence of the rains and the thunder. Theophilus echoed *precisely the same sequence* of imagery as that of Job 38, with all elements in the very same chronological order.

Yet out of all of these copious resonances of Job, it is those carrying the speech of the Lord to Job that sound most loudly. This should not surprise

---

Hebrew text of Genesis.

68. I am not using this Mosaic language to make any claims about Pentateuch authorship, for which readers may consult a vast literature.

69. Hollander, *Figure of Echo*, 67

70. *Autol.* 1.6.2.

71. *Autol.* 1.6.12.

us. Here is another instance of the privileging of the voice of the Lord in Scripture that Kannengiesser noticed in Irenaeus.[72] He observed that when Irenaeus represented Gnostic arguments he quoted narrative portions of Genesis, but when he expressed his own argument, in nearly every case, he used the voices of speakers in Genesis, especially that of the Lord. We might be tempted to think that this parallel between Theophilus and Irenaeus could be caused by a simple transmission of an exegetical tradition. After all, while scholarship has not followed Loof's argument that Irenaeus produced his *Adversus haereses* by importing, in a fairly thoughtless and uncreative way, ideas from Theophilus and from an unnamed presbyter, it has accepted Loofs' demonstration of how greatly Theophilus influenced Irenaeus's thinking about theology and about the interpretation of certain passages.[73] However, this cannot be a mere transmission of an exegetical tradition, since Theophilus echoed the voice of the Lord in Job while Irenaeus quoted the voice of the Lord in Genesis. That we find Theophilus also expressing his argument through the Lord's voice in Job signals that the tendency to privilege the voice of the Lord in Scripture was more widespread in the second century than previously suspected.

Considering that he exposited God's creation, why might Theophilus have had Job in view rather than the Genesis creation account? Perhaps the answer emerges when we consider Job's concern about seeing God. In one place Job complained about God, "Were he to pass beyond me, I would in no way see him; Were he to go past me, I would not know."[74] Later Job complained again, "When he acts on the left, I do not understand; he surrounds on the right, I do not see."[75] Elihu mirrored Job's concern, declaring about God, "He will conceal his face, and who will see him?"[76] Job demanded to *see* God. This is why Theophilus was using the account of Job to answer his pagan friend Autolycus' demand to see God. The demand to see God is essential for understanding Theophilus's first letter. It is obvious from Theophilus's explicit acknowledgment, both at the beginning of letter one and also again at the end, that he was responding to the demand

---

72. Kannengiesser, "The 'Speaking God,'" 337–52.

73. Loofs, *Theophilus von Antiochen Adversus Marcionem*; Hitchcock, "Loof's Theory of Theophilus of Antioch as a Source of Irenaeus"; Rousseau, "Plan du livre v."

74. Job 9:11.

75. Job 23:9.

76. Job 34:29. Elihu claimed explicitly to offer an argument differing from those of the first three friends. The Lord himself agreed with his point that Job sinned by justifying himself rather than God. Perhaps this is why Elihu was not rebuked by the Lord but the first three were.

by Autolycus to show his God.⁷⁷ Clearly, these acknowledgments create an instance of *inclusio* that encloses letter one and supplies its rhetorical and apologetic context. What it means to perceive God, and how this can be done, is precisely the question that the first letter answers. Autolycus' demand to see God runs throughout the letter as an insistent challenge. We find confirmation of this suspicion by considering again the first of Job's demands to see God in Job 9:11. Theophilus neither quoted not alluded to Job 9:11. But in his proof from creation, he alluded three times in close succession to one of its neighboring verses, as we have seen. Job's demand to see God in 9:11 lingered in Theophilus's mind with a persistence that he could never ignore, just as a new mother cannot bare to ignore the background cries of her hungry infant.

Where on the one hand, Elihu put Job into the shoes of a doubting mocker for justifying himself but not God, on the other hand, Theophilus put his doubting friend Autolycus into Job's shoes. When Autolycus demanded to see God, Theophilus knew he had a ready-made answer in the Scriptures. It was the answer that both Elihu and the Lord himself gave Job after Job made the very same demand. Theophilus recognized that the Lord's answer to faithful Job could also serve the doubtful pagan, Autolycus.

Not only for literary echoes but also for allusions, their non-obvious character adds a potent impact. When a passage is merely echoed or alluded to, rather than explicitly cited, biblically-informed readers and hearers are forced to engage in the process of locating the parallel in Scripture.⁷⁸ Theophilus's non-obvious allusions and echoes would have served as transient puzzles, carrying intrigue and delight, which his listeners could not leave untouched. This need for active intellectual engagement by readers surely endows allusions with greater literary power than citations. Perhaps this is why allusions are at least as important as quotations or citations for patristic writers, as Becq argues. So as to alert us more fully to the rich rhetorical impact of biblical allusions, some representative examples of literary echoes of Scripture in *Ad Autolycum* feature in this chapter.

Finkelpearl reminds us that the ancients truly valued unconscious recollection of classic texts.⁷⁹ She reminds us of Seneca's analogy of the bees.⁸⁰ Just as bees gather pollen from various flowers and then produce honey in a somewhat mysterious way, so aught a writer imitate various works, but not

---

77. *Autol.* 1.2; 1.14.

78. Hays, *Echoes of Scripture*, 23.

79. Finkelpearl, "Pagan Traditions of Intertextuality," in MacDonald, *Mimesis and Intertextuality*, 83.

80. Seneca, *Epistulae* 84.

simply by way of deliberate copying. Rather, a writer should gather textual insights along with one's own insights and brood on the mixture, allowing it to "ferment" over time. This involves not merely what is conscious and deliberate, but also what is sometimes unconscious, even mysterious since its details may not be completely understood.

We have seen early in this chapter an initial survey of Theophilus's use of Scripture in terms of modern literary categories. Just as sunrise exposes features of a previously-dark landscape, this survey alerted us to the prevalence of allusion in his writings. It thus provided us a helpful first step towards transcending our highly-literate culture's fixation on quotations of written texts.

We have also seen objective evidence for frequent memory recall of Scripture in Theophilus's world. To this end, I have used insights from Skarsaune, McIver and Carroll to show that Theophilus's heavy use of biblical allusions and reminiscences indicates that he had a deeper knowledge of Scripture than most early- and mid-second-century Christian writers, and that he could easily and even unconsciously access it from memory, often apart from strict and laborious reliance on written biblical texts. While early- and mid-second-century Christians often provided large blocks of biblical quotations hand-copied from biblical manuscripts of only some of the Hebrew Scriptures, he recalled many of his biblical texts from memory, as indicated by the typically short lengths of his many allusions, reminiscences, and even of most of his quotations.

Even as we have thus explored the role of memory in the life of Scripture in second-century Antioch, I have in no way attempted to supply a comprehensive treatment of orality and literacy there. Rather, my aim has been more limited: I have shown the inadequacy of the typical treatment of Scripture in early apologetic writings which attends only to full or partial *quotations* of Scripture. Tellingly, we would never have seen how deeply Job shaped Theophilus's little argument from creation if we only looked at full- and partial-biblical quotations. But if we want to take seriously the highly-illiterate setting of second-century Antioch, then we cannot merely deal with exact quotations of biblical phrases. We must go beyond, dealing also with literary echoes and reminiscences (which often recall biblical passages without quoting any phrases from them), the stuff of highly-oral cultures. We simply must look beyond the blinders of our own highly-literate, written-document-rich, modern culture with its demands for exact quotation, so that we can investigate how Scripture truly functioned in Antioch's oral culture. Indeed, we have seen in the little three-page argument for the existence of God from the witness of his creation, that although Theophilus only partially quoted Job a mere five times, this paucity of Job usage was actually just the "tip of the iceberg," and a massive iceberg at that. These few partial quotations acted as spurs which immediately and automatically brought to the minds of his illiterate but biblically-aware hearers a mass of biblical echoes of Job. These echoes comprise those dozens of remembrances of Job passages which remained unquoted but which are proximate to those few partially quoted portions. Upon this mass of unquoted remembrances rested the structure and details of Theophilus's argument for the existence of God. They, not the few fully- or partially-quoted portions of Job, determined the course and content of the argument.[81] Studies of patristic exegesis simply must take such realities seriously.

While these few examples of how unquoted Scripture echoed in Theophilus's world are not intended to provide a comprehensive treatment of biblical echoes in early apologetic writings, they *are* sufficient for justifying a call to research. Patristic studies simply *must* take far more seriously the illiteracy of the apologetic age and the rich ways that biblical allusions and reminiscences functioned in that age. In the largely-illiterate early Christian world, biblical *quotations* were not the main course of the biblical feast, merely a side-dish. All too frequently, studies of exegesis in the apologetic age taste from that side-dish, but leave the main course of that ancient, savory, biblical feast completely unnoticed, unappreciated, and untouched.

Even as an educated and highly literate bishop, Theophilus nonetheless operated skillfully in a world of high illiteracy, tapping into memory- and imagery-based effects that lent power to his appeals, for the benefit of both literate and illiterate alike. But another component of his intellectual world was his judicial rhetoric. It is a foreign rhetoric to us, because the modern age has forgotten it. Yet it can expose historical weaknesses of the typical stereotype of Theophilus as a disorganized and shallow thinker. To this we now turn.

---

81. While this biblically-rich argument for the existence of God may initially appear nonsensical, since we are tempted to wonder why people soaked in the Scriptures should need convincing that God exists, it ultimately emerges as a quite sensible argument. First, it would be natural for Theophilus, as a devotee of Scripture, to impacted by Scripture in his thinking. Second, even his biblically-enriched but illiterate hearers would appreciate knowing how to argue for the existence of God on the basis of an argument that was soaked in the biblical account of Job. They also were profoundly shaped by Scripture.

4

Scripture and a Forgotten Coherence

THE PROBLEM OF THE COHERENCE OF THEOPHILUS'S THOUGHT

To some, the order of topics in the three letters that Theophilus wrote to his friend Autolycus may appear haphazard, curious, incoherent, or simply less than adequate. Walter Bauer, reacting to Friedrich Loofs' high estimation of Theophilus as a theologian, states "To me, there is no comparison between the superior theologian Irenaeus and the shallow babbler of the *Apology to Autolycus*."[1] No less an authority on *Ad Autolycum* than Robert M. Grant remarked after describing its topical order, "Theophilus's arrangement of his materials thus leaves something to be desired, and his insistently didactic tone often fails to retain the reader's interest."[2] David Runia takes the same view of Theophilus's arrangement.[3] But this dissatisfaction with the arrangement of *Ad Autolycum* in Theophilus studies is surprising and suspect right from the start, given that ancient Greco-Roman education consistently and

---

1. Bauer, *Orthodoxy and Heresy*, 18n38.

2. Grant, *Ad Autolycum*, xi. Grant's "Scripture, Rhetoric and Theology in Theophilus," 33–45, deals with rhetoric in *Ad Autolycum* tangentially but helpfully. In retard to rhetoric, the focus of Grant's essay is on passages in 1.3 and 3.15 and on the Logos doctrine of the second letter, but specifically to illumine the theological and polemical setting of exegetical moves rather than to expose specific rhetorical τόποι or the overall rhetorical structures of the letters.

3. Runia, *Philo in Early Christian Literature*, 110.

strongly stressed arrangement (τάξις) of topics.⁴ We shall see that the arrangement of *Ad Autolycum* would actually have been well-appreciated by Theophilus's audience. It delivered precisely what they would have expected and admired.

While scholarship has begun to understand some other figures in the early church in deeper and more historically-informed ways through a renewed interest in ancient rhetoric which has transformed New Testament studies at the end of the twentieth century and which has begun to transform patristic studies, it has only examined Theophilus this way in a few small studies, none of which deals with his rhetorical moves in great detail. Perhaps this is why scholarship is typically (and unfortunately ahistorically) less than satisfied with his argument, and mis-characterizes it as being unfocused and even somewhat incoherent. In historical view, nothing could be further from the truth.

My aim here is to transcend this anachronistic picture of Theophilus. I want to make evident the very coherent arrangement of *Ad Autolycum*; to show the central and essential role of Scripture in its rhetoric; and against prior anachronistic views, to argue that carefully constructed and highly effective rhetorical structures underlie each of the three letters of *Ad Autolycum* and even pervade their every detail. Scholarship has not yet appreciated this kind of detailed rhetorical analysis of Theophilus's writings, but such is mandatory for a true historical understanding.

ANCIENT RHETORICAL HANDLING OF TEXTUAL WITNESSES

What exactly did the ancients expect when their orators used authoritative texts? Recent scholarship has helped us answer this question. Margaret M. Mitchell argues that patristic exegetes were not trained to read texts in predominantly literal or predominantly allegorical ways, contra impressions from some textbook descriptions of Bible use in the early church.⁵ Rather, they learned a range of classical manners of speaking which enabled them to present their cases effectively, either in the courts or lecture halls. Accord-

---

4. Cf. *Rhetorica Ad Herennium* 1.2.3; 3.8.16–10.18; Aristotle, Τέχνη ῥητορική 3.13–19.

5. Mitchell, "Biblical Interpretation as a Trial." She presents a later version of this study in Greer and Mitchell, *The "Belly-Myther" of Endor*. Other important works which look in ancient rhetoric and philology for keys for understanding patristic exegesis include Young, *Formation of Christian Culture*; Schäublin, *Methode und Herkunft der antiochenischen Exegese*; Clark, *Reading Renunciation*; Dawson, *Allegorical Readers*; and Mitchell, *Heavenly Trumpet*.

ingly, when they discussed biblical passages, they often put Greco-Roman judicial rhetorical techniques into play.⁶ For example, Mitchell shows that the fourth-century argument of Eustathius of Antioch against the exegesis of 1 Samuel 28 by Origen of Alexandria, often regarded as a prime example of dichotomy between an Antioch school of interpretation and an Alexandrian one, branded Origen as a foolish allegorist, even though it can be shown that Eustathius actually allegorized 1 Samuel 28 to a greater extent than did Origen. In other words, she shows that the familiar Alexandrian/Antiochene dichotomy, found in textbook descriptions of patristic exegesis, is not always very descriptive of actual exegetical moves in the early church.

Now admittedly, her discussion of fourth-century texts does not inform the present study of Theophilus and second-century apologetic exegesis. Nevertheless, it makes one wonder if second-century use of Scripture can be similarly illumined through attention to classic Greco-Roman rhetoric. Of course, I am not suggesting that later developments such as an Alexandrian or Antiochene school of exegesis necessarily existed during Theophilus's lifetime. Rather, I am merely using Mitchell's study to show how patristic exegesis scholarship is beginning to bypass anachronistic ways of describing use of the Bible by church fathers and to achieve higher levels of precision and historicism. These anachronistic ways have lingered far too long.

This new attention to rhetorical features in patristic exegesis, for the sake of better understanding exegetical moves, is a by-product within patristics of an important resurgence of interest among New Testament scholars in rhetorical features of the biblical text. This resurgence owes much to the work of Perelman and Olbrechts-Tyteca, which reminds scholars that the content of ancient writings cannot be reliably understood apart from analysis of their classic rhetorical features and how these features were carefully structured so as to persuade a quite specific audience of a particular writing.⁷

Burton L. Mack explains that since the beginning of the twentieth century, New Testament scholars generally no longer received rhetorical training, based on Greco-Roman classics, in their own educations. As a result,

---

6. Kennedy points out that the common scholarly term "forensic rhetoric" is troublesome, since all species of classical rhetoric, and not only judicial rhetoric, were used in the forum. Furthermore, "forensic" can be falsely associated with "forensics," a term that describes modern activities not strictly concerned with judicial rhetoric. Therefore, I follow his lead in using the more historically precise terms, "judicial rhetoric" or "ancient judicial rhetoric." See Kennedy, *On Rhetoric*, 47n73.

7. Perelman and Olbrechts-Tyteca, *New Rhetoric*, a translation of their *Traité de l'argumentation; la nouvelle rhétorique* (1958).

they were largely uninterested and unequipped to notice the significance of rhetorical features in the New Testament. In prior years, it was common for biblical scholars to give attention to such features.[8] Mack notes for example, that during the time of the Reformation, both Heinrich Bollinger and Martin Bucer took for granted that Pauline literature must be understood by reference to the rules of classic rhetoric recorded by Quintilian. Mack identifies two especially influential spurs to the rediscovery of the importance of ancient rhetoric. The first was the presidential address by James Muilenburg, presented to the Society of Biblical Literature in 1968, entitled, "After Form Criticism What?" The second was the publication in English translation of the above-mentioned work of Perelman and Olbrechts-Tyteca.[9] Perelman and Olbrechts-Tyteca contribute to the resurgence in two notable respects.[10] First, they remind scholarship that ancient rhetoric was more than a collection of techniques for mere ornamentation, but that it was at its essence "the art of persuasion." Second, they uncover many nuances in social contexts of speaker-audience settings that explain the persuasive power of the various ancient rhetorical devices.

As it turns out, there is currently a basic disagreement in scholarship regarding rhetorical analysis of the New Testament. One camp views rhetoric as being inherently and markedly conditioned by the culture and historical position of the given speaker or writer. The methodological implication of this view is that rhetorical moves in an ancient text are misunderstood unless they are judged strictly by the rhetorical standards of culture and age which produced that text.[11] The other scholarly camp believes that parallel rhetorical moves develop in all cultures. Therefore, modern rhetorical analysis, though informed by ancient rhetorical conventions, is legitimately applied to ancient texts as well as modern ones. Those advocating this approach claim that studies employing the categories of modern rhetorical

---

8. Mack, *Rhetoric*, 9–17.

9. On the decline and subsequent recent rediscovery of rhetoric in New Testament scholarship, see Mack, *Rhetoric*, 10. For an influential introduction to this approach, see Kennedy's *Rhetorical Criticism*.

10. On the main areas of influence of Perelman and Olbrechts-Tyteca in subsequent scholarship, see the discussion in Mack, *Rhetoric*, 14–16.

11. Perhaps the best recent detailed critical survey of this approach to rhetorical analysis is the introduction chapter of Mitchell's *Paul and the Rhetoric of Reconciliation*. She advances the practice by considering not only rhetorical moves championed in the ancient handbooks but also those discovered with surveys of actual Greco-Roman speeches and letters. She also insists on persuasively demonstrating that a given ancient species is indeed present, and critiques the prevailing tendency to show such in a perfunctory way.

analysis are strengthened by the high level of nuance afforded by highly-developed modern rhetorical theories.[12]

However scholarship eventually settles this basic disagreement, it is sufficient in this present study to consider ancient Greco-Roman rhetoric. Here, the aim is not to produce a comprehensive understanding of Theophilus's rhetorical maneuvers. Rather, the goal is to use second-century standards to understand and appreciate how *Scripture* bolstered Theophilus's claims. While Zeegers explores Theophilus's general use and comprehension of the NT in her 1975 essay, "Les citations du Nouveau Testament dans les Livres Autolycus de Théophile d'Antioche," she does not treat his use of the NT in connection with ancient judicial rhetorical standards.[13] However, she does discuss his use of the rhetorical device of "agreement" (σύγχρισις) in her earlier monograph on the citation of the poets by the Greek apologists.[14] The present study aims to extend prior scholarship by showing how Theophilus's pervasive use of certain formal τόποι (lit. "places," but understood in a metaphorical sense to denote standard rhetorical topics or strategies) neatly explains the shape of his argument and the central role of Scripture in it.

Zeegers, following Geffcken, has shown that Theophilus had only a superficial understanding of Greco-Roman philosophical and poetic treatises and that many of his citations of them were taken from anthologies.[15] If his education regarding this literature was evidently shallow, then was he truly skilled in classical rhetoric? As it turns out, we have reason to think so. There are several reasons. First, such rhetoric was on daily display in his culture.[16] Even those having only a basic education could observe and mimic its use. Second, Zeegers herself argues that Theophilus could have accessed a measure of classical learning either from pagan teachers or from classically-informed rabbis with whom he likely conversed. Third, while only advanced students studied the philosophers and poets in depth,

---

12. For a brief survey of major voices in this methodological disagreement, see Isacson, *To Each Their Own Letter*, 25–27.

13. Zeegers, "Citations du Nouveau Testament," 371–82.

14. Zeegers, *Citations des poètes grecs*, 118–19, 137.

15. Geffcken, *Zwei Griechische Apologeten*, 250–52; Zeegers, *Citations des poètes grecs*, 120–21, 27–28, 303–4; and Zeegers, "Les trois cultures," 136–38.

16. Although the corpus of Greco-Roman literary classics which formed the models for rhetors ceased to grow after the decline of the old Greek and Roman city-states, the use and importance of rhetoric itself remained strong even during Theophilus's age. This is why it would be natural for Theophilus to imbue his writings with a rich array of rhetorical devices, since writing in his day was used as a supporting prompt for oration more than as a product in its own right. Writing was intended mainly for oral performance, not reading per se. See Habinek, *Ancient Rhetoric and Oratory*, 75–76, 84.

it was common for less-advanced students to study rhetoric, including in Theophilus's own region.[17]

A second question arises, related to Geffcken's and Zeegers' above-mentioned demonstrations that Theophilus's shallow and in some places erroneous knowledge about the details of Greco-Roman philosophical and poetic treatises. Was Theophilus able to build a truly persuasive appeal using judicial rhetoric that depended on a mass of citations of authors whose writings Theophilus knew only to a shallow decree? As it turns out, there is good warrant to think that he could. The majority of the educated of his culture was like Theophilus himself—equipped with a basic knowledge of the poets and philosophers, knowledge that was shallow or erroneous in places. As discussed immediately above, only advanced students studied the poets and philosophers in depth.[18] If Theophilus himself knew the poets and philosophers mainly through anthologies, there is no reason not to think that his friend Autolycus, and many others like him, likewise knew these great writers mainly through anthologies. And we shall see in chapter 5 that use of anthologies was not uncommon in the second century. For Autolycus and others, Theophilus's citations of the poets and philosophers had the ring of truth, even despite occasional inaccuracies which only highly-educated readers might notice. And indeed, the majority of his citations would have borne the weight of his argument. We will see in the remainder of this chapter that his rhetoric would have been indeed highly persuasive, in large part because of the sheer mass of his detailed and skillful moves.

If the resurgence of interest in rhetoric has led to a better understanding of New Testament writings and of the writings of early church fathers such as Origen and Eustathius, how might it clarify our knowledge of Theophilus? I suggest that the particular rhetorical τόποι functioning most frequently in *Ad Autolycum* in connection with uses of Scripture are those described in the rhetorical handbook addressed to Gaius Herennius concerning judicial examination of witnesses.[19] I intend to demonstrate

---

17. For Theophilus's classical and/or Jewish education and the possibility of his oral interaction with the rabbis, see Zeegers, "Les trois cultures," 167–70. Regarding opportunities for formal and informal exposure to rhetoric in Antioch near the time of Theophilus, see Kennedy, *Rhetorical Criticism*, 8–10.

18. Kennedy, *Rhetorical Criticism*, 8–10.

19. *Rhetorica Ad Herennium* 2.6.9. The treatise was ascribed to Cicero beginning in the fifth century CE, although internal and external evidence does not support this ascription. Among prominent rhetorical handbooks, this handbook is notably helpful for analysis of *Ad Autolycum*, since it takes good notice of the importance of leveraging a witness' authority or lack thereof. Since Theophilus profoundly understood this importance, as we shall see, he was well in accord with rhetorical traditions described in this handbook. By contrast, Aristotle failed to treat adequately factors impacting the

the relevance to *Ad Autolycum* of these particular τόποι by progressively accumulating sheer weight of evidence and showing their consistent presence and role throughout virtually every one of the many portions of *Ad Autolycum*. Against the charge that its author was a Latin not necessarily known to a Greek writer such as Theophilus, it may be easily answered that this handbook described venerable Hellenistic rhetorical arts which the Romans appropriated.[20] Furthermore, they would have been well known in a major Roman city such as Antioch, both through curriculum in the higher schools and by rhetorical standards in the courts. This handbook gives a helpful view of traditional Greco-Roman rhetorical practices for examining witnesses.

Its writer instructed advocates to promote the trustworthiness of witnesses by the following "promoting τόποι":

1) discoursing on their "authority" (*auctoritatem*),

2) discoursing on the "life of witnesses" (*vitam testium*),

3) discoursing on their "consistency of testimony" (*constantiam testimoniorum*).

He next instructed advocates to challenge the veracity of witnesses by the following "challenging τόποι":

1) discoursing on their "foulness of life" (*vitae turpitudinem*),

2) discoursing on their "inconsistency of testimony" (*testimoniorum inconstantiam*), or by

3) showing that what witnesses claim to have happened either could not have happened or

4) showing that it did not happen, or

5) showing that they could not have known, or

6) showing that they speak out of partiality.

All of these judicial rhetorical τόποι, with the possible exception of the sixth challenging τόπος, were used abundantly by Theophilus as he exhorted Autolycus to read the Scriptures and other inspired texts so that he might come to know the true God. He applied the challenging τόποι to the pagan

---

authority of witnesses and associated rhetorical consequences. In this regard, see the assessment of the limitations of Aristotle's theory of rhetoric in Kennedy, *On Rhetoric*, 21–23, 39n41. For what little Aristotle wrote about witness interrogation τόποι, see Τέχνη ῥητορική 1.15.13–19.

20. Caplan, "Introduction," in *Cicero*, vii.

philosophers and poets, and applied the promoting τόποι to the prophets and inspired Christian writers.

Mitchell has warned that those performing Greco-Roman rhetorical analysis must not only employ the ancient handbooks but also show that the given rhetorical devices were used in actual Greco-Roman speeches and letters that have content similar to the text in question, in this case, *Ad Autolycum*, a set of apologetic texts.[21] Happily, it is easy to show that the witness interrogation τόποι are not merely advocated in the ancient rhetorical handbooks, but that examples of their use can be found in actual Greco-Roman apologetic texts. A few examples can suffice.[22]

Plato, *Letters* 3:
Since the argument answers two charges which stand upon what Plato understands to be a faulty memory of events, it uses judicial rhetoric. It is no surprise then that we can find within it examples of classic witness interrogation rhetoric:

Promoting τόποι for friendly witnesses:
3.318d-e—discoursing on the life of witnesses: Here the commendable witness is Plato himself, testifying on his own behalf. He applies the τόπος by noting he did not betray his friend, a noble man, out of fear. Rather, he upheld virtue by his faithfulness to his friend, even in the face of threat, and also by avoiding the mere pursuit of monetary gain. His courage would have been considered a virtue.

Challenging τόποι for hostile witnesses:
3.319b-c—discoursing on their foulness of life: Here the testimony of Dionysius is challenged by showing Dionysius's lack of virtue displayed in his mocking of Plato's program of education, a plan that recent events vindicated. Thus Dionysius's mocking proved to be a

---

21. Mitchell, *Rhetoric of Reconciliation*, 13–14.

22. In regard to Plato's third letter with its apologetic theme, Betz (see his groundbreaking 1989 *Galatians*) and others argue that the apologetic letter was a recognized ancient genre. However, there is a difference of opinion among New Testament scholars whether such was indeed a recognized genre. But here, I am not trying to show, nor is it necessary to do so, that it was so recognized by Greeks and Romans. Rhetorical specialists generally will acknowledge that even if the rhetorical handbooks did not have much to say about letter writing, nonetheless rhetorically-trained individuals were known to write letters and thus, rhetorical features clearly made their way into ancient letters, even if these features had no formal part in letter-writing training. Regardless, I offer Greco-Roman examples in this chapter which are in the form of both treatises and of letters.

foolish response, and sign of a foolish and therefore untrustworthy witness. The implication for the larger perspective is clear: Dionysius is a foolish witness, not a virtuous one, who levels unjustified charges.

3.319d-e—showing that what witnesses claim to have happened did not happen: Here Plato refers to his previously-recounted dialogue with Dionysius which puts to the lie Dionysius's charge that Plato hindered him from colonizing the Greek cities in question.

Plato, *Apology*:

Although Socrates, speaking in his own defense, does not take an apologetic emotional tone in this treatise, he provides indeed a judicial defense speech nonetheless, set in a court trial setting.[23] This treatise is very much an apology, in a technical sense. For the sake of brevity, I consider here only Socrates' interrogation of Meletus in 24b–28a. Meletus gives testimony both verbally and in written affidavit form. In Plato's day, written witness testimony was regarded as being more reliable than spoken witness testimony.

Here I do not assume the historicity of the actual words spoken by Socrates and Meletus. The *Apology* is of course Plato's reconstruction of the trial. Rather, my intent here is to show the classic witness interrogation τόποι which Plato used in this section of his *Apology*.[24]

Challenging τόποι for hostile witnesses:

24d-e—discoursing on their foulness of life: Meletus' silence concerning who is the improver of youth is offered as testimony that Meletus has no interest in improving the youth. His lack of interest in such would have been regarded as base. Accordingly, Socrates calls it disgraceful.

24d-e—showing that what witnesses claim to have happened they could not have known: Socrates shows that Meletus, having claimed to have discovered the corruptor of the youth, ought to know their improver. He then by his interrogation shows that Meletus does not know. The implication then is that Meletus actually does not know who corrupted the youth but has dared to testify to this.

24e-25c—showing that what witnesses claim to have happened could not have happened: Socrates skillfully and gradually leads Meletus into a corner from which he cannot escape by having him admit that he believes that the judges, the audience, the Council members,

---

23. This setting is explicitly mentioned in 17d.
24. Specialists generally agree that Plato is indeed the author.

the assembly members, and even every single Athenian except Socrates improves the youth and Socrates is the only one who corrupts them. Socrates then springs his trap by showing the court that when creatures are trained and improved, the general and expected setting is one in which there are multiple corruptors but merely one master, trainer, or teacher. His trap depends upon a premise upon which the court will grant the truth, since it is a generally accepted axiom. This dynamic was not unusual in Greco-Roman rhetoric. Enthymeme theory depended upon the use of just such an axiom.

24e-25c—discoursing on their foulness of life: Having led Meletus to display his foolishness in regard to his ludicrous belief that every Athenian except Socrates is an improver of the youth, Socrates then displays Meletus' evident lack of thought and concern for the improvement of the youth. The court would assume that this is evidence of Meletus' foul life.

25c-26a—showing that what witnesses claim to have happened could not have happened: As in the prior portion, Socrates employs a trap. Here, he leads Meletus to admit that bad neighbors do evil to their neighbors, and that no one likes to be injured, and that he believes that Socrates intentionally corrupted the youth. Socrates then springs his trap by pointing showing the court the inconsistency of Meletus' claims. If Socrates corrupted the youth, then they are corrupt and evil. If so, they must therefore do harm to their neighbors. But if this is so, why should Socrates choose to continue to interact with the youth, since they would only do him harm, and Meletus has admitted that no one likes to be harmed.

25c-26a—discoursing on their inconsistency of testimony: The inconsistency of Meletus' official testimony in the above-mentioned trap in which Socrates ensnared him is an additional classic witness interrogation τόπος in this portion.

26a—discoursing on their foulness of life: At the conclusion of the above-mentioned trap, Socrates again reminds the court that Meletus' incoherent grasp of the implications of the matter prove that Meletus has no concern for the improvement of the youth. In the eyes of the court, this is evidence of Meletus' foul life.

26b-28a—discoursing on their inconsistency of testimony: Socrates leads Meletus to admit in the court that Meletus accuses Socrates of believing in some sort of spiritual agencies, but not in the gods of Athens. He then leads Meletus to admit that Meletus accuses

Socrates of not believing in any actual gods. He then leads Meletus to admit that no one can believe in demigods and supernatural humans (which are spiritual agents by their nature) without also believing in gods. After this string of interrogation, Socrates springs his trap by showing that Meletus has testified that Socrates does not believe in the gods, but he has also testified that Socrates must believe in the gods.

The present study is akin to Mitchell's above-mentioned study, but where Mitchell focused on application by Origen and Eustathius of standard rhetorical rules for interpretation of texts such as laws or wills in courtroom settings, my approach is slightly different. We shall see how Theophilus applied rhetorical τόποι meant specifically for handling witness testimony. Accordingly, alternate rhetorical τόποι come into play here than those which Mitchell discusses. Where Origen and Eustathius each applied judicial rhetoric so as to show that their own interpretations of a text, 1 Samuel 28, were correct, and that contrary interpretations were erroneous, Theophilus used standard judicial rhetoric for a different end. He specifically sought to parade the reliability and trustworthiness of his own friendly witnesses, the biblical prophets, over against that of the pagan poets and philosophers, whom he considered unworthy of trust. In this way, he wanted his pagan friend Autolycus to realize that the Christian body of literature is true, and pagan literature is not.

Against the objection that the Romans did not really use written records of witness testimony, and that they did not value testimony of dead witnesses in the same way that they valued that of living witnesses in the courts, one must answer to the contrary, they truly did indeed. Tatian explicitly mentioned the practice.[25] Furthermore, Young points out that the ancients typically treated texts as records of speech. Texts were typically read aloud, and thus were considered devices for recreating an author's speech.[26] Contrary to modern practice, ancient texts were typically received audibly rather than optically. They were primarily used as devices for re-performing audible speech, not as records in their own right. Thus in antiquity, oral rhetorical standards indeed applied to written media. Hearers of *Ad Autolycum* then would have taken it for granted and even expected that it would contain oral rhetorical τόποι applied to trusted ancient authors.[27]

25. *Oratio ad Graecos* 31.

26. It goes too far to claim, as some NT scholars have, that Greco-Roman readers always read aloud. See Rodríguez, *Oral Tradition*, 43.

27. Young, "Apologists of the Second Century," 90. She notes that judicial rhetoric includes defense (ἀπολογία), that is, apology. She points out that apology (= defense)

Indeed, written records of ancient witness testimony commanded greater authority that the words of living witnesses, at least concerning issues outside of the mere occurrence or non-occurrence of an event. We see this in the rhetorical views of Aristotle. In his *Art of Rhetoric*, written after he had already written about rhetoric in his dialogue *Gryllus*, and after he himself become a teacher of rhetoric at Plato's Academy, Aristotle commended the use of long-dead witnesses over recent ones for testifying about the quality, justness, or advantage of an action. Orators and audiences trusted venerable and already-dead witnesses over living ones, because it was impossible to corrupt them.[28]

This appeal to ancient rhetoric finds support also in Loveday Alexander's observation that ancient apologetic is not itself a category of genre, but rather is an application of judicial rhetorical genre.[29] Therefore, it should be expected that the instruction represented in *Rhetorica ad Herennium* about judicial rhetoric should apply to an apology such as *Ad Autolycum*. All the more warrant for understanding the function of Greco-Roman rhetoric, and its impact on exegesis, in second-century apologies such as *Ad Autolycum*.

But to understand this, we must look beyond his use of classic τόποι at a micro level. We must also demonstrate that Theophilus followed ancient conventions for arranging judicial discourses, speeches about past events, at a macro level. Let us then consider the over-all rhetorical arrangement of *Ad Autolycum*.

Both Aristotle and Quintilian instructed that judicial discourses must consist of an introduction (προοίμιον, *prooemium*), then a narrative (διήγησις, *narratio*, which, according to Aristotle, may substitute for the thesis statement, πρόθεσις, used in non- judicial speeches), then a proof (πίστις, *probatio*), and finally, a conclusion (ἐπίλογος, *peroratio*), although the

---

is a type of speech that could be manifested in a variety of surface genres, including epistolary genre such as the three letters which Theophilus addressed to Autolycus. According to this analysis of Greco-Roman categories, *Ad Autolycum*, an apology in the form of three letters, resides securely within the realm of ancient judicial literature.

28. Aristotle, Τέχνη ῥητορική 1.15.17. This assertion appears in the chapter in which Aristotle enumerated and evaluated the various types of witnesses which a speaker might use. It represents Aristotle's comprehensive assessment of the value of the various kinds of witnesses available for speakers seeking support for an argument. See also Τέχνη ῥητορική 1.15.13–15.

29. Alexander, "Acts of the Apostles," in Edwards et al., *Apologetics in the Roman Empire*, 24. However, Young points out that second-century apologetic writings actually used a variety of "surface genres," including oration, appeals to the emperor, dialogue, and letter (Young, "Apologists of the Second Century," 82). Therefore, it seems even more precise to say that second-century apologetic is an application of Greco-Roman judicial rhetoric, manifested in varieties of surface genre. See also Bergjan, "How to Speak about Early Christian Apologetic Literature," 177–83.

conclusion was sometimes omitted.³⁰ At the beginning of each discussion of each letter of *Ad Autolycum*, it will be shown how that letter conforms to the typical four-fold arrangement of introduction, narrative, proof, and conclusion.

Indeed, this arrangement does not merely appear in the ancient handbooks as if it were merely an ideal way of structuring arguments, but one which was never actually used in any Greco-Roman apologetic texts. Rather, we can easily find various surviving examples of its use:

Isocrates, *To The Rulers Of The Mytilenaeans* (*Letters* 8):
The apologetic content of this letter defends the exiled musicians Agenor and his relatives, and advocates conferral of citizenship upon those who contribute to the glory of a city by means of music and "those spreading abroad any of the noble occupations" (οἱ διαφέροντοι περί τι τῶν καλῶν ἐπιτηδευμάτων). Yet in a broader sense, it also offers an apology for music and other arts and sciences which benefit the city.

I. προοίμιον—*Letters* 8.1.1–5³¹

II. διήγησις—*Letters* 8.1.5–8.2.15

III. πίστις—*Letters* 8.3–8.10.81

IV. ἐπίλογος—*Letters* 8.10.81–83 Here it is barely present, almost an afterthought containing merely of a few words intended for some personal acquaintances. But this near absence should be no surprise, for the ἐπίλογος was often omitted in Greco-Roman rhetoric when the proof was brief, which is certainly true here.³²

---

30. Aristotle, Τέχνη ῥητορική 3.13; Quintilian, *Institutionis oratoriae* 4.Pr.6, attest to the accepted arrangement for judicial discourses. However, there is sometimes variation in its description. For example, Aristotle, Τέχνη ῥητορική 3.13, evidences disapproval that Theodorus and Licymnius further sub-divided the same fourfold arrangement that he himself advised. As another example of this variety, *Rhetorica ad Herennium* 1.3.4 advised rhetoricians to compose discourses using an arrangement consisting of introduction, recitation of facts, division (of issues so as to separate those on which parties agree from those on which parties disagree), proof, refutation of objections (which some, such as Aristotle, considered an element of proof), and conclusion. It is evident that these variations are not actually divergences from the four-fold division of introduction, narration, proof, and conclusion, but simply more detailed versions of it. Aristotle, Τέχνη ῥητορική 3.13, advised that the ἐπίλογος could be omitted if a speech was short or if the matter was so easy to remember that no summation would be required. For narrative, see also Quintilian, *Institutionis oratoriae* 4.1.9–132. For thesis statement, see also Quintilian, *Institutionis oratoriae* 4.4.

31. Unless noted, line numbers in this section are based on the given Greek critical edition in the bibliography.

32. Aristotle, Τέχνη ῥητορική 3.13.

Plato, *Letters* 3:

I. προοίμιον—*Letters* 3.315a–315c

II. διήγησις—*Letters* 3.315d–316b

III. πίστις The proof consists of a defense against two charges leveled against Plato, these explicitly mentioned in the διήγησις. The defense against the first charge appears in *Letters* 3.316c–318e. The defense against the second charge appears in *Letters* 3.319a–319d.

IV. ἐπίλογος—*Letters* 3.319e. The epilogue is barely present, consisting only of a closing appeal to renounce the second false charge. The short length of the letter justifies the near lack of any epilogue, which the handbooks allow, as mentioned above, for Plato's brief arguments would be still fresh in Dionysius's mind.

The structure of these apologetically-themed letters by Isocrates and Plato demonstrate that this standard arrangement promoted in the ancient handbooks, and even used in actual ancient letters, could easily have been applied by Theophilus in his letters to his friend Autolycus.[33]

If the present study successfully shows how Theophilus used inspired texts as documentary witnesses, then it will confirm Young's assertion that Theophilus is the apologist who makes the second-century pagan/Christian "battle of literatures" most evident.[34] Similarly, Margaret Mitchell observes that patristic exegetes functioned in a combative oratorical setting, facing off in duels involving standard rhetorical (specifically judicial rhetorical) weapons.[35] Accordingly, the present study seeks to show how profoundly Theophilus relied on these tools as he challenged the written witness testimony of Greek religion, from the pagan poets and philosophers, and argued the veracity of his Christian witnesses, who were the Jewish and Christian writers inspired by the Holy Spirit.

---

33. The surveys of Greco-Roman apologetic texts in this section are not meant to be exhaustive.

34. Young, "Apologists of the Second Century," 94.

35. Mitchell, "Biblical Interpretation as a Trial," 21.

COHERENCE AND RHETORICAL USE OF SCRIPTURE IN THE FIRST LETTER

Rhetorical Structure

A judicial rhetorical structure undergirds Theophilus's first letter to Autolycus. Deirdre Good has exposed its telling features.[36] While her discussion of the three letters as a whole is helpful and insightful, it is brief and suggests the usefulness of a more extensive rhetorical analysis of each individual letter. Additional structural details emerge when it is clearly kept in mind that the three letters of *Ad Autolycum* were written as three separate epistles on separate occasions, with each one of them being structured according to ancient judicial structural standards.

It is apparent that *Ad Autoycum* 1 as a self-contained unit follows standard conventions for structuring a judicial address. An introduction (προοίμιον, *prooemium*) is found in *Autol.* 1.1. When Dionysius of Halicarnassus praised Lysias for his skillful introductions, he remarked that Lysias used all of the introductory devices recommended by the handbooks of rhetoric. One of the introductory devices that he mentioned is self-praise. Another is to recite an opponent's accusation, and then provide a refutation.[37] Theophilus used both in *Autol.* 1.1. He employed self-praise when he implied that Autolycus used "fluency" (στωμύλον στόμα, literally "a chattering mouth") "and eloquent speech" (καὶ φράσις εὐεπής), but did not understand the truths of the matter as Theophilus himself did. He used the accusation/refutation device towards the end of *Autol.* 1.1 when he related that Autolycus called Theophilus a Christian as if that name were evil. He refuted the intimation of associating with evil by turning the charge on its head and showing that the name "Christian" signifies "goodness."[38]

The narrative (διήγησις, *narratio*) of a judicial speech typically involved reciting the facts and events behind a case, hence the name of this structural feature. Its purpose was to declare the main question of the dispute (*quaestio*), or the central issue to be resolved (*constitutio*).[39] However, Cicero instructed that the narrative should be omitted when the events of a case are well known, or when their recitation does not help one's own case. Whenever the narrative is thus omitted, then the orator may simply state the

---

36. Good, "Rhetoric and Wisdom in Theophilus." Such judicial rhetorical structures are no strangers to early Christian apologetic texts. Cf. Neyrey, "Forensic Defense Speech," 210–24; Winter, "Forensic Speeches in Acts," 305–36.

37. Dionysius of Halicarnassus, *Lysias* 17. Cf. *Thucydides* 19.

38. This refutation is discussed further in the following "Challenging τόποι" section.

39. Cicero, *De inventione* 1.8.10; 1.13.18.

problem upon which the court must focus its concern.[40] In such a case, the problem statement served as the beginning of the next standard component of a judicial speech, the proof (πίστις, *probatio*).

Theophilus provided such a problem statement at the beginning of *Autol.* 1.2.1. He announced Autolycus' challenge "Show me your God" (Δεῖξόν μοι τὸν θεόν σου). What it means to perceive God, and how this can be done, is precisely the problem which *Ad Autoycum* 1 solves. The entire letter is concerned with how the true God can be perceived, and why the act of looking at the familiar statues of Greco-Roman gods, is actually a false vision of gods because they are indeed false gods.

Theophilus provided the proof in *Autol.* 1.2.2–13. He intended it to show that the Christian God is the only true God, and that Autolycus' gods are false gods. While some ancient handbooks described a five-fold structure for judicial speeches, where proof and refutation were separate components, other handbooks combined proof and refutation and presented a four-fold structure, as was also typical for Theophilus. For example, in *Rhetorica Ad Herennium*, proof and refutation are treated in the same breath, as inseparable entities.[41] Refutation is subsumed under proof in *Rhetorica Ad Alexandrum*.[42] Similarly, Aristotle's *Art of Rhetoric* subsumes refutation under proof and asserts that the required parts of a judicial speech at most consist of prooemion, proposition, proof, and epilogue, the same four-fold structure that we will find in each letter of *Ad Autolycum*.[43]

Finally, Theophilus closed *Ad Autoycum* 1 with the last standard component of a judicial speech, the conclusion (ἐπίλογος, *peroratio*).[44] Here, he provided a final encouragement to believe in the one true God, along with a recapitulation of the argument of *Ad Autoycum* 1. There is a concluding exhortation: "Because you asked, oh friend, 'Show me your God,' this is my God, and I advise you to fear him and to believe in him" (Ἐπειδὴ προσέθηκας ὦ ἑταῖρε, "Δεῖξόν μοι τὸν θεόν σου," οὗτός μου θεός, καὶ συμβουλεύω σοι φοβεῖσθαι αὐτὸν καὶ πιστεύειν αὐτῷ).

Challenging τόποι

Letter one of *Ad Autolycum* conforms to classic rhetorical expectations not only by its organization, but also at a detailed level. In contrast to the other

---

40. Cicero, *De inventione* 1.21.30–22.31.
41. *Rhetorica ad Herennium* 1.10.18; 2.1.2.
42. *Rhetorica ad Alexandrum* 13 (1431a).
43. Aristotle, Τέχνη ῥητορική 3.13.4.
44. *Autol.* 1.14.

two letters of *Ad Autolycum*, this first letter relies almost completely on those τόποι that challenge hostile witnesses, and only rarely on those promoting friendly ones. This shows that the focus of letter one is on weaknesses of Greco-Roman claims about divinity.

We see this right from the start. We saw above that a rhetorical device suitable for an introduction involved reciting an accusation by an opponent and then refuting it. Theophilus applied this device in his introduction in *Autol.* 1.1. He referred to two charges that Autolycus leveled. The first one was unstated. Theophilus only related that it was a byproduct of Autolycus' boasting of Roman gods. He refuted the charge by recalling Ps 113:12–14 so as to emphasize the impotence of Autolycus' idols.

Whatever the actual language of any pagans who challenged Theophilus's message, in *Autol.* 1.1, he expressed their challenges with the language of Scripture. He expressed this pagan demand, "Where is your God?," in the words of Ps 113:10, "Let not the nations say 'Where is their God?,'" and then looked to the larger context of the verse for the direction of his response.[45] He used not Ps 113:10, but a later passage, vv. 12–14, to argue the foolishness of idolatry. This theme was common in early Christian apology. The setting was lively. Autolycus boasted of his gods, and denigrated the biblical God. Theophilus had to make his defense, and to do so, he recalled these words of the psalmist about the impotence of idols. This was a paraenetic reading of Ps 113:12–14. Theophilus used the language of the psalm to point out the powerlessness of Autolycus' gods in the course of exhorting him to heed the Scriptures. Theophilus knew from personal experience that the Scriptures have the potential of opening Autolycus' eyes to the true God.

---

45. Perhaps he followed the lead of the *Apocalypse of Abraham*. The *Apocalypse* twice recalls Ps 113:13–15 in relating that Abraham considered the power of the gods of his father and brother and concluded that they were merely objects fashioned out of wood, stone, gold, silver, copper, and iron (*Apocalypse of Abraham* 1.1–3; 7.1–2). And yet it is unlikely that Theophilus drew from this work for his description of idols since (1) he did not seem to be influenced by other portions of the work; and (2) there is no real agreement in the actual textual details. Rather, a passage in John's Apocalypse may well be the intertext informing Theophilus's reading of Ps 113:12–14. This is not improbable, since Eusebius testified that Theophilus knew John's Apocalypse (*Historia ecclesiastica* 24.1). While the passage in Psalms could have supplied the language in *Autol.* 1.1 about idols being the works of human hands, and about the inability of idols to see or hear, it could not have supplied Theophilus's specific language about idols being formed out of stone, wood, or metal. However, Rev 9:20 could have, since it speaks of idols of gold, silver, bronze, stone, and wood, which can not see, hear, or walk. Theophilus did not quote directly from this or any other of the possible intertexts, since he altered the spelling of wood and stone, specifying the dative forms of these words (λιθίνοις καὶ ξυλίνοις). Other possible intertexts include Deut 4:28; 28:36 and 64; 2 Chron 2:13; Ezek 20:32; Wis 14:21. Deut 4:28 is the closest. No Jewish or Christian predecessor presented these words in the same order and spelling.

Theophilus himself came to believe after he had encountered the writings of the prophets.[46]

The second charge is that Christians are evil because the name "Christian" is somehow evil. A century before Theophilus, Emperor Trajan advised Pliny the Younger to punish those who did not deny their Christianity.[47] Autolycus perhaps considered the name "Christian," Χριστιανός, derogatory because it had become scandalous after long use in Roman interrogations, or perhaps because the title "Christ," Χριστός, is a homophone of a name frequently given to slaves, Χρηστός, and of the adjective, χρηστός, that while it typically is translated as "serviceable," can also carry the sense of "simple," or "silly."[48]

Theophilus responded to this charge by exploiting those same phonic parallels that Autolycus seems to have used. Christians, Χριστιανοί, he claimed, are indeed useful, χρηστός, to God. Therefore, they are pious. The implication is that Autolycus was self-deceived about his own piety. This is rhetorical over-powering, a venerable move known by the substantival adjective βίαιον (lit. "violent," but used by the ancients in its substantival sense, "violence").[49] In this, a speaker seizes an opponent's argument and turns it against him. It also applied a standard judicial rhetorical device for challenging hostile witnesses. By questioning whether Autolycus himself was useful to God, Theophilus thus challenged Autolycus' manner of life, sowing suspicion that Autolycus practiced a foul lifestyle, and was therefore untrustworthy. It served to undercut Autolycus' own testimony about the Roman gods. The appearance within just a few lines of so many rhetorical devices (the introductory practice of citing then refuting an opponent's accusation, rhetorical "over-powering," and the challenge of a witness' foul life) signal that Theophilus was a most skilled rhetorician.[50]

---

46. *Autol.* 1.14. The sense of "paraenetic" owes to its Greek root, παραινέω, "I exhort, recommend."

47. Pliny the Younger, *Epistulae* 10.97.

48. Greco-Roman religionists commonly associated this slave name with Jesus because of the phonic similarity. See Hurtado, "Christ," 108. On χρηστός, see the fourth definition in Liddell and Scott, *Greek-English Lexicon*.

49. This term appears as a neuter substantival adjective along with a description of its rhetorical function in Ps.-Hermogenes, Περὶ εὑρέσεως 3.3. The writer indicates that this adjective is indeed the traditional name for the rhetorical device. Thus, despite being formally an adjective, it was traditionally used substantivaly as the technical name of this rhetorical move. The unknown teacher of rhetoric likely wrote around the time of Theophilus or shortly after. His language about this rhetorical move indicates that it had already become tradition by the time he wrote his handbook. For the age of this handbook, see Davis, "Violence in the Schools of Rhetoric," 199.

50. Another indication of this appears roughly a page later in *Ad Autolycum*. Ziegler

The τόπος of reminding an audience of a hostile witness' foulness of life remains in play in *Autol.* 1.2. Theophilus charged that Autolycus is impure, and that his sin has blinded the eyes of his soul. He was quite explicit: "your impieties obscure (ἐπισκοτοῦσιν αἱ ἀσέβειαι) so that you cannot see God." Theophilus's charge drew force from common notions about atheism. His very language recalled that assertion in the treatise on superstition attributed to Plutarch that an atheist cannot see God because the soul is debilitated, as if "its turning of its many brightest and most powerful eyes to the perception of god has been extinguished."[51] In short, Theophilus shifted the blame. Autolycus intimated that God is of no account, and therefore invisible. But Theophilus laid the problem on Autolycus. He cannot see because he is a self-blinded atheist. This, of course, is another application of rhetorical "over-powering," for Theophilus stayed Autolycus' attack by again seizing Autolycus' own rhetorical weapon.

He also applied judicial τόποι. In charging that Autolycus cannot perceive God because of his own blinding sin, Theophilus raised the specter that Autolycus is an immoral witness, and therefore unreliable.

The τόπος involving showing that a witness dares testify about what he cannot know raised the stakes. Autolycus dared boast of his own gods. However, if Theophilus's claim about Autolycus' impurity held, then Autolycus was doubly unreliable on account of testifying too rashly about what he cannot possibly perceive with his blinded soul. It would have been better if he had not spoken of his own gods.

Thus, as he had just done, Theophilus again combined several rhetorical devices into a single rhetorical parry. The only inspired text involved, 2 Cor 7:1, appeared when Theophilus used five words from it to tell Autolycus that he must cleanse himself of his defilement before he can see the true God.[52]

---

shows that, in accord with ancient rhetorical practices of creating discourses with pleasing phonic patterns, especially rhymes, Theophilus crafted the first few lines of *Autol.* 1.4 with six infinitives, all ending with the typical ειν. While Ziegler addresses only the beginning of *Autol.* 1.4, he raises the possibility of similar phonic patterns in following lines (Ziegler, "Erklärung des Gottesnamens bei Theophilus," 333). As it turns out, there are indeed other patterns. In the center of *Autol.* 1.4 Theophilus invested his allusions to Gen 1:14, 26 with two different rhyming patterns. The first consists of three recurrences of "of the universe" (τῶν ὅλων), followed by "of everything" (τῶν πάντων). The second has three recurrences of "because of his being" (either διὰ τὸ εἶναι αὐτὸν or διὰ τὸ αὐτὸν εἶναι). Dionysius of Halicarnassus prescribed such phonic craftsmanship in his handbook, not only for works of poetry, but also for historical treatises (*De compositione verborum* 5).

51. Plutarch, *De superstitione* 167b.

52. The "all defilement" of 2 Cor 7:1 was for Theophilus two things. First, it was the kind of ethical failing he had just enumerated, such as adultery, fornication, theft,

The charge that Autolycus dared to testify about what he could not have known seems to reappear a few pages later, in *Autol.* 1.5. At least a suggestion can be made that *Autol.* 1.5 may present a complex and perhaps unconscious μίμησις of the Greek idea of heavenly ascent, certainly famous in Plato but also found elsewhere. If so, then it would have intimated that Autolycus is like those who cannot see heavenly reality and who mock true philosophers. *Autol.* 1.5 would thus reinforce Theophilus's ten applications elsewhere of the τόποι challenging Autolycus' testimony about what he could not have known.[53]

In *Autol.* 1.7, Theophilus again challenged Autolycus' testimony about Roman gods through standard judicial approaches by showing that the witness testified concerning what he could not have known (how could Autolycus with his blind heart know who is the true God?), and by suggesting that he is an untrustworthy witness by reminding the audience of his foulness of life. Where Theophilus discussed Autolycus' blind soul and deaf heart in *Autol.* 1.2, he used similar language in *Autol.* 1.7, here implying that Autolycus' heart is blinded. The figure of the blinded heart was not unique to Theophilus. We also encounter it in *Acts of Peter* 28.

The rhetorical challenge of a hostile witness on the basis of his or her foulness of life that was used in *Autol.* 1.1–2, and 7 reappears in *Autol.* 1.9. This time the hostile witness is not Autolycus. Rather, the poets and philosophers are mustered as hostile textual witnesses. He recited the scandalous deeds and characteristics of the gods: incest, adultery, pederasty, drunkenness, insanity, ignorance and weaknesses. If the gods are so disreputable, then so are the witnesses who champion them, the poets and philosophers. He used a second judicial τόπος when he challenged inconsistent testimony of the poets and philosophers about the god Osiris.

The very same devices appear again in *Autol.* 1.10, where the inconsistent testimony concerns the identity of Zeus, and the scandalous deeds recalled are those of the mother of the pagan gods. Theophilus concluded these challenges of hostile witnesses by conflating Ps 95 and Ps 113 to state that these pagan gods are no true gods at all.

He also used the τόπος of challenging inconsistent testimony in neighboring portions, applying it in *Autol.* 1.8 to Autolycus' testimony about the gods and to his denial of resurrection. Theophilus pointed out on the one

---

swindling, and the like. Such ethical appeals were characteristic of early Christian apologetic. Secondly, it was the taint of idolatry mentioned in 2 Cor 6:15–18, which sounds only through allusive echo, since he did not explicitly quote that passage. The echo fits perfectly with his aim of awakening Autolycus to the true God, so that he might forsake the false gods of wood, stone, and metal, mentioned in *Autol.* 1.1.

53. *Autol.* 1.2, 7; 2.5, 12, 30, 32–33; 3.2, 16, 30.

hand that Autolycus' testimony about the divinity of idols entails a fairly high level of credulity. On the other hand, Autolycus' denial that the true God who created him can easily remake him in resurrection depends on what is by comparison a low, and thus, inconsistent level of credulity.

Theophilus used this τόπος also in a discourse on resurrection in *Autol.* 1.13.[54] Here he applied the device of ἀντιπαραστάσις, literally "standing in contrast," which involves depicting an opponent as having a certain view and then refuting it.[55] Autolycus' view is indicated by his mocking challenge to show even a single person raised from death. Theophilus offered two refutations.

The first one applied the inconsistent testimony τόπος. On the one hand, Autolycus denied that resurrection is possible. On the other, he granted that Heracles, burnt to death, and that Asclepius, killed by lightening, were both later found alive.

The second refutation is Theophilus's suggestion that even if he did show Autolycus someone raised from the dead, he would still disbelieve. This is an echo of Luke 16:31. Theophilus merely alluded to this verse and did not explicitly quote or cite it, but its content and surrounding context, the narrative of Lazarus and the rich man, informed him. It would have

---

54. *Autol.* 1.13 provides an answer to pagan objections to the concept of resurrection. The inspired texts that Theophilus used, John 12:24 and 1 Cor 15:37, were used also in close proximity in a discussion about resurrection in the Bodmer Papyrus text of *3 Corinthians* (Anonymous, "Correspondance apocryphe des Corinthiens et de l'apôtre Paul," 40). It should be no surprise that both *3 Corinthians* and *Autol.* 1.13 evidence use of John 12:24 with 1 Cor 15:37, since they both use the metaphor of a seed buried in the ground like a corpse, which sprouts up to figuratively rise from the dead. It is not necessary to infer any common source relating *3 Corinthians* and *Ad Autolycum*. But both writings show the popularity of this natural metaphor in early Christianity.

Near the end of the first century, Clement of Rome had argued the plausibility of resurrection using analogies of the cycles of day and night, on the life springing out of bare seeds buried in the earth, and on the life of the phoenix bird (*1 Clem.* 24–26). Theophilus used the first two of these analogies in *Autol.* 1.13, although not with the same wording as in Clement. In the course of this, he recalled 1 Cor 15:37, bringing more of the wording of that passage into his discussion than did Clement. He then used additional natural analogies of resurrection: the waxing and waning of the moon; the decline and regeneration of human health; the termination and rebirth of the seasons; the cycles of day and night. The rhetorical power of natural analogy modeled by 1 Cor 15:35–38 motivated both Clement and Theophilus to develop or appropriate additional natural analogies. That both writers included the analogy of the cycles of day and night and that of the burial and rebirth of seeds, and that both analogies lie adjacent to each other, and in the same order, suggests either that Clement particularly influenced Theophilus in this regard, or that these two analogies had become traditional supports on behalf of the concept of resurrection.

55. The device of ἀντιπαραστάσις was a standard topic in the rhetorical schools. See Clark, *Reading Renunciation*, 62.

spontaneously brought to the minds of Theophilus's Christian audience features of that narrative, such as the words from the mouth of Abraham out of Hades that the unbelieving brothers of Lazarus would continue in unbelief even if they were to see someone raised from the dead, since while they have sufficient cause for faith in Moses and the prophets, they still disbelieve. The application of this echo to the second century is that mockers such as Autolycus would behave the same way, even if they also witnessed someone raised from the dead.

Promoting τόποι

After mustering throughout *Ad Autoycum* 1 these various τόποι which "softened the ground" by undermining the testimonies of Autolycus, the poets, and the philosophers, Theophilus was now ready to launch his full frontal assault. Thus, we find the only judicial promoting τόποι anywhere in the first letter only at its very conclusion.[56] This was merely his initial offensive wave. His full force would land with unrestrained power in his next two letters.

As it turns out, this initial offensive wave included every one of the τόποι that we have seen in *Rhetorica ad Herennium* for championing the testimony of friendly witnesses. Characteristically, Theophilus's friendly witnesses are the prophets and apostles. He again used the same complete set of judicial τόποι in *Autol.* 2.9–10 when he was about to present a major piece of testimony from one of his witnesses, namely, his lengthy exposition of Moses' narrative of the Creation. More than once then, Theophilus availed himself of every possible promoting τόποι for championing friendly witnesses before he employed his witnesses in a major way.

Here at the end of his first letter, he claimed that the poets and philosophers stole from the Scriptures, and therefore declared that eternal punishment will come to the impious. But since notice of eternal punishment appears both in the Scriptures and in the writings of poets and philosophers, then no one can claim "we did not hear or know" (οὐκ ἠκούσαμεν οὐδὲ ἔγνωμεν).[57] By reminding his audience that his own textual witnesses all provide consistent testimony on this matter, he applied the τόπος of emphasizing the consistency of his friendly witnesses. He applied the device

---

56. *Autol.* 1.14.

57. This phrase may be a quotation from the fragment of *Kerygma Petri* preserved by Clement of Alexandria, although this is not certain. See Clement of Alexandria, *Stromata* 6.5.43. Paulsen, "Kerygma Petri und die urchristliche Apologetik," 12n67, observes that Elze, Quispel, and Grant all take the phrase as a quotation from *Kerygma Petri*. However, Paulsen, following Köster and Robinson, asserts that textual differences are such that it is uncertain whether *Autol.* 1.14 actually quotes *Kerygma Petri*.

of displaying the authority of his own witnesses when he commented that their writings are divine (ἱεραῖς). He reinforced their authority by pointing out that they can predict future events. He unleashed the remaining possible τόπος for promoting friendly witnesses when he reminded his audience of the virtue of his witnesses by repeatedly disassociating them from the impious and unrighteous who will be punished in the final judgment.

COHERENCE AND RHETORICAL USE OF SCRIPTURE IN THE SECOND LETTER

Ad Autoycum 2 represented a skirmish in the literary battle waged between Christians and Greco-Roman religionists in the second century. Theophilus announced in *Autol.* 2.1 that he would use some of Autolycus' own history books in order to convince him of the truth. As in *Ad Autoycum* 1, Theophilus again used conventional judicial rhetoric whereby the prophets and inspired Christian writers functioned as friendly textual witnesses, and the poets and philosophers functioned as hostile textual witnesses. However in *Ad Autoycum* 2, their testimony concerned what was the true history.

Rhetorical Structure

To argue that Theophilus used biblical passages rhetorically as textual witnesses, it is not enough merely to discuss rhetorical roles of particular passages. We must also show that the separate letters of *Ad Autolycum* were structured according to rhetorical standards. As it turns out, just as it was possible to identify a rhetorical structure beneath the first letter, so it is possible to demonstrate that one undergirds the second as well.

Theophilus located his introduction (προοίμιον, *prooemium*) in *Autol.* 2.1. He used three of the standard introductory forms in Dionysius of Halicarnassus' handbook.[58] The first form consists of gathering sympathy for one's case by praising or flattering the listener. Theophilus did this when he called Autolycus "noble" (ἀγαθώτατος), appreciated his patience in listening, and mentioned the great friendliness that they enjoyed during their prior discussion.

The second introductory device that Theophilus used involves praise of self. He combined both devices by adding that the great friendship appeared even through Autolycus had been initially hostile to Theophilus's case. Theophilus thus implied that he had triumphed in the earlier exchange.

---

58. Dionysius of Halicarnassus, *Lysias* 17.

His specific language in this regard recalls 1 Cor 1:18. This verse describes his perception of their earlier dialogue: his Roman friend, because he is among those who are perishing, considered the gospel message to be folly.

The third conventional introductory device is self-depreciation. Here also Theophilus recalled a phrase from the inspired writings, quoting from 2 Cor 11:6a. In this verse, Paul gained sympathy by depreciating his own skills of oratory, but was quick to add, lest his readers doubt his knowledge, that this did not detract from his insight into the gospel. Likewise, Theophilus gathered sympathy also by depreciating his own rhetorical skills, but he also implied that this did not detract from his knowledge of the true religion which he was about to discuss. He also gathered sympathy by indicating his willingness to accommodate his friend while at the same time turning aside any suspicion that he was unduly partial (thus recalling the τόπος of emphasizing the untrustworthiness of witnesses swayed by partiality) when he mentioned that he presented this second treatise only in response to Autolycus' own request.

In a judicial speech, the narrative (διήγησις, narratio) typically appeared after the introduction. It typically recited facts and events underling the given case. But Cicero allowed that the narrative could be omitted if the events of a case are well known, or if their recitation would not help persuade. Whenever it was omitted, the orator could simply state the problem upon which the court must focus its concern, or the line of argument that would follow.[59]

These statements would prepare the court for the next standard component, the proof (πίστις, probatio). In *Autol.* 2.1.8, Theophilus claimed to provide a διήγησις, but this was either false modesty, or probably more likely a reflection of his explicit intention to prove whose witnesses provide true history. The great historian Thucydides used a verbal cognate of διήγησις (lit. "setting out in detail") to describe his own historical writing.[60] Perhaps Theophilus wanted to use the same language to speak of historiography that was used in the history books that Autolycus knew. After all, Theophilus had already informed Autolycus at the beginning of the letter that he would use Autolycus' own history books to prove whose witnesses relate true history.[61] But in a rhetorical sense, this διήγησις is actually a πίστις, and so Grant translates the term. While some handbooks described a five-fold structure for judicial speeches, where proof and refutation were separate components, other handbooks combined proof and refutation and presented a four-fold

---

59. Cicero, *De inventione* 1.21.30–22.31.
60. Thucydides, *Historiae* 6.54.1.2.
61. *Autol.* 2.1.

structure. This is what we find in the second letter to Autolycus, just as we also found it in the first letter.⁶²

The ancient handbooks asserted that it is fitting for a rhetorical proof to be introduced by brief mention of the thesis and central argument.⁶³ This was exactly what Theophilus provided at the end of *Autol.* 2.1. His thesis was that the Roman religion of Autolycus is for naught, but Christianity is worthy and true. His announced line of argument was to prove his case using the same pagan histories read by Autolycus himself. This approach is reasonable, given that Greco-Roman histories of the cosmos relate activities of the gods. After arguing the absurdity of pagan histories, he would then maintain the trustworthiness of biblical history. He would use standard judicial rhetoric throughout *Ad Autoycum* 2, showing the inconsistencies and untrustworthiness of hostile witnesses to history, the pagan poets and philosophers, and the trustworthiness of his friendly witness, the prophet Moses. And in this way, he would produce one of the oldest Christian commentaries on the early chapters of Genesis.

The final standard component of an ancient judicial speech was its conclusion (ἐπίλογος, *peroratio*). The conclusion of *Ad Autoycum* 2 appears in 2.38. Theophilus had announced by his thesis statement in *Autol.* 2.1 that he would use the same histories which Autolycus himself read to argue that Greco-Roman religion is for naught, while Christianity is invaluable. Having contended this throughout *Ad Autoycum* 2, he concluded with a short recapitulation followed by exhortations to seek faith, righteousness, and good works. His exhortations end on a telling note: Autolycus should meet him and other Christians more frequently, "so that also giving ear to a living voice you might be accurately learning the truth" (ὅπως καὶ ζώσης ἀκούσας φωνῆς ἀκριβῶς μάθης τἀληθές). His specific language is a judicial rhetorical "tip-off": having heard Theophilus's trustworthy dead witnesses throughout *Ad Autoycum* 2, Autolycus should find confirmation by "also giving ear to" (καὶ . . . ἀκούσας) testimonies by second-century Christians, those trustworthy witnesses not yet dead.

Challenging τόποι

One cannot say with any degree of certainty that Theophilus used any inspired texts in *Autol.* 2.2–8. There is not a single one for *Autol.* 2.2–8 listed in the biblical indexes in both Biblia patristica and Marcovich's edition of

---

62. For details on proof and refutation, see the discussion of the structure of the first letter to Autolycus, earlier in this chapter.
63. Aristotle, Τέχνη ῥητορική 3.13; Quintilian, *Institutionis oratoriae* 4.Pr.6.

Ad Autolycum. Nonetheless, this portion is important because it challenged Autolycus' textual witnesses promoting Greco-Roman religion. Once their testimony was undercut, Theophilus could present his major witness, Moses, starting in *Autol.* 2.9.

In *Autol.* 2.2, Theophilus used a τόπος for challenging hostile witnesses that involved showing inconsistencies in their testimony. He applied it to two classes of witnesses representing Greco-Roman religion. The first were the craftsmen who constructed statuary of the gods. He pointed out that while these craftsmen are forming such statues, they considered the statues to be nothing.[64] However, their inconsistency emerged once the statues were fully formed, for these craftsmen suddenly considered them to be gods. Theophilus applied this inconsistency τόπος a second time in *Autol.* 2.2, only this time the inconsistency was in the testimony of Autolycus himself. Theophilus observed that when Autolycus read the genealogies of the gods, he read of their births and considered them to be mere humans. Later, he considered them gods, forgetting that he had previously considered them to be mere mortals.

In *Autol.* 2.4, Theophilus made use of a different judicial τόπος, the strategy of showing that the testimonies of hostile witnesses contradict. Accordingly, he enumerated a number of contradictory opinions of the philosophers concerning the existence of God and concerning the origin of the cosmos. He noted that some Stoics believed that God does not exist. Others thought that he does but is unconcerned about the created realm. Others explained the existence of the cosmos without reference to God, believing that the cosmos has eternal existence and that the processes of nature are spontaneous. Others asserted that God is the animating and organizing spirit resident throughout the cosmos. Theophilus made much of apparent disagreement among Stoics.

He was not finished. He next demonstrated that Platonists also disagreed, not only among themselves, but also with the previously-mentioned Stoics. On the one hand, Platonists alleged that God is uncreated and is the Creator of the cosmos. On the other hand, they also alleged that matter is eternal. However, if these things are true, their testimony concerning the nature of God was contradictory because God cannot truly be the Creator of the cosmos if he does not create matter.

Theophilus mentioned an additional inconsistency. Platonists held that God is immutable since he is uncreated. However, if this is true, matter must also be immutable since it is eternal and uncreated, according to

---

64. Grant considering Theophilus's language, "they consider them nothing" (οὐδὲν αὐτοὺς ἡγοῦνται), reminiscent of 1 Cor 8:4, notes a use of it in *Autol.* 2.2 in his edition of *Ad Autolycum*.

Platonists. This contradicted the Platonic doctrine that the material world is mutable. Furthermore, if matter is uncreated and thus immutable, it is equal to God who is likewise uncreated and immutable. If such is the case, the Platonic teaching the God is sovereign was contradicted.

Theophilus in *Autol.* 2.5 continued to use the conventional judicial τόπος of showing inconsistencies of hostile witnesses. He maintained that the statements of the philosophers are inconsistent with those of earlier writers, namely poets such as Homer and Hesiod.[65] On the surface, one might question how effective this argument could be, since it does not seem unreasonable that various philosophers and poets have a diversity of views concerning origins. Still, there was a certain force to his argument, for three reasons. First, Theophilus proceeded on the basis of contemporary judicial rhetoric by which opposing cadres of textual witnesses differ over a matter. Again bearing in mind that texts in late antiquity were typically read aloud and regarded as means for re-performing spoken language, thus being bound by the same expectations used to judge orations, including legal orations, all of the testimony supporting a particular case would be relevant. Since the words of both poets and philosophers carried at least some authority for Theophilus's audience, and since both groups spoke on behalf of the traditional gods, the testimony of both groups would be considered to be at least somewhat relevant. Second, Theophilus considered it significant that by contrast, all of his own witnesses, the prophets and inspired Christian writers, spoke consistently about the nature of God and about origins, because they were all inspired by the one Spirit of God. Third, philosophy in his day at the popular level was quite eclectic. It was quite typical for individuals such as Autolycus to draw insights simultaneously from a variety of philosophical streams without feeling compelled in any way to align exclusively with only one single philosophical tradition.[66] Thus in all likelihood, Autolycus would never have considered responding to Theophilus's argument about contradictory origins theories with the rejoinder that such an argument fails since he (Autolycus) only agreed exclusively with one particular philosopher and no others, nor with any earlier poetic writers.

---

65. For an overview and analysis of Theophilus's philosophical rejoinders throughout *Ad Autolycum*, see Perendy, "Judging Philosophers." While Perendy does not discuss the function of these rejoinders in Theophilus's judicial rhetoric, his contribution is helpful particularly because he surveys the literature on Theophilus and philosophy, assembles his philosophical statements, and discusses the historical backgrounds and teachings of philosophers named by Theophilus.

66. Armstrong, *Introduction to Ancient Philosophy*, 142; Perendy, "Judging Philosophers," 213.

Theophilus initiated his demonstration in *Autol.* 2.5 that the testimonies of the philosophers are inconsistent with testimonies of earlier writers by considering Homer's statement that Ocean is the "origin of the gods" (θεῶν γένεσις).⁶⁷ This testimony contradicted Platonic testimony already presented in *Autol.* 2.4 that God created everything. Theophilus made the point explicit: "But God, if he is Maker of everything, just as he is, then he is Creator of the water and the seas also" (ὁ δὲ θεός, εἰ τῶν ὅλων ποιητής ἐστιν, καθὼς καὶ ἔστιν, ἄρα καὶ τοῦ ὕδατος καὶ τῶν θαλασσῶν κτίστης ἐστίν).

Theophilus then cited Hesiod's testimony to similar effect. He reminded his audience that while Hesiod stated that the world is created, the poet could not identify the Creator. Theophilus then led his audience into speculation concerning which god Hesiod might have had in mind as the Creator. He recalled that Hesiod mentioned the gods Kronos, Zeus, Poseidon, and Pluto. However those gods, "we discover came into existence after the cosmos" (μεταγενεστέρους εὑρίσκομεν τοῦ κόσμου). Theophilus notes that Hesiod also implored the Muses, Zeus' daughters, to tell him about origins. But they could not, they and their father Zeus having come into existence only after the creation.

Theophilus's point was that the testimony of Hesiod, like that of Homer, contradicted testimonies of later pagan writers. Homer and Hesiod claimed that the gods came into being after the cosmos, but the later pagan writers claimed that the gods existed before the cosmos. Like any courtroom advocate, Theophilus did not need to produce an elaborate and balanced analysis of statements from hostile witnesses such as Hesiod. He merely needed to undermine the testimonies of hostile witnesses by noting inconsistencies.

Having argued in *Autol.* 2.5 that Hesiod contradicted philosophers such as Plato, he contended in the next portion that Hesiod even contradicted himself. His further citations of Hesiod simply reinforced what he had already argued concerning Hesiod's belief that the gods came into being after the cosmos.⁶⁸ Near the end of *Autol.* 2.6 Theophilus explicitly noted

---

67. Zeegers, *Citations des poètes grecs*, 113, notes that Theophilus paired this statement by Homer about Ocean with a verse from a separate song of the *Illiad*, and was apparently the only author to associate these two verses.

She also observes that while Grant argues in his "Problem of Theophilus" that Theophilus used an anthology for his citations of the poets in *Autol.* 2.5–7, this conclusion is not certain (112–14). Grant concluded such because two of the citations in *Autol.* 2.5–7 are also used in Athenagoras, *Leg.* 18. Zeegers points out that the two common citations are very famous, and could have been obtained from a text other than an anthology, or from memory. She believes that some of the short citations in *Autol.* 2.5–7 were cited from memory, and that Theophilus consulted a text of Hesiod for his use of *Theogenia* 73–74, 104–33.

68. Hesiod, *Theogenia* 116–23; 126–33.

that Hesiod contradicted himself. He meant by this that the creative activity that Hesiod described requires a Creator. However, Hesiod did not know who the Creator is. It had to be a god. But in Hesiod's thought, the gods come into being after the created realm. The contradiction is that at least one god had to come before the created realm in Hesiod's system, but none did.

Theophilus in *Autol.* 2.7 amplified his claim in *Autol.* 2.1–8 that later pagan testimonies about history contradict earlier ones. To this end, he quoted the poet Aristophanes' assertion that the cosmos came out of a primal egg.[69] He quoted a genealogy of the descendants of Dionysus, and mockingly explained that if the gods have genealogies, it is because they are begotten like mere mortals. These examples also helped Theophilus emphasize inconsistency since they differ from Plato's account of a heavenly "craftsman" (δημιουργός) who built both the natural realm and the gods themselves.[70]

At the beginning of *Autol.* 2.8, he summed up his arguments in *Autol.* 2.1–7. This tactic of recapitulating (ἀνακεφαλαίωσις) was itself a standard rhetorical device. It served to remind a judge of an argument's key points, by a concluding restatement.[71] He brought the judicial τόπος to mind when he explicitly called their statements about origins "inconsistent" (ἀσύμφωνος). His recapitulation included a litany of testimony designed both to remind Autolycus of the argument, and also to drive it home by recalling the sheer number of inconsistencies in testimonies advocating pagan gods. In rapid succession, Theophilus cited Aratus concerning the providential care of Zeus; Sophocles' claim that providence does not exist; Homer's that Zeus fosters human virtue; the testimonies of Simonides, Euripides, Menander, Euripides again, and finally (a false citation of) Thestius concerning providence.[72] After showing the witnesses contradicting one another, Theophilus next sought to show one of these witnesses caught in self-contradiction. He reminded Autolycus that Sophocles taught that providence does not exist. It hardly needed mentioning since he had just cited Sophocles to that effect.

---

69. Aristophanes, *Aves* 695.

70. Plato, *Respublica* 596a–c.

71. On recapitulation as a Greek literary convention, see *Rhetorica ad Herennium* 2.30.47.

72. For the false citation of Thestius, see Geffcken, *Zwei Griechische Apologeten*, 251. Likewise, Zeegers shows that Theophilus either did not know or else he forgot the context of his Sophocles and Euripides citations, and that he modified his Menander quotation in support of monotheism. See Zeegers, *Citations des poètes grecs*, 121–22.

But he then cited Sophocles supporting the contrary idea that God strikes all mortals.[73]

He then explained why these hostile witnesses were inconsistent: these hostile witnesses did not know the truth, they were inspired by demons (δαίμονες), they were unduly proud, they testified on the basis of their imaginations rather than true knowledge, and that they testified "not by means of a clean spirit but by means of a spirit of error" (οὐ καθαρῷ πνεύματι ἀλλὰ πλάνῳ). This last accusation reflected the language of the gospels about the unclean spirits which Jesus exorcised. Indeed, Theophilus explicitly mentioned Christian exorcism of unclean demons in the very next few lines. He explained his religious epistemology. Namely, that those promoting false gods were possessed by the same sort of unclean demons of which the gospel writers spoke. By contrast, the prophets and the Christians were not inspired by unclean demons, but by one clean Spirit, who is the Spirit of God. As a result, they were true and consistent.

When Theophilus emphasized the contradictions of Homer and Hessiod, or the contradictions of the poets as he did in *Autol.* 2.4–8, by simply quoting their views one after another without analysis or nuance, so as to highlight every sense of contradiction, he employed a standard rhetorical technique. Numerous Greek writers employed this same technique, including Plato, Aristotle, Isocrates, Chrysippus, Cicero, Lucianus, and Sextus Empiricus.[74] Regardless of whether modern readers find convincing his arguments that pagan writers contradicted both themselves and one another, second-century Romans evidently did, at least somewhat, since various famous Greco-Roman writers used this same technique. Moreover, Jews such as Josephus and other Christians, such as Justin and Tatian used it as well.[75]

Theophilus also undercut the trustworthiness of the poets and philosophers in *Ad Autoycum* 2 by showing that what they attested could not have happened. In so doing, he applied one of the standard τόποι for challenging hostile witnesses. He proceeded by observing that the genealogies of the gods speak of much begetting.[76] He reasoned that this begetting would naturally continue up to the present, but it had not. He laid out two explanations for the cessation of begetting. Either the gods became old and could no longer reproduce, or they had died. Quoting the Sibyl, he observed

73. Sophocles frg. 876.
74. Zeegers, *Citations des poètes grecs*, 118.
75. *Oratio ad Graecos* 31 describes the rhetorical method of using textual witnesses. And Tatian's *Oratio ad Graecos* 26 evidence the approach of citing texts one after another to support a point. For similar examples, see Zeegers, *Citations des poètes grecs*, 119nn1–3.
76. *Autol.* 2.3.

that if the gods indeed could still beget because they neither die nor become old and weak, then there ought to be more gods then humans. But no one claimed that.

Then he deftly turned from the τόπος of showing that what a hostile witness claimed *could* not happen, to that of showing that what a hostile witness testified indeed *did* not happen. He proposed that if the gods are immortal and resident in certain places as the poets and philosophers testified, then they ought to be still located in these places. But they are not. According to Homer and others, Zeus resides on Ida. Theophilus noted that Zeus is no longer seen there. Mount Olympus formerly hosted numbers of supposedly immortal gods according to the poets. But it is now deserted. He adopted a mocking tone as he took up the later history of Zeus, speculating that perhaps he went to Crete, where his tomb could still be seen.

He applied the same τόπος again in *Ad Autoycum* 2, in his assessment of pagan writings on origins.[77] Those histories, he claimed, lack "any spark" of truth. He offered two evidences that pagan accounts of origins are false. First, he noted that people call the seventh day the "hebdomad," but they do not know why it is called this. He subtly explained why using wordplay from his prior phrase, "what the Hebrews call 'Sabbath' . . ." (παρ᾽ Ἑβραίοις ὃ καλεῖται σάββατον . . .). This is "assonance," literally "resemblance of sounds," a technique from the classical world for explaining the meaning of a word based on the meaning of another word that sounds similar.[78] He in this way drew the meaning of "hebdomad" (ἕβδομος) from the similar sounding word "Hebrews" (Ἑβραίος). His implication was that the name of the seventh day derived from the origins account of the Hebrews, their "Hexaemeron" in Genesis 1–2. His rhetorical challenge was that the philosophers, poets, and historians, those textual witnesses for the traditional gods, gave false testimony about what happened at the beginning, for if they actually knew the true history of origins, then they would have known the reason that the seventh day is called "hebdomad."

Clearly the second-century Christian/pagan contest concerning whose body of literature is most true formed the setting for these remarks. Immediately before declaring that pagan histories of origins lack the barest hint of truth, he sang the praises of the "supreme stature" (ὑπερβάλλον μέγεθος) of the Genesis Hexaemeron. In so saying, he first observed that many writers imitated it. While this remark might not greatly impress modern readers, it meant much in Theophilus's day. Ancient writers sought not to innovate as much as to imitate a classic text, thus adding to a body of venerable literature,

---

77. *Autol.* 2.12.
78. For assonance, see Clark, *Reading Renunciation*, 62.

extending its riches in new directions. Thus, he subtly conferred classic status upon Moses' Hexaemeron. This played into his rhetorical strategy, since a text having the status of a classic automatically possessed great authority. And according to rhetorical standards, an authoritative textual witness was therefore trustworthy.

As a second evidence that pagan historians, poets, and philosophers testified falsely about origins, he offered Hesiod's account of origins, which he considered "foreign to every truth" (ἀλλότριος πάσης ἀληθείας). In that origins account, the supposed god Eros is ruled by pleasure. But no true god would be ruled by pleasure, for it was axiomatic that wise and virtuous people shun shameful lust. How much more should a god shun lust?

The final classic τόπος for handling hostile witnesses that Theophilus used in letter two was that of showing that witnesses testified about what they could not have known. It appeared in the challenge of Hesiod's account of origins in *Autol.* 2.5. Theophilus presented statements by Hesiod claiming that the Muses are born of Zeus, and that the gods, presumably including father Zeus, are born of earth and heaven. Theophilus's point is that the Muses could not have seen the origins of either the gods or of the cosmos. Furthermore, neither could Zeus. Neither Hesiod, nor the Muses to whom he appealed, nor their forebears could have seen or known what they claim occurred.

The τόπος next appears in the discussion of the six days of creation in *Autol.* 2.12. There he claimed that since philosophers, historians, and poets used Moses' Hexaemeron as a source for their own histories, they call the seventh day the "hebdomad," but they do not know why it is called this.[79] If they could attest truly concerning earliest history, they would have known. They do not know, but with overconfidence, they brazenly present their account of origins nonetheless.

This τόπος resurfaces near the end of letter two. Theophilus asserted that pagan writers cannot speak truthfully about the creation or inhabitation of the world because they simply do not know the truth about such things.[80] His use of the device could not be more explicit. He then explained why the testimonies spoken "by the supposed wise-men and poets or historiographers" (τῶν καλουμένων σοφῶν καὶ ποιητῶν ἢ ἱστοριογράφων) attested to what they could not have actually known. They lived so long after the creation of the world and the initial establishment of cities and nations and the earliest spread of humanity that their histories of antiquity amount

---

79. He refers to the etymological explanation of "hebdomad" discussed above.
80. *Autol.* 2.32.

Promoting τόποι

Little by little, Theophilus thus built his case against the Greco-Roman gods using judicial rhetoric. Against the inconsistencies of witnesses who testified on behalf of the traditional gods, he repeatedly emphasized consistencies running though the testimonies of his friendly witnesses, the prophets. Against perceived temerity of poets and philosophers, whom he depicted attesting to what could not have happened or what they could not have known, he emphasized the virtue and authority, and thus trustworthiness, of the prophets.

When he emphasized the authority of the prophets, he enlisted a standard judicial τόπος. He did this in various ways in *Ad Autoycum* 2. He made oblique reference to the authority of his own witnesses, the prophets, by his assertion that these prophets are possessed "by a Holy Spirit" (πνεύματος ἁγίου), as well as his explanation that they are inspired and instructed "by God himself" (ὑπ αὐτοῦ τοῦ θεοῦ).[82] This language appealed to the type of authority granted to oracles in the ancient world.[83] Theophilus's audience associated a measure of authority to a prophetess who spoke on behalf of a god at an oracle site. That Theophilus's textual witnesses likewise were prophets who spoke on behalf of a God automatically imbued them with a certain measure of authority.

In *Autol*. 2.18–22, 30, and 35, he applied the same τόπος through fleeting references to the religious authority of his friendly witnesses. He referred to their words as the "divine Scripture [or: writing]" (θεία γραφή)[84]

---

81. Ibid., 2.33.

82. Ibid., 2.9. He made a similar claim in 2.33.

83. Fontenrose presents the types of responses given by the oracle at Delphi as revealed by surviving historical records, as opposed to legendary responses given in literature. See his *Delphic Oracle*. He also shows that this oracle was consulted in regard to a wide variety of concerns, including occasions of sickness, crime victimization, war, selecting political leadership, founding cities and colonies, marriage, pregnancy, death, business turning-points, worship, diplomatic events, and family crisis. See Fontenrose, *Delphic Oracle*, 53–55. This oracle exerted influence. While the oracle at Delphi had its own particularities, nevertheless it was typical of various local oracles in the empire. It was common for the ancients to associate certain degrees of authority to various oracles. See Ferguson, *Backgrounds of Early Christianity*, 213.

84. *Autol*. 2.18–19.

or "divine law" (θεῖος νόμος).⁸⁵ The adjective θεία suggested utmost authority to his audience, typically signifying "from the gods," although this was not what Theophilus himself had in mind. The τόπος also appears with reference to Moses' authority. He characterized Moses' testimony by the terms "divine" (ἱερός)⁸⁶ and cognates of "sacred" (ἅγιος).⁸⁷ He used these terms in a traditional Christian sense, yet alternate senses of "super-human" for ἱερός and "devoted to the gods" for ἅγιος would nonetheless signify utmost authority even to pagan ears. In *Autol.* 2.22 the relevant phrase was "the holy Scriptures" (αἱ ἅγιαι γραφαί), but the effect was similar.

This τόπος is also hinted in *Autol.* 2.28 where his witness was Adam, cast in the role of a prophet. Citing Adam's words in Gen 2:23–24, he exclaimed that this prophecy is fulfilled in the present-day by the action of newly married men when they separate from their parents and cleave to their wives so closely that they are willing to suffer death for the sake of their spouses.⁸⁸ The appeal of such fulfilled prophecy would have resonated

---

85. Ibid., 2.35.

86. Ibid., 2.20.

87. Ibid., 2.21, 30.

88. Modern editions of Genesis often use indenting to attribute Gen 2:24 to the narrator rather than to Adam. By contrast, Theophilus explicitly attributed Gen 2:24 to Adam, and regarded it as prophecy.

Theophilus's treatment of Gen 2:23–24 contrasts with gnostic treatment in the *Apocryphon of John* (*Apocryphon Ioannis* BG 8502.2.59.17–60.8). The writer of that treatise used the verse to argue that both men and women are composed of similar natures, partly psychic and partly spiritual, yet the manner of the creation of the woman is "not according to the manner [learned] from Moses" (*Apocryphon Ioannis* BG 8502.2.59.17–18). That is, the woman was not created as Moses claimed, from a rib of Adam. The writer used the exact same phrase earlier to dispute Moses' account of the trance given to Adam at the formation of the woman (*Apocryphon Ioannis* BG 8502.2.58.17–18). Rather that mere sleep, he claimed, Adam's trance is actually the veiled perception of those without knowledge. Thus, the writer of the *Apocryphon* used both Gen 2:21 and Gen 2:23 in ways that undercut the veracity of the Genesis narrative. Indeed, the writer used this phrase elsewhere, such as when he disputed the account of Noah's ark (*Apocryphon Ioannis* BG 8502.2.73.4). This writer thus repeatedly disputed the Genesis narrative. Regarding Gen 2.21–24, it may be that a desire to show that woman, like man, has a spiritual component motivated the writer to reject the words from Gen 2:21, "of ribs" (τῶν πλευρῶν) and assume that the emendation "of fullness" (τῶν πληρωμῶν) represented the true phrase. Theophilus would not contest that women possess spiritual capacity. However, in contrast to the purpose for which Gen 2:21–24 was used in the *Apocryphon of John*, Theophilus used Gen 2:23 for precisely the opposite purpose, which was to argue *in favor* of the veracity of the Genesis narrative.

The reason why Theophilus so differed from the writer of the *Apocryphon of John* as to his use of Gen 2:21–24 is not that he used a differing exegetical method, for both writers engaged in deductive expansion in order to explain the reasons way the woman was formed in a particular way. Rather, the reason Theophilus used Gen 2:21–24 as he did owes not to method, but to his theological and religious convictions that (1) there

with the contemporary hunger to know the future that was attested by widespread practices of divination.[89]

Besides the above-mentioned fleeting references to Moses and the prophets' authority appearing via cognates of ἅγιος, we also find repeated explicit mention of their superior authority.[90] Theophilus claimed that their books were more ancient (and thus more trustworthy and therefore more authoritative, according to Greco-Roman literary standards) than the writings of the historians and poets.

In *Ad Autoycum* 2, he also used the τόπος of emphasizing his friendly witnesses' virtue, and thus their trustworthiness. However, his use of it was selective, appearing only a few times, when he presented his early history of the cosmos.[91] But this was entirely fitting. The first eight chapters of *Ad Autoycum* 2 rhetorically consist of challenges to Autolycus' witnesses, the poets and philosophers. In the next chapters, Theophilus shifted attention to his own witnesses. So it is no surprise that he emphasized their virtue at this point.

Theophilus accomplished this by his assertion that after the prophets were possessed by a Holy Spirit and instructed by God himself, they "became pious and righteous" (ἐγενόμενοι . . . ὅσιοι καὶ δίκαιοι). While even on the surface, this is a strong claim of virtue in Theophilus's witnesses, it emerges even stronger in light of Greco-Roman standards. Piety and righteousness were often regarded as principal virtues, not only in Hellenistic Jewish circles, at least as attested by Philo, but also in the wider Greco-Roman world as well, as attested by the renowned Roman rhetorician Dionysius of Halicarnassus.[92] Other Christians also framed ethics by reference to these two Roman virtues. For example, when Justin Martyr related to Trypho the virtues which Christians cultivate, he began with piety and righteousness.[93] Theophilus's claim loomed even larger in view of the scandalous deeds of pagan gods, which he had mocked in the prior portion, quoting Greco-Roman histories which portrayed the gods as drunkards, fornicators, and murderers.

---

is one true God (hence Theophilus's point that no one can conclude that one god made man and another god made woman); and (2) Moses' narrative of creation is true and trustworthy (hence Theophilus's appeal to the great affection between husbands and wives as a consequence of the original unity of the sexes).

89. Ferguson, *Backgrounds of Early Christianity*, 220–21.

90. *Autol.* 2.30, 32, and also indirectly in *Autol.* 2.31.

91. Ibid., 2.9, 14–16.

92. Philo of Alexandria, *De praemiis et poenis* 53; *De Decalogo* 52, 119; Dionysius of Halicarnassus, *Isocrates* 7; *Epistula ad Pompeium Geminum* 6.

93. *Dialogus cum Tryphone Judaeo* 110.

Shortly after this, he made oblique references to the virtue of his friendly witnesses.[94] He judged that the prophets' words gush with sweetness, compassion, and righteousness. He asserted that his own witnesses are like the brightest stars, because they obey the commandments of God.[95] By contrast, the philosophers are "impious" (μάταιος). The same τόπος came into play in *Autol.* 2.16 where he produced testimony from one of his key witnesses, the prophet Moses, as a spur to live "by piety" (ὁσίως) and "by righteousness" (δικαίως). While some of his witnesses' virtues in *Ad Autoycum* 2 are implicit, here he explicitly named those two principal virtues so prized by Dionysius and others.

The third and final τόποι in *Rhetorica ad Herennium* for promoting a friendly witness involved emphasizing the consistency of the witness' testimony. Theophilus used this device far more extensively in *Ad Autoycum* 2 than in the other two letters he sent to Autolycus. Perhaps he did so because *Ad Autoycum* 2 relies so extensively on the words of a single key witness, Moses. This should be no surprise, since his aim was to show that Christianity is the true religion by demonstrating the trustworthiness of Christian primal history, this being Moses' account, over against the absurdity of pagan primal histories.

He reminded Autolycus that there are "not [merely] one or two" (οὐχ εἷς ἢ δύο)[96] prophets who testified "in agreement" (συμφώνως),[97] but all of them. They did not reside all in a single age or culture, where they might have met so as to "get their story straight." Rather, they consistently testified "throughout times and seasons" (κατὰ χρόνους καὶ καιροὺς), not only among the Jews, but also among the Greeks and other Gentiles through the voice of the Sibyl.[98]

He produced examples. Regarding claims that God can sometimes be found localized in a particular place,[99] he cited Moses and John.[100] He added Isaiah as a collaborating witness for Moses' account of primal creation in *Autol.* 2.13.[101] He believed that all the prophets confirm Moses' account of

---

94. *Autol.* 2.14.
95. Ibid., 2.15.
96. Ibid., 2.9.
97. Ibid., 2.10.
98. He claimed in ibid., 2.36 that the Sibyl functioned as a prophetess among the Greeks and other Gentiles.
99. Ibid., 2.22.
100. Genesis 3; John 1:1, 3.
101. Isa 40:22.

early generations.¹⁰² Summarizing Moses' testimony about cities built after the Deluge and about Babel, he added supporting testimony, from the treatise he called "Genesis of the World" and from the Sibyl.¹⁰³ It should be no surprise that his citations from the third book of the Sibyl were especially consistent with Gen 11:1-9, since that particular Sibylline was certainly composed by Jewish writers for apologetic purposes.¹⁰⁴

A striking example is the discourse on idolatry and monotheism in *Autol.* 2.35. Here Theophilus produced testimony after testimony, supporting his point that there is one true God. Theophilus cited in succession Moses (Exod 20:13-17), Solomon (Prov 4:25), Hosea (13:4), Isaiah (Isa 42:5-6, 12; 40:28), Jeremiah (Jer 10:12-13, 14-15; 6:29), David (Ps 13:3), Habakkuk (2:18-19).¹⁰⁵ Twice, he explicitly pointed out that they spoke in agreement with one another. Several times he introduced citations with the formula "in like mind . . ." (ὁμοίως . . .).

If this lengthy string of citations were not long enough, Theophilus further exclaimed, "And why should I recount the throng of prophets?" (Καὶ τί μοι τὸ πλῆθος καταλέγειν τῶν προφητῶν;). Answering his own question, he asserted that there are many prophets, and "countless" (μυρία) are their lines of agreement. In other words, he could have gone on and on with even more examples of consistent friendly testimony.

Still he added one more, the testimony of the Sibyl, who for him was a prophetess among the Greeks and other Gentiles.¹⁰⁶ Through this he

---

102. *Autol.* 2.30.

103. Ibid., 2.31; *Sib. Or.* 8.1; 3.97-103, 105; 8.5. Theophilus also referred Autolycus to "Genesis of the World" (Γένεσις κόσμου) in *Autol.* 2.29. Grant, *Theophilus of Antioch*, 73, notes that Theophilus may possibly have meant the biblical book of Genesis. If so, his appeal to this book would not constitute independent confirmation of the truth of Moses' testimony, but it at least would confirm the accuracy of Theophilus's citation of Gen 4:1-2. It could also be that Theophilus was referring to a commentary on Genesis that he had written, separate from *Ad Autolycum*.

104. For the Jewish provenance of *Sib. Or.* 3-5, see Ciholas, *Omphalos and the Cross*, 149-50; Collins, *Between Athens and Jerusalem*, 96-97, 165-67.

105. In connection with idolatry, though in a different portion of *Ad Autolycum*, his use of the great commandment concerning idols, Exod 20:5, was diametrically opposed to the use of the verse in the *Apocryphon of John*. The *Apocryphon* recalled the phrase from Exod 3:5b, "a jealous God," so as to argue for the existence of another god (lit., "I am a god of jealousy," *Apocryphon of John* BG 8502.2.44.14; Waldstein and Wisse, NHMS, 78). Specifically, the logic was that since the divine jealousy exists, then there must exist another god who triggers it. But Theophilus had argued in *Autol.* 2.28 that other gods do not really exist. In *Autol.* 3.9, he used Exod 20:3-5 to teach that piety consists of fidelity to the one true God. Each writer used the same verse to opposing ends, one writer against monotheism, and the other writer on behalf of it.

106. *Autol.* 2.36; *Syb. Or.* frg. 1.

showed that his witnesses are not all hidden in the small corner of the world that is Palestine.

Zeegers-Vander Vorst comments that his use of this sibylline text was typical of his tendency to cite classical works without a great deal of reflection on their content.[107] She has rightly characterized him. One might therefore be tempted to conclude that he did not reflect deeply on the words of the Sibyl simply because he was ignorant of their depths. However in this instance, one would misunderstand him apart from noting his reliance on judicial rhetoric. The fragment served him not at all as an object of commentary, but rather, as a textual witness supporting his argument. To break the words up with commentary would dull their value as supporting testimony. They had to stand alone, undiluted. His audience had to hear an unbroken stream of consistent witnesses supporting his case.

He even provided a theological explanation for the harmonious testimonies of his friendly witnesses. They agreed because the Logos, a participant in the Creation, spoke about it consistently through all the prophets.[108] By contrast, polytheists with diverse, antagonistic gods necessarily produce dissonance. His explanation dampened suspicion that his witnesses' consistency was merely illusionary.

He next added a further layer of supportive testimony about monotheism and final judgment.[109] Surprisingly, he appropriated it away from Autolycus, citing Aeschylus, Pindar, Euripides, Archiloches, Dionysius, Aeschylus again, Simonides, Euripides again, and finally Sophocles, all to one effect.[110] His phrase "some of the poets" was a backhanded reminder that not every poet so testified. Therefore, besides applying the τόπος of emphasizing consistency among supportive witnesses, he also implicitly invoked the τόπος of challenging opposing testimony.

The consistency of these particular pagan witnesses was more apparent than real. Diels shows that there are subtle alterations in the citations, vis a vis the original poetic treatises, enhancing apparent consistency, such as the missing μή from the Archiloches citation.[111] One wonders if Theophilus

---

107. Zeegers, *Citations des poètes grecs*, 142.

108. *Autol.* 2.10, 35, recalling 1 Cor 12:11.

109. *Autol.* 2.37.

110. Zeegers, *Citations des poètes grecs*, 123–30, shows that Theophilus did not access the poets whom he cited in *Autol.* 2.37 in the work of another writer, or by accessing the treatises of these poets directly. Rather, he used some lost collection of fragments.

111. The Archiloches fragment is found in *Ioannis Stobaei anthologium* 1.3.24. See also Zeegers-Vander Vorst, *Les citations des poètes grecs*, 128n3.

changed the wording, but Zeegers-Vander Vorst provides evidence that these alterations already existed in the lost anthology consulted by Theophilus.[112]

This was the first time he cited the poets on his own behalf. Therefore, he had to explain how at least sometimes they spoke truth. So he admitted that although they are much more recent than Moses, they can nonetheless relay true primal history "by stealing" (κλέψαντες) from Moses and other prophets.[113] He thus repeated a traditional Christian claim that poets and philosophers plagiarized Septuagint texts.[114]

He concluded his case with another string, citing Malachi (3:19); Isaiah (30:30, 28);[115] Solomon (Prov 3:8); David (Ps 50:10); Timocles (*Ioannis Stobaei anthologium* 4.57.8); Homer repeatedly (*Odyssey* 11.222; 16.856=22.362; *Iliad* 23.71), and Hosea (14:10).[116] By judicial rhetorical conventions, this was a formidable series of testimony supporting his case for monotheism, providence, and divine punishment.[117]

COHERENCE AND RHETORICAL USE OF SCRIPTURE IN THE THIRD LETTER

Rhetorical Structure

Just as for *Ad Autoycum* 1 and 2, so also one can demonstrate the overall judicial structure of *Ad Autoycum* 3. The introduction (προοίμιον, *prooemium*) is contained in *Autol.* 3.1. Theophilus used a conventional rhetorical device that was especially prevalent in the introductions of ancient judicial orations, namely the device of "προκατασκευή," lit., "a thing arranged beforehand," or rendered more metaphorically, "anticipation." Anticipation gives

---

112. Zeegers, *Citations des poètes grecs*, 127–28.

113. *Autol.* 2.37.

114. See, for example, Justin Martyr, *Apologiae* 1.44.

115. When he mentioned (but did not quote) the Sibyl just earlier, he referred to *Sib. Or.* 3.669–701. In this section of the oracle, the writer not only supplied a chilling description of the judgment, but also recalled Isa 30:30 as support, just as Theophilus did.

116. Zeegers, *Citations des poètes grecs*, 129–32, argues that the three citations of Homer are taken from some unknown writer, since all three are also found together in other writings. The Timocles citation is found in the anthology of Stobaeus. Zeegers also observes that the Timocles citation is the first of a couplet. The two elements of the couplet express the mercy of God toward the dead and his malevolence toward the living. Since the second element does not support Theophilus's argument, Zeegers concludes that he himself may have omitted it.

117. Theophilus did not use Hos 14:10 judicially, but paraenetically, to urge Autolycus to seek wisdom and righteousness and eventually find the true God.

the audience a hint of what is to come, in order to smooth its way.[118] An example of it can be seen in Isaeus' legal discourse against Aristogeiton and Archippus, where legal arguments appear in summary form in the introduction before their detailed expression in the narrative.[119] Anticipation in *Autol.* 3.1 consists of a "thumbnail sketch" of the historical and chronological arguments for the antiquity and trustworthiness of the Scriptures which reappear later in full flower.

The purpose of the narrative (διήγησις, *narratio*) of a judicial speech was to explain the main question of the dispute (*quaestio*), or the central issue to be resolved (*constitutio*).[120] However, the narrative was to be omitted if events of a case were well known, or if such recitation would not help the case. Whenever the narrative was omitted, then the orator simply stated the problem upon which the court must focus.[121] In such instances, the problem statement served to introduce the next standard component of a judicial speech, the proof (πίστις, *probatio*). Theophilus supplied his problem statement at the end of *Autol.* 3.1 where he observed that Autolycus thought the Scriptures are "silly talk" (λῆρος), and that they are only recent, and thus lack trustworthiness and authority. Since Autolycus was misinformed, Theophilus sent *Ad Autoycum* 3 to show him the antiquity of the Scriptures. Theophilus stated this explicitly.

He also embraced another aim. As he stated at the end of *Autol.* 3.1, he also wanted Autolycus to perceive the corresponding inferiority of other writings, meaning works of Greco-Roman poets, philosophers, and historians. *Ad Autoycum* 3 truly was a salvo in the Christian/pagan literary confrontation.

After a lengthy proof, Theophilus supplied the final standard component of a judicial speech, its conclusion (ἐπίλογος, *peroratio*).[122]

Here he recapitulated his argument, a common way of concluding.[123] He recapitulated the three main arguments of *Ad Autoycum* 3 but in reverse

---

118. Dionysius of Halicarnassus praised this device as a feature of Isaeus's rhetoric that ought to be imitated. See Dionysius of Halicarnassus, *Isaeus* 3.

119. Ibid., 15.

120. Cicero, *De inventione* 1.8.10; 1.13.18.

121. Ibid., 1.21.30–22.31.

122. While some ancient handbooks described a fivefold structure for judicial speeches, where proof and refutation were separate components, other handbooks combined proof and refutation and presented a four-fold structure, the very structure of all of the three letters to Autolycus. For details on proof and refutation, see the discussion of the structure of the first letter to Autolycus, earlier in this chapter.

123. *Autol.* 3.28–30.

order: Christians have the most ancient and trustworthy literature, the surest path to virtue, and the true philosophy.

We see that none of the letters of *Ad Autolycum* are thoughtlessly or foolishly structured, assertions by some modern critics notwithstanding. Rather, each was carefully organized according to ancient judicial rhetorical standards. While these structures might not sway modern audiences, they would please ancient ones.

Challenging τόποι

Ad Autoycum 3 opens with an introduction typical of a judicial discourse, as we have seen immediately above. After this introduction, Theophilus's first declaration was that writers ought to be eyewitnesses of the events they describe, or at least, should have accurately learned about the events from eyewitnesses of them. His following words make clear that he was indicting the poets and philosophers. Why should he have insisted that they should have restricted their accounts to what they personally witnessed or to what they learned directly from eyewitnesses? His use of judicial rhetoric supplies the answer. This was a clear application of the standard τόπος of showing that hostile witnesses have testified about what they could not have known. Since they had, it is no wonder to him that their writings were not conducive of virtue, like worthy literature, but was "unprofitable" (ἀνωφελής) and "impious" (ἄθεος).[124] This was a harsh judgment. Piety ranked quite highly among Greco-Roman virtues.[125] By so indicting the words of the poets and philosophers, he struck a bold blow against pagan literature.

He used the τόπος twice more in this letter. Introducing his own historical chronology, he charged that the poets and historians produced things written "from ignorance" (ἐπ' ἀδήλῳ).[126] He tried to bolster this attack by arguing that Plato's chronology relied on conjecture, and therefore, it is false.[127] Then after his chronology, he asserted that Greek writers provide erroneous history, because by their own admission, they only relatively

---

124. Ibid., 3.2. Promotion of virtue is noted as a characteristic of worthy literature in Dionysius of Halicarnassus, *Isocrates* 6, 9.

125. Regarding this, see the discussion of the priority of piety and righteousness in Greco-Roman thought, in the above discussion of Theophilus's promotion of his friendly witnesses' virtue in the early portions of *Ad Autolycum* 2.

126. Ibid., 3.16.

127. He provided a strained analysis of *Leg* 3.683c. Plato merely sought to introduce his audience to a deeper analysis of laws, but Theophilus took *Leg* 3.683c as an admission of conjecture.

recently learned writing.[128] If so, their claims about origins come not from eyewitnesses who truly knew primal history, but merely from recent writers testifying about what they could not have really known.

Theophilus used in *Ad Autoycum* 3 two other τόποι for challenging hostile witnesses, that of highlighting inconsistent testimony and that of emphasizing a witness' foul life. Interestingly, even though they are essentially unrelated devices, he used them in concert nearly everywhere in this letter. For this reason, in some places I will discuss them jointly.

The τόπος of displaying inconsistencies in hostile testimony sometimes surfaced in *Ad Autoycum* 3 only in passing. In *Autol*. 3.30, he cited Greek claims that the alphabet was discovered by Chaldaeans, or by Egyptians, or by Phoenicians, thus exhibiting the pagan historical inconsistency. However, his central aim here was merely to establish that the Greeks themselves knew they only learned the art of writing recently.

Elsewhere, not wanting Autolycus to have any doubt about inconsistent pagan testimonies, he supplied abundant examples. In *Autol*. 3.3, he connected the τόπος with his indictment of the poets and philosophers when he asserted explicitly, "they have spoken inconsistencies" (ἀσύμφωνα εἰρήκασιν). He applied the τόπος on two levels. On one level, they contradicted one another. On another, some voices even contradicted their own testimony. He then illustrated by breathlessly enumerating a string of pagan testimonies: for theism; against theism; about spontaneous generation of the cosmos; for providence; against providence; promoting purity; denying purity by allowing licentiousness, fornication, adultery, and "abominable" (ἀρρητοποιός) expressions; tolerating fornication among the gods and the cannibalism of Kronos and Zeus who ate their children; and tolerating the incest and obscenities of Hera, and the offenses of the gods Poseidon, Apollo, Dionysus, Heracles, Athena, and Aphrodite. This litany by Theophilus was itself an application of a standard rhetorical device. It was common for Greco-Roman writers, including some of the greatest, to emphasize contradictory assertions by opponents by means of simply citing their contrasting views one after another in rapid succession, so as to impress readers by the magnitude of an opponent's inconsistency.[129]

This litany not only applied the τόπος of emphasizing the inconsistent testimony of hostile witnesses. It also applied the judicial τόπος of showing the foul lives of hostile witnesses. Theophilus accomplished this in a subtle way by repeated mention of foul acts which poets and philosophers

---

128. Here he referred to their assertions that the alphabet was discovered by Chaldaeans, or by Egyptians, or by Phoenicians.

129. Zeegers, *Citations des poètes grecs*, 118.

tolerated as they promoted licentious gods. His rhetorical acumen was evident, for this single, dense litany implemented three distinct rhetorical devices simultaneously.

Theophilus also employed βίαιον (lit. "violent," but used by the ancients in its substantival sense, "violence" to denote rhetorical "over-powering" of an opponent's argument in order to use against him for one's own rhetorical advantage) in *Autol.* 3.4–6.[130] He applied the device by reciting various charges leveled against Christians: having wives in common, incest, cannibalism, that their teaching had been only recently made known, which is to say that it was by second-century standards untrustworthy, and that Christians had no proof of the veracity of their own teachings. Theophilus initiated the rhetorical "over-powering" when he accused Autolycus of not bothering to investigate the truth of these charges. His implication was that it was not Christians who could not prove their claims, but their pagan opponents. He amplified the rhetorical "over-powering" in *Autol.* 3.5, demonstrating that it was not Christian writers who promoted immoral behaviors such as cannibalism. Rather, the pagan poets and historians advocated these scandals. Theophilus cited to this effect Zeno, Diogenes, and Cleanthes who allegedly asserted that those who refuse to eat their fathers must themselves be eaten. He also cited Herodotus who recorded that a child of Harpagus was killed and placed before him as food, and who also related that it was a practice of the "Indians" (Ἰδοί) to eat their own fathers. Theophilus did not cite these examples to prove that pagans rather than Christians practiced cannibalism. Rather, he cited them to prove that Greco-Roman poets and historians rather than Christian writers advocated cannibalism in their writings.

Having considered cannibalism, he dealt with incest and having wives in common in *Autol.* 3.6. He reminded his audience that Plato advocated that wives ought to be the common property of all so that populations would increase, and so that widowers would be comforted. He cited Epicurus, and Solon as examples of philosophers who advocated incest. Solon recommended incest with sisters and mothers so that children would not be produced from adultery and so that fathers would not be dishonored, presumably also from acts of adultery.

Autol. 3.7 brings more τόποι. Nicole Zeegers-Vander Vorst observes that the successive and rapid citing of contrary views here in *Autol.* 3.7 was

130. This term appears as a neuter substantival adjective along with a description of its rhetorical function in Ps.-Hermogenes Περὶ εὑρέσεως 3.3. Despite being formally an adjective, it was traditionally used substantivaly as the technical name of this rhetorical move. See the more detailed discussion of this move in the above discussion of challenging τόποι in *Autol.* 1.1.

an application of the standard rhetorical device of σύγχρισις, "comparison," applied in order to discredit the poets and philosophers as a group.[131] In a broader sense, this was simply the standard judicial τόπος of showing inconsistency in testimonies of unfriendly witnesses. Theophilus cited Greco-Roman claims that the gods are composed of atoms; that the gods have no greater power than humans. He cited Pythagoras to the effect that the gods exist; that the cosmos emerged spontaneously; and that the gods do not care for humanity. He cited the philosopher Clitomachus on behalf of atheism; Critias and Protagoras on behalf of agnosticism; Euhemerus on behalf of the gods, and then in denial of the gods, on behalf of spontaneous providence; Plato on behalf of the immortality of the soul, and then on behalf of the transmutation of souls into other humans and into animals; Pythagoras in agreement with Plato, then disagreeing with him over the existence of providence; the poet Philemon on behalf of the gods; Euthemerus, Epicurus, and Pythagoras again in denial of providence; Ariston on behalf of providence.

Zeegers-Vander Vorst shows that these citations drew partly from a standard list of atheistic citations.[132] While she rightly notes[133] that Theophilus was rather uninformed about the content of Greco-Roman treatises which he cited by way of anthologies, still he knew enough about typical citation anthologies used by professional rhetors.

Autol. 3.7 also provides examples of a dynamic to which Theophilus had referred in *Autol.* 3.3. There, he stated that most of the philosophers demolished their own doctrines. The examples in *Autol.* 3.7 concern doctrines about the traditional gods. Plato both affirmed the gods and also implied they must be composed of matter. Pythagoras affirmed the gods, and then seemed to deny their power when he affirmed spontaneous generation of the cosmos. Theophilus cited a statement by Protagoras affirming that he did not know whether or not the gods exist. This mocking litany by Theophilus created an instance of the early Christian apologetic motif of idolatry's folly.

Autol. 3.8 served to recapitulate (thus employing a standard rhetorical device, as we have seen) Theophilus's indictment of inconsistent and unsavory philosophy of Greco-Roman religionists.[134] He began by summarizing the two charges against the poets and philosophers which he leveled in the prior portions. First, the poets and philosophers testified in-

---

131. Zeegers, *Citations des poètes grecs*, 137.

132. Ibid., 132–37.

133. Ibid., 303.

134. Theophilus also used the rhetorical device of recapitulation in *Autol.* 1.14; 2.8, 33; 3.9, 28–29.

consistently concerning the gods, on the one hand, denying their existence, and on the other hand, admitting it. Second, the poets and philosophers are to be dismissed because of their foul lives. He was quite explicit here, asserting that the poets and philosophers assented "to accomplish unlawful acts" (πράξεις ἀθέσμους ἐπιτελεῖν). He reminded his audience that the poets were not at all ashamed of the shameful acts of Zeus, but rather, "they sing all the more euphoniously" (εὐφωνότερον ᾄδουσι) of them. He enumerated various acts of the gods concerning which the poets showed no embarrassment. Hera had sexual intercourse with her husband Zeus "with a disgusting mouth" (στόματι μιαρῷ, perhaps implying that she engaged in oral sex). Zeus Latiaris thirsted for human blood. Theophilus next raised more general criticism of the gods. Attis was castrated. Zeus the Tragedian burnt his own hand, but yet is worshipped. The temples of Antinous are ridiculed. At the end of *Autol.* 3.8, Theophilus completed his recapitulation with yet another summary of his indictments against the poets and philosophers. They teach atheism, promiscuity, unlawful sexual intercourse, and cannibalism. He even asserted that the poets and philosophers themselves cannibalize. Needless to say, Theophilus laid heavy charges against the poets and philosophers. Having undercut their textual witness in *Autol.* 3.1–8, he would next emphasize the trustworthiness of his own textual witnesses, the prophets, starting in *Autol.* 3.9.[135]

Major thematic shifts take place at *Autol.* 3.9. Within the first Greek sentence, he both summarized his Christian metaphysic and introduced his moral values: Christians affirm a God, yet only one, the cosmic legislator who "with foresight" (προνοίᾳ) governs all things, and they have learned from him a holy law and are being taught justice, piety, and beneficence. From here through the end of *Autol.* 3.15, ethics take center stage.

There is also a rhetorical shift, a focus on promoting his own witnesses rather than attacking those of Autolycus. Still, he could not resist challenging Autolycus' witnesses a few more times. He used a series of citations in *Autol.* 3.16 to highlight inconsistency among the poets and philosophers. The first citation is of an unnamed group who claimed that the cosmos always existed and always will exist. The second is Apollonius declaring to the contrary that the cosmos came into existence 153,075 years prior. The third is a Platonic citation stating that if the cosmos truly is unchanging, then on the one hand, those who lived long ago must have failed to notice that things then were as they are at present, and on the other hand, some of the ancients actually did report things made clearly (καταφανῆ) evident since

---

135. For which, see the following section on promoting τόποι.

the time of Daedalus.¹³⁶ This charge of pagan cosmological inconsistency with even some of the same evidences reappears in the discussion of chronology at the end of letter three.¹³⁷

Theophilus also seized opportunities to further undercut the ethical credibility of Autolycus' textual witnesses a few more times in letter three. In *Autol.* 3.15, he cleverly enumerated false charges laid against the Christians and provided for each an example of its performance in the poets and philosophers, Autolycus' textual witnesses. There was a ring of familiarity here: he had already throughout *Autol.* 3.9–14 accused the poets and philosophers of legitimizing these same foul behaviors. For the charge of cannibalism, Theophilus implied that it is not the Christians who murder, but the Greco-Roman religionists, as they glory in the murder constantly exhibited in the gladiatorial shows. Christians are not accomplices in these murders, since they are forbidden by their religion to witness such atrocities. Furthermore, it is the poetic account of Thyestes and Tereus rather than Christian literature that glorifies cannibalism. For the charge of adultery, Theophilus cited the tragedies with their accounts of adultery among humans and among the gods. His discourse in *Autol.* 3.26 on the inconsistency of hostile witnesses is simply a restatement of some of the same examples of inconsistency which appeared earlier in *Autol.* 3.7 and 16. He reminded his audience of greatly differing ages of the cosmos produced by Plato and by Apollonius, and of differing Greek views about the generation of the cosmos. Some such as Pythagoras, claimed that the cosmos was generated spontaneously. Others, such as Ariston, affirmed the existence of providence.¹³⁸ In *Autol.* 3.30, he reminded Autolycus that pagan writers eagerly discussed what is "frivolous" (μάταιος) and "unprofitable" (ἀνωφελής), rather than promoting virtue. Not only so, their readers slandered the one true God, daily persecuted those who worship him, stoning and killing those eager for virtue and living holy lives.

Promoting τόποι

As we have seen, Theophilus turned from attacking the credibility of Autolycus' witnesses to bolstering that of his own in *Autol.* 3.9. From here on, he marshaled all three standard τόποι for supporting one's own witnesses.

---

136. Plato, *Leges* 677c-d.
137. *Autol.* 3.26.
138. Ariston is not explicitly cited in ibid., but he and other Greeks who affirm providence are clearly in view, since the charge of Greek inconsistency does not hold otherwise. Theophilus had cited Ariston in ibid., 3.7.

The first to appear is that of emphasizing a witness' virtue. Theophilus pursued this masterfully by showing how the Mosaic law exemplifies the finest of the Greco-Roman virtues.

He connected the Mosaic law to the most prominent Greco-Roman virtues by presenting the Decalogue as a legal summation. He concluded *Autol.* 3.9 with a summary statement partaking of a Hellenistic Jewish exegetical tradition of referring to the Decalogue as ten summations of all of God's commandments. As Philo put it, "the ten words are summaries of the particular laws extending through the entire legislation registered in the holy books" (οἱ δέκα λόγοι κεφάλαια νομων εἰσὶ τῶν ἐν εἴδει πὰρ ὅλην τὴν νομοθεσίαν ἐν ταῖς ἐραῖς βίβλοις ἀναγραφέντων).[139] He then indicated the supreme rank of these ten over other divine commandments by pointing out that the many particular commandments were given through a human prophet, but the ten chief commandments heading up the lot came not through a human prophet but directly from God himself, here referring to the finger of God that wrote them on Moses' stone tablets at Sinai.[140] Indeed, he referred to these Ten Commandments of Deuteronomy 5 as "ten summations" (κεφάλαια ... δέκα) numerous places in his writings.[141] Theophilus likewise called them "ten summations" (δέκα κεφάλαια).[142]

This tradition of referring to the Decalogue as ten κεφάλαια also indicates Philo's and Theophilus's rhetorical world, since κεφαλή is a cognate of the rhetorical technical term signifying the device of recapitulation, ἀνακεφαλαίωσις.[143] Their rhetorical training and literary culture made them predisposed to understand the Decalogue as a recapitulation of Moses' entire legal code. Autolycus would have understood this.

The categories under which Theophilus arranged these ten summations offer further evidence of his shrewd use of rhetoric for explaining God's commandments to his pagan friend. Grant finds himself at a loss to explain the organization of the Decalogue within *Autol.* 3.9. He maintains that Theophilus divided his discussion of the elements of the Decalogue

139. Philo of Alexandria, *De Decalogo* 154.

140. Exod 31:18.

141. Philo of Alexandria, *De praemiis et poenis* 2, where the description of the Ten Commandments as ten summations appear in an overview of the Pentateuch in the introduction in his treatise; *De Decalogue* 154–75, where Philo explained how the Ten Commandments are general and supreme commandments under which the many particular commandments fall; and *De congressu quaerendae eruditionis gratia* 120, where he asserted that the ten commandments are not only the heads but also the source of every imaginable particular commandment, there being an infinite number of these.

142. *Autol.* 3.9.

143. For recapitulation as a Greco-Roman literary convention, see *Rhetorica ad Herennium* 2.30.47.

into two parts, the first dealing with piety and doing good works, and the second dealing with justice. Concerning this division, Grant exclaims, "the division Theophilus makes, into three and seven, is difficult to understand, especially since in II 35 the last five are quoted in a slightly abbreviated form, and no allusion is made to Exod 23 6–8."[144] However, this can be easily explained in light of the sensitivity of Theophilus for Greco-Roman aretegenic concerns.[145]

It is no coincidence that Theophilus summarized the teaching of divine law under the aretegenic categories of justice, piety, and doing good works, and further that he turned first to piety (εὐσέβεια). Two of these are traditional Hellenistic Jewish aretegenic categories. Philo asserted that piety is the most esteemed virtue.[146] Elsewhere, he called piety the source or chief (ἀρχή) of virtues and their sovereign (ἡγεμονίδας).[147] He explained that the very order of the Ten Commandments, which begin with commandments concerning piety and later deal with those concerning mortal humans, mirror reality in that God is the beginning of all created things. Therefore, the ten summations of all divine commandments and even of all imaginable commandments have piety as their chief and origin.[148] He not only made piety the sovereign of virtues, but also stated that justice is akin to it.[149] Thus, Philo elevated the same two virtues by which Theophilus organized his discussion of every element of the Decalogue save one. Theophilus may also have had these two virtues in mind in *Autol.* 1.7 when he informed Autolycus that he can see God if he lives in "holiness and sanctity and righteousness" (ἁγνῶς καὶ ὁσίως καὶ δικαίως).

Indeed, justice and piety were not only traditional Hellenistic Jewish aretegenic categories but also in a broader sense, traditional Hellenistic categories. The renowned rhetorician Dionysius of Halicarnassus, writing in Rome a few decades before the birth of Jesus, recommended the imitation of the discourse by Isocrates entitled "On the Peace," because it effectively exhorted both individuals and entire communities towards justice and

---

144. Grant, "Bible of Theophilus," 176.

145. The meaning of "aretegenic" derives from the Greek root word, ἀρετή, meaning "goodness" or "excellence," and in a moral sense, "virtue." For an impressive discussion of aretegenic concerns in the New Testament and in the church fathers, see Charry, *By the Renewing of Your Minds*, 3–152.

146. Philo of Alexandria, *De praemiis et poenis* 53. Philo asserted that piety "is the finest in the chorus [of the virtues]" (κάλλιστεύει . . . ὡς ἐν χορῷ).

147. Philo of Alexandria, *De Decalogo* 52, 119.

148. Ibid., 52; cf. *De congressu quaerendae eruditionis gratia* 120.

149. Philo of Alexandria, *De specialibus legibus* 4.134–35.

piety.[150] Justice and piety again were singled out for praise among the virtues when Dionysius discussed philosophical comments in historical writings of Theopompus of Chios.[151] Dionysius claimed piety and justice are for historians qualities "worthy of imitation" (ζηλωτά). This also signaled that the goal of Greek history was not dispassionate documentation as with modern history, but rather, exhortation towards virtue.

Thus, Theophilus and Philo both presented ethical treatments which derived their content from the inspired writings, but were organized according to two major ethical categories of Hellenistic culture, piety and righteousness. While Theophilus's use of the inspired writings was abundant, his presentation followed the rhetorical standards of his day.

Even his third category, beneficence, the execution of good works, had a place among Greco-Roman virtues. It was attested, for example, in the high honor accorded to those who became great benefactors.[152] With the fifth commandment, Theophilus probably turned to beneficence because honoring one's parents does not solely belong to either piety or justice. Philo came the closest to Theophilus's three aretegenic categories in his treatise on the Decalogue, since he placed the first four commandments under the category of piety, the last five under the category of justice, and the fifth commandment on the borderline separating piety and justice.[153] It is not surprising that one would separate the Ten Commandments into two sets given that the narrative of their reception by Moses depicts half of the commandments on one tablet and half on a second tablet. However, what is distinctive of both Philo and Theophilus's treatments is firstly, that they used the same identical terms, piety and justice, to label the two main sets, and secondly, that they treated the fifth commandment, the injunction to honor one's parents, in a category of its own.

While this aretegenic category of beneficence did not enjoy a supreme place among Greco-Roman virtues, the other two aretegenic categories

150. Dionysius of Halicarnassus, *Isocrates* 7.

151. Dionysius of Halicarnassus, *Epistula ad Pompeium Geminum* 6.

152. For the honor associated with benefactors and its connection with the development of the ruler cult, see Ferguson, *Backgrounds of Early Christianity*, 202–3.

153. Philo of Alexandria, *De Decalogo* 106–10. He reasoned here that the fifth commandment concerning one's parents deals both with the immortal realm (since parents by their capacity for generation are thereby similar to God who is the Father of the cosmos) and with the mortal realm (since mortal parents have relationship with other mortals). Therefore, the fifth commandment fittingly occupies the border between first four commandments dealing with the immortal God and the remaining five dealing with behavior towards mortals. Similarly, *Quis rerum divinarum heres* 172 presents the idea that the fifth commandment is on the borderline (μεθόριος) between commandments dealing with devotion to God and those dealing with justice per se.

which Theophilus used in *Autol.* 3.9 did. By so connecting the Mosaic law to these supreme Greco-Roman virtues, Theophilus brought into play the judicial τόπος of emphasizing the virtuous life of his own witness, Moses the law-giver.

Theophilus continued his use of this τόπος in *Autol.* 3.10. Taking up the history of the exodus which he began relating at the end of *Autol.* 3.9, he arrived at the point where the children of Israel were about to leave Egypt. Here he cited a statement from his witness, Moses, concerning sojourners.[154] Since the Israelites were sojourners for 430 years, they knew the world of a sojourner. Accordingly, they were commanded to abstain from oppressing them. Here is a high contrast with Roman political ethics. The empire depended much on slave labor, drawn in great part from involuntary sojourners taken in conquest. However, Moses attested to an ethic which made a sore point of Roman dependence on foreign captives. Thus Moses was presented in *Autol.* 3.9–10 as a witness who was virtuous and thereby trustworthy.

Theophilus emphasized his witnesses' virtuous lives a few more times in letter three. The chorus of prophetic voices elaborating details of a high social ethic in *Autol.* 3.12 and a high sexual ethic in *Autol.* 3.13 presented a brilliant contrast to the dark and scandalous deeds Theophilus cited in *Autol.* 3.1–8 from the writings of the poets and philosophers. He illustrated this sexual ethic, with its prohibitions not merely against adulterous behaviors but also against even the most fleeting thoughts of lust, by means of a string of examples taken from Proverbs and from Matthew 5. He referred to the prohibition in Matt 5:28 against lusting after another man's wife. He then cited Solomon's injunction of Prov 4:25–26 to keep one's eyes directed straight (and presumably not to the side in a lustful leer) and to make straight the paths of one's feet. He next cited the "gospel voice" (Matt 5:28, 32) concerning adultery and divorce; and Solomon again (Prov 6:27–29) on adultery. We have seen in chapter 3 that he engaged in a rich use of link words for unifying Prov 4:25–26 and 6:27–29.

Theophilus also used in letter three the standard judicial τόπος of emphasizing the consistency of the testimony of friendly witnesses. In *Autol.* 3.11, he successively cited the testimony of Isaiah (Isa 55:6–7), Ezekiel (Ezek 18:21–23), Isaiah again (Isa 31:6; 45:22), Jeremiah (Jer 6:9) all in support of his point that the one true God wants all people to repent and quickly pours out mercy whenever they do. After this citation string, he claimed that additional prophetic testimonies supporting this same point, beyond those he has just cited, are in number many, or "rather more truly countless"

---

154. Exod 23:9.

(πᾶλλον δὲ ἀναρίθμητά). So saying, he further emphasized the consistency of his own witnesses, the prophets, by intimating that he could go on and on with additional consistent prophetic citations.

Having shown the consistency of his witnesses in *Autol.* 3.11, concerning repentance, Theophilus proceeded similarly in *Autol.* 3.12 regarding justice. He cited a lengthy string of supporting textual witnesses from among the prophets, including Isaiah (1:16–17; 58:6–8); Jeremiah (6:16); Hosea (13:4); Joel (2:16; 1:14); and Zechariah (7:9–10). The judicial rhetorical nature of *Autol.* 3.12 is emphasized by the almost total lack of commentary by Theophilus on these biblical citations. Between each citation appears only a mere citation formula generally consisting of the word "ὁμοίως," "in like fashion," followed by the name of the next witness. Repeated, rapid-fire citation was enough for demonstrating consistency.

Grant asserts that the gospel passages relating to justice in *Autol.* 3.12 have been lost and that they would probably have come from Matthew.[155] He notes that Theophilus alluded to Matt 3:15 in his discussion of the Ten Commandments, minus the third and fourth, in *Autol.* 3.9. This reasoning holds some force, since Theophilus stated at the beginning of *Autol.* 3.12 that both the prophets and the gospels are consistent in their teaching on justice. However, an alternate explanation seems simpler. The gospel passages are not lost as Grant thinks. Their omission is explained by Theophilus's use of the inspired texts as supporting textual witnesses. Even though he stated at the beginning of *Autol.* 3.12 that both the prophets and the gospels are consistent regarding their teaching on justice, he only needed to demonstrate a great consistency among a number of his own friendly witnesses, regardless of whether they are prophets or gospel writers. He simply needed to maintain the sharp contrast that he had highlighted among the poets and philosophers (demonstrated in *Autol.* 3.1–8), and the great consistency of his own textual witnesses (demonstrated in *Autol.* 3.9–15). Furthermore, Autolycus had not in his objections to Christianity (these being indicated by the responses given by Theophilus) demonstrated any great familiarity with either the prophets or the gospels. Therefore, Autolycus was not likely to distinguish between gospel voices and prophetic ones upon reading *Autol.* 3.12.

The opening sentence of *Autol.* 3.12 is significant for seeing Theophilus's theory of inspiration. Here he asserted that the OT prophetic writing and the NT gospels are consistent because one single Spirit of God produced both. I discussed in chapter 1 Harnack's view that Theophilus did not consider NT texts to be Scripture, Grant's point by point refutation of Harnack,

---

155. Grant, *Theophilus of Antioch*, 117n1.

and Zeegers' case in support of Grant in this regard. I also observed that the crucial issue is not really whether Theophilus *referred* to the NT epistles as Scripture, but whether he indeed *considered* them such, notwithstanding his terminology. And the burden of proof is on Harnack, since Theophilus implied here in *Autol.* 3.12 that the prophets and the gospels exist on the same level in regard to both inspiration and authority. And indeed his use of both OT and NT texts in his judicial rhetoric throughout all three letters bears this out. The percentage of his uses of Scripture by way of citation, so vital for his judicial rhetoric, since *citations* of friendly and hostile witnesses are so prominent in it, is virtually identical for OT and NT texts. Of his OT uses of Scripture, 26% are citations.[156] Of his NT uses of Scripture, 25% are citations. This signals that both the OT and NT were equally valuable as sources of citations of friendly witnesses in his judicial rhetoric. As a rhetor, he favored neither over the other.

Theophilus continued to highlight the consistency of his witnesses in his discussion of utmost chastity in *Autol.* 3.13. This portion consists mostly of a citation string of the words of Solomon intermingled with those of Matthew, all mandating utmost chastity even in hidden thoughts. His strategy here is very similar to that of the prior portion.

He emphasized consistency of his supporting witnesses also in his discussion of goodness in the following portion. He championed good deeds by citing one prophet (Isa 66:5), three texts from Matthew (5:44, 46; 6:3) introducing them with the formula, "and the gospel:" (τὸ δὲ εὐαγγέλιον·), and two other Christian inspired texts (1 Tim 2:1–2; Rom 13:7–8), introducing these with the formula, "the Divine Word commands us" (κελεύει ἡμᾶς ὁ θεῖος λόγος).[157] Theophilus implied through this citation string the constancy of the component voices. Indeed, throughout *Autol.* 3.9–15, he demonstrated in detail his explicit claim that the words of the prophets are consistent with those of the gospel writers.[158]

He was similarly explicit in *Autol.* 3.17 where he asserted, "All the prophets spoke in harmony and pleasing one another" (σύμφωνα καὶ φίλα ἀλλήλοις οἱ πάντες προφῆται εἶπον). He explained how the prophets alone could speak consistently. They alone were inspired by one unique Holy Spirit of God. Therefore, they all testified consistently. His argument is subtle, for he admitted that Homer, Hesiod, and Orpheus claimed to have learned from divine providence. Yet his language about prophetic truthfulness, "with how

---

156. The scripture usage tables in the appendices provide the details.

157. Harnack argues that this formula does not refer to 1 Tim 2:1–2 and Rom 13:7–8. However, Grant rightly corrects him in this regard. See Harnack, "Theophilus von Antiochien und das Neue Testament," 17–18; Grant, "Bible of Theophilus," 183–84.

158. He makes this explicit claim in *Autol.* 3.12.

much exceeding measure" (πόσῳ ... μᾶλλον), indicates his perception that the divine worked more profoundly in the prophets than in the poets.

His concept of inspiration supports the unity of his third letter. For Theophilus, divine inspiration of the prophets explains both the superiority of their ethics which he argued in *Autol.* 3.9–15, and the superiority of their chronology which he argued in *Autol.* 3.16–30. His thoughts about inspiration therefore fittingly appear near the border of these two major portions of the letter, in *Autol.* 3.17.

The third standard τόπος for supporting friendly witnesses involves emphasizing their authority. Theophilus frequently employed it in letter three. He used it first in his discussion of inspiration in *Autol.* 3.17, in conjunction with a deft application of rhetorical βίαιον (lit. "violent," but used by the ancients in its substantival sense, "violence" to denote rhetorical "over-powering" of an opponent's argument in order to use against him for one's own rhetorical advantage).[159] He applied it by citing Plato's assertion that "accurate learning" (ἀκριβὲς μαθεῖν, the infinitive functioning as a substantive) only comes through perception of divine law.[160] He then reminded Autolycus that Homer, Hesiod, and Orpheus claimed to have received accurate learning, and that the historians similarly learned from diviners and seers. He exclaimed that Christians know the truth even more, since they learn not from diviners and seers but from the holy prophets, the ones in whom the Holy Spirit of God dwells. If the poets and historians spoke with a measure of authority because they relied on diviners and seers who perceived something of the divine, how much more authority did the prophets carry, since they did not contact the divine in a second-hand way?

In *Autol.* 3.20–23, Theophilus made veiled reference to the authority of his friendly textual witnesses when he asserted that the (OT) Scriptures are older, and thus by ancient standards, more trustworthy than other writings. He also emphasized their authority by describing them as "holy" (ἱερός).[161] Autolycus likely understood it in the sense of "divine." Therefore, the term carried a weighty import for him, even if he was unfamiliar with its typical biblical sense. Theophilus emphasized the antiquity of Moses, his primary textual witness, in several ways. In *Autol.* 3.21, Theophilus used the chronology of Manetho to argue that Moses lived nine hundred or a thousand

---

159. This term appears as a neuter substantival adjective along with a description of its rhetorical function in Ps.-Hermogenes Περὶ εὑρέσεως 3.3. Despite being formally an adjective, it was traditionally used substantivaly as the technical name of this rhetorical move. See the more detailed discussion of this move in the above discussion of challenging τόποι in *Autol.* 1.1.

160. Plato, *Meno* 99e.

161. *Autol.* 3.20.

years prior to the Trojan War.¹⁶² In *Autol.* 3.22, Theophilus used the writings of Josephus and of Menander of Ephesus to argue that Moses lived seven hundred years before the founding of the city of Carthage. In *Autol.* 3.23, he recapitulated what he has argued in *Autol.* 3.21–22 by reminding his audience that the ancient Greco-Roman writers whom he has cited, Manetho, Manander, and Josephus attested that other chronologies were more recent than the chronologies of Moses and the other prophets.¹⁶³ He also added another layer of evidence, arguing that all of the Greco-Roman legislators (οἱ νομοθέται πάντες) legislated after the time of Moses. To this effect, he cited examples. Solon the Athenian lived during the time of the prophet Zacharias, who lived long after Moses. The legislators Lycurgus and Draco, and Minos lived long after Moses, since the Scriptures of Moses were penned prior to the rule of Zeus in Crete and prior to the Trojan War.¹⁶⁴

Having thus demonstrated the inferiority of Greco-Roman chronologies in *Autol.* 3.21–23, Theophilus introduced his own chronology at the end of *Autol.* 3.23. As he puts it, his goal was that "we might make a more accurate proof of exact times and periods" (ἀκριβεστέραν ποιήσωμεν τὴν ἀπόδειξιν τῶν καιρῶν καὶ χρόνων). Even this purpose statement suggests use of judicial rhetoric. It is relevant that he used the word ἀπόδειξις, "exhibition" or "proof." It is equivalent to πίστις, used in the rhetorical handbooks to denote a judicial proof.¹⁶⁵

In *Autol.* 3.24–25, he made allusion or reminiscence to over eighty separate texts, from the historical narratives of Genesis, Exodus, Judges, 1 Samuel, 1 and 2 Kings, 2 Chronicles, and Ezra. They compose his chronology of the period from the time of Adam through the rebuilding of the Jewish temple under King Cyrus. Not one of these uses of OT Scripture is a citation. Therefore, it may not seem evident that he used them as textual witnesses in his argument. But the claims of *Autol.* 3.26 immediately following this primal chronology show that they indeed served as such.

---

162. Tatian, *Oratio ad Graecos* 31, 36–39, also argued that Moses is more ancient than Troy. However, Tatian used the testimony of different Greek historians than that of Theophilus.

163. Geffcken claims that while Theophilus gave the appearance of having studied Manetho's and Manander's chronologies directly, he simply learned them from Josephus. See Geffcken, *Zwei Griechische Apologeten*, 251.

164. Tatian, *Oratio ad Graecos* 41, presents a similar argument concerning the greater antiquity of Moses over these legislators, only in greater detail. It is even plausible that Theophilus studied the argument in this very text, given that Epiphanius reported that Tatian's writings were influential in Antioch around 170 (Epiphanius, *Haeres.* 46.1).

165. Aristotle, Τέχνη ῥητορική 3.13; and Quintilian, *Institutionis oratoriae* 4.Pr.6, attest to the necessity for a proof (πίστις, *probatio*) in judicial discourses.

In *Autol.* 3.26, it was easy for him to emphasize the authority of his witnesses. He simply pointed out that the historians Herodotus, Thucydides, and Xenophon began the detailed and accurate portions of their histories with events which occurred during or close to the days of King Cyrus, who appeared not at the beginning of Theophilus's own detailed chronology, but far into it, at the end of *Autol.* 3.25. But Theophilus had produced a detailed chronology in *Autol.* 3.24–25 of events prior to Cyrus. Only a truly ancient chronology could have dealt so thoroughly and precisely with events which took place long before the time of Cyrus. Therefore by ancient literary standards, the prophets were more trustworthy and authoritative on account of their superior antiquity.

Theophilus had argued[166] that his witnesses did not conjecture as did Autolycus' in part by reference to their detail and precision concerning events from Adam to Cyrus. Therefore, he could not give an impression of ignorance about events after Cyrus. Accordingly, he completed his chronology in *Autol.* 3.27 with a detailed account of recent rulers, and deduced that 741 years elapsed from Cyrus to the then recent death of Emperor Verus.[167]

STRATEGIC MOVEMENTS AND AD AUTOLYCUM'S META-LOGIC

We have seen that Theophilus frequently employed a judicial rhetorical technique that we do not often find in modern courtrooms but which was often used in ancient ones. He devoted great attention and trust to the testimony of dead witnesses recorded in written form. It is important to understand how pervasive this specific ancient technique is throughout *Ad Autolycum*. The following charts indicate its extent.

---

166. *Autol.* 3.18–19.

167. Verus was the adoptive brother and co-regent of Marcus Aurelius. Verus died in 169 CE.

Promoting Τόποι for Friendly Witnesses	Chapters of *Ad Autolycum* 1	Chapters of *Ad Autolycum* 2	Chapters of *Ad Autolycum* 3
authority	14	9, 18–22, 28, 30, 32–33, 35	17, 20–23, 26–27
virtuous lives	14	9, 14–16	9–10, 12–13
consistency	14	9–10, 13, 22, 29–31, 35–38	11–14, 17
Challenging Τόποι for Unfriendly Witnesses	Chapters of *Ad Autolycum* 1	Chapters of *Ad Autolycum* 2	Chapters of *Ad Autolycum* 3
foul lives	1–2, 7, 9–10	none	3, 6–8, 15, 30
inconsistency	8–10, 13	2, 4–8, 37	3, 7–8, 16, 26, 30
could not have happened	none	3	none
did not happen	none	3, 12	none
could not have known	2, 5, 7	5, 12, 32–33	2, 16, 30
partiality	none	none	none

As it turns out, when Theophilus was not drawing on promoting τόποι to champion testimony of prophets and apostles, then he typically employed challenging τόποι to contest testimony of poets and philosophers. Representing τόποι with asterisks (*) and dividing them by whether they promoted friendly witnesses or challenged hostile ones, we can see just how true this is.

Τόποι	Ad Autolycum 1	Ad Autolycum 2	Ad Autolycum 3
promoting τόποι for friendly witnesses	*	** **** *****	****** **** ****** * **** ****** * ****
challenging τόποι for hostile witnesses	** * **** *	******* *	** * ** *** ** ** * *

There is hardly a chapter of *Ad Autolycum* where we do not find interrogation of dead witnesses, a very trusted ancient judicial rhetorical approach, involving prophets on one side and poets and philosophers on the other. Witness interrogation serves as the "meta-logic" of Theophilus's apologetic.

These charts also depict appropriate strategic rhetorical shifts within *Ad Autolycum*. Letter one prepared the way for Theophilus's attack, "softening up the ground." Therefore, it is no surprise that almost all of the τόποι in letter one challenge Autolycus' witnesses. Theophilus only turned to the trustworthiness of his friendly witnesses at its conclusion, as a suggestion of what was to come in the next letter. Letter two argued historical matters by both challenging the *historical* reliability of Autolycus' witnesses and also emphasizing the *historical* trustworthiness of his own. This explains why mainly it is in letter two that we find recourse to τόποι used for false or overconfident eyewitnesses. Letter three is a discourse on true literature, in three categories: philosophy, ethics, and chronology. Here Theophilus wanted to show the foolishness of pagan writings in comparison with the truth of Christian ones. Accordingly, here we find very balanced recourse to both challenging τόποι directed to Autolycus' witnesses and promoting τόποι directed to his own witnesses.

But we also see that his strategy of only promoting his own witnesses after he had first challenged Autolycus' appears not only across *Ad Autolycum* as a whole in the sense that letter one challenges hostile witnesses and later, letters two and three promote friendly ones, but also at a smaller scale within each individual letter. Furthermore, at the end of each letter, each one a personal letter, he appealed to his friend, exhorting him to embrace Christianity, with his most detailed exhortation at the conclusion of his final letter.

The Greeks and Romans, including the Hellenistic Jews, used protreptic approaches. Aune observes that their methods for composing protreptic speeches, λόγοι προτρεπτικοί, are not described in any surviving ancient rhetorical handbook. Therefore, the typical structure of protreptic appeals can only be discerned by inductive examinations of the fairly few surviving protreptic speeches. Aune's survey of these notes that a protreptic appeal was typically twofold or threefold, consisting of a attack on a competing philosophy or way of life, a promotion of the preferred one, and sometimes a concluding appeal to embrace the preferred philosophy or way of life.[168] This is exactly what we find in *Ad Autolycum*. And we find a hint of this strategy in Aristotle's *Art of Rhetoric* 3.17.14 in the instruction that if an opponent's case contains a multitude of good points, an attack should be made first before presenting one's own case. Considering both judicial and protreptic features of *Ad Autolycum*, its meta-logic then can be visualized as a garment woven of classic witness interrogation structures and τόποι that is draped over a traditional protreptic literary framework. This is why it was essential in chapter 2 to establish, despite some contrary claims in scholarly literature, that *Ad Autolycum* is protreptic through and through, and to establish in this present chapter that its second-century judicial rhetoric, where Scripture plays a central role, was fully coherent and even masterful. The arrangement of *Ad Autolycum* is anything but confusing or unsatisfying. To second-century eyes, it would have appeared lucid and very rhetorically compelling.

168. Aune, "Protreptic literature," in *Early Christian Literature*, 383–86.

AFTERWORD: A NEW OUTLINE OF *AD AUTOLYCUM*

Since the organization of *Ad Autolycum* is quite coherent according to the judicial rhetorical standards of Theophilus's day, it is fitting to propose a new outline of the three letters in light of those standards. The new outline provided here offers several benefits.[169] First, it reflects well Theophilus's own words indicating his purpose for each letter. Second, it shows how the sub-themes in each letter relate to its stated purpose. Third, it is informed by rhetorical standards of Theophilus's own day.

The title of letter one, "Argument concerning the True God," draws from Theophilus's acknowledgment at the beginning of letter one, in *Autol.* 1.2, and at the end, in *Autol.* 1.14, that he was responding to the request of Autolycus that he show his God. Clearly, these acknowledgments create an instance of *inclusio* that encloses letter one and supplies its rhetorical and apologetic context. The title of letter two, "Argument concerning the True History," draws from the admission at the beginning of letter two, in *Autol.* 2.1, that Theophilus intended to provide a further defense of his religion by recourse to Greco-Roman history books.[170] The title of letter three, "Argument concerning the True Literature," draws from the denigration in *Autol.* 3.1 of pagan literature, and the stated intent to defend the antiquity (and thus, according to second-century values, the trustworthiness) of Christian writings vis-à-vis "the nonsense of the rest of the writers" (τῶν λοιπῶν συνταξάντων τὴν φλυαρίαν).

Sub-titles in the outline have been chosen so as to describe the theme of each letter section. However, it is also evident that the sub-titles all fit easily under the respective letter titles chosen for the three letters of *Ad Autolycum*. This harmony between letter titles and sub-titles, each chosen by differing methods, the letter titles chosen on the one hand by examination of certain statements in the introductions and conclusions to the letters, and the sub-titles chosen on the other hand by examination of thematic content in the various letter sections, confirms the coherence of this new outline of *Ad Autolycum*.

LETTER ONE: ARGUMENT CONCERNING THE TRUE GOD
προοίμιον: *Autol.* 1.1
διήγησις: *Autol.* 1.2.1
πίστις: *Autol.* 1.2.2–1.13

---

169. Citations of *Ad Autolycum* here and below refer to the book (letter), chapter, and Greek text line number in Grant's edition.

170. Droge insightfully argues, primarily on the basis of book two, that Theophilus attempted to provide a christianized cultural history. See Droge, *Homer or Moses*, 102–23.

    Autol. 1.2–5: The True God
    Autol. 1.6–8: God as Creator and Ruler
    Autol. 1.9–10: Folly of False Gods
    Autol. 1.11–13: Objections Answered
ἐπίλογος: *Autol.* 1.14

LETTER TWO: ARGUMENT CONCERNING THE TRUE HISTORY
προοίμιον: *Autol.* 2.1.1–8
"διήγησις"[171] (πίστις): *Autol.* 2.1.8—2.37
    Autol. 2.2–8: Origin of the Gods and of the Cosmos
    Autol. 2.9–19: Genesis and Creation
    Autol. 2.20–33: Genesis and Early Generations
    Autol. 2.34–37: Idolatry and the Coming Judgment[172]
ἐπίλογος: *Autol.* 2.38

LETTER THREE: ARGUMENT CONCERNING THE TRUE LITERATURE
προοίμιον and problem statement: *Autol.* 3.1
πίστις: *Autol.* 3.2–27
    Autol. 3.2–8: Philosophy
    Autol. 3.9–15: Ethics
    Autol. 3.16–27: Chronology
ἐπίλογος: *Autol.* 3.28–30

---

171. As discussed earlier in this chapter, Theophilus claimed to give a διήγησις, but this was probably a reflection of his explicit intention (*Autol.* 2.1) to prove whose witnesses relate true history. Thucydides used similar language to describe his own historical writing (Thucydides, *Historiae* 6.54.1.2). In a rhetorical sense, it is actually a πίστις, and so Grant translates the term.

172. For ancient Jews and Christians, the great coming judgment and other future prophetic fulfilments were entirely pertinent to historical discussions. See Wilken, "*In novissimus diebus.*"

5

Scriptural Anthologies and Testimonia (Excursus)

THE SEARCH FOR TESTIMONIA AND TESTIMONY SOURCES

Students of patristic use of Scripture are interested in the various media through which ancient writers accessed the Scriptures. Theophilus lived close to the heyday of one particular biblical medium, the testimonia collection.

To my knowledge, we have not yet seen any published studies of Theophilus's use of biblical anthologies and other testimony sources. But I believe that he used them in various portions of *Ad Autolycum*.

A helpful way of understanding testimonia collections is to review a bit of the history of their discovery. The "Testimony Hypothesis" was influential in New Testament research in the early part of the twentieth century, but has since been largely ignored. While not many New Testament scholars are convinced that testimonia collections were used in the first century, good evidence for use of small testimonia collections in the second century has been presented by Bousset, Kraft, Skarsaune, and others. Frequent use of anthologies in the ancient world, and surviving testimonia collections from Qumran, and in the writings of Cyprian and Pseudo-Gregory of Nyssa also remind second-century scholars to be alert to the presence of testimonia collections and "testimony sources." The term, "testimony source," is used to denote a treatise containing various biblical quotations that is not an anthology of biblical passages per se, but that nevertheless was used as one.

Testimonia scholarship has a long history. In 1838, C. Credner proposed that certain Old Testament passages, which he called "testimonia," were used by Christians. His term derives from the use of these passages as points of evidence in judicial arguments. While Credner was the first to write about such Christian use of testimonia, the most influential early testimonia scholar was J. Rendel Harris.[1]

Harris posited in 1916–1920 that certain testimonia texts were compiled under the authority of the apostle Matthew into a single, widely distributed anthology, a "testimony book."[2] Harris believed that such testimonia were useful to early Christians in their debates with Jews, thus explaining the prominence of these same Old Testament texts in the New Testament.

More recent scholars recast the testimonia theory. C. H. Dodd argues that certain Old Testament texts provide "regulative ideas" for the first-century church, which are transmitted through exegetical traditions, rather than through a single testimony book, as Harris had argued.[3] Likewise, Barnabas Lindars argues that anthology books of certain Old Testament texts may have indeed been assembled, but only after the writing of the New Testament, rather than before, which Harris had posited.[4] Dodd and Lindars represent an English slant on testimonia that emphasized their oral rather than written transmission. Harris had been unsuccessful in arguing for the use of a single testimony book. Therefore, Lindars and later scholars henceforth speak of either orally transmitted testimonia or multiple written testimonia collections.

Recent scholars are more successful presenting evidence for use of testimonia collections in the second century than in the first. Regarding Pseudo-Barnabas, Robert Kraft shows that the writer in some cases used Jewish testimonia which were adapted by Christians. Pierre Prigent's study of Pseudo-Barnabas similarly shows that the writer used several collections of testimonia. This should not be surprising, for it was likely common in antiquity for writers to use such collections. Scholars have viewed Pliny the Elder's habit of compiling his own personal anthologies of documents that

---

1. For an assessment the of work of Credner and Harris, see Osborn, *Justin Martyr*, 116.
2. Harris, *Testimonies*.
3. Dodd, *According to the Scriptures*.
4. Lindars, *New Testament Apologetic*.

he studied as being probably representative of a widespread practice in the ancient world.[5]

In contrast to most studies of testimonia, which focus on the NT or on a particular patristic writer's works, Daniélou offers a history of the development of traditions of interpretation of ten OT citations that figure most prominently in Christian tradition.[6]

Much of recent testimonia research addresses Justin Martyr. Prigent, in a monograph entitled *Justin et l'Ancient Testament*, initially intended to uncover use of testimonia in Justin as he had in his earlier monograph on testimonia in the *Epistle of Barnabas*.[7] However, Prigent abandoned this intent after suspecting that Justin's lost *Syntagma* (Treatise) *Against All Heresies* is the source behind his still extant *Apologies* and *Dialogue*. Prigent supports this thesis by also identifying passages in Irenaeus and Tertullian that he understands to be quotations of the same *Syntagma* material. Prigent thinks that Justin used testimonia in the *Syntagma* but not in the extant writings. Rather, the extant writings merely use quotations of the *Syntagma*.

Skarsaune highlights the importance of "testimony sources," treatises which functioned as biblical anthologies. His *Proof from Prophecy, A Study in Justin Martyr's Proof-Text Tradition* has become the standard work on testimony sources in Justin.[8] He critiques Prigent's study in several ways. First, he wonders why Justin would not have had access to the testimony sources for his later works if he had access to such sources for his earlier work. Second, he finds unconvincing Prigent's explanation that Justin wrote a well-organized *Syntagma*, which explains the well-organized use of the source in Irenaeus and Tertullian, but later was unable to similarly organize the *Syntagma* quotations in his *Apologies* and *Dialogue*. Third, Prigent consistently identifies sources as being from the *Syntagma* even apart from evidence in the details of the given extant text. Even though he does not

---

5. Kraft, "Barnabas' Isaiah Text"; Kraft, "Epistle of Barnabas"; Prigent, *Les testimonia dans le christianisme primitif*, 117–18.

6. Daniélou, *Études d'exégèse judéo-chrétienne (les Testimonia)*.

7. Prigent, *Justin et L'Ancien Testament*. There are a number of helpful overviews as well as more detailed evaluations of Justin's thought including Bammel, "Justin der Märtyrer"; Barnard, *Justin Martyr*; idem, "Justin Martyr in Recent Study"; Edwards, "Justin's Logos"; Goodenough, *Justin*; Guerra, "Conversion of Marcus Aurelius and Justin Martyr"; Nahm, "Debate on the 'Platonism' of Justin"; Osborn, *Justin Martyr*; Piper, "Nature of the Gospel according to Justin"; Price, "'Hellenization' and Logos Doctrine in Justin." Osborn's *Justin Martyr* is an especially helpful recent analysis. On Justin's use of Scripture, besides Skarsaune's *Proof from Prophecy*, discussed below, also see Hagner, "Sayings of Jesus"; Manns, "L'exégèse de Justin"; Simon, "The Bible in the Earliest Controversies"; and Shotwell, *Exegesis of Justin Martyr*.

8. Skarsaune, *Proof from Prophecy*.

accept Prigent's thesis, Skarsuane appreciates his work. He accepts Grant's assessment that even though Prigent does not convincingly reconstruct Justin's lost *Syntagma Against All Heresies*, he very much advances our comprehension of the extant writings of Justin.[9] Skarsaune finds two main sources in Justin, a "recapitulation source," which was perhaps the lost *Controversy between Jason and Papiscus*, and a "kerygma source." Where Bousset proposes that the kerygma source consists of a number of tracts from a school tradition, Skarsaune proposes that there may also be an alternate or additional kerygma source which consists of a single treatise since there are explanations and fulfillment narratives which are added to particular Scripture extracts more than once.[10] Based on his analysis of OT quotations, he concludes that the lost *Kerygma Petrou*, portions of which are preserved in Clement of Alexandria's *Stomata*, may well be this kerygma source treatise. Skarsaune is not the only scholar to use the concept of a testimony source. Prigent uses it as well.[11]

Martin C. Albl presents a recent comprehensive treatment of the history and current state of testimonia research in his *'And Scripture Cannot Be Broken': The Form and Function of the Early Christian Testimonia Collections*.[12] He helpfully refines terminology and identifies strengths and weaknesses of prior approaches. He also notes that while J. Rendel Harris' "Testimonia Hypothesis," which insisted that a single testimony book was widely used in the first century, has not been accepted, plausible arguments are provided by Bousset, Kraft, and Skarsaune that many small written testimonia collections were used in second-century Christian school settings.[13] A conclusion of his relevant to second-century testimonia research is that standard methods for detecting use of testimonia remain valid today.[14]

---

9. Skarsaune, *Proof from Prophecy*, 4–5. For Grant's assessment, see his review of *Justin et l'Ancien Testament*.

10. Skarsaune, *Proof from Prophecy*, 136. Skarsaune judges that Bousset's analysis "as a whole is hardly surpassed by any later writer."

11. Prigent, *Les testimonia dans le christianisme primitif*, 218. Prigent argues that the writer of the *Epistle of Barnabas* used some testimony sources (not necessarily testimonia) when he wrote of Christology and universalism. These testimonia traditions had similar authority as Scripture for Pseudo-Barnabas and had to do with the passion and the resurrection, at least initially.

12. Albl, *And Scripture Cannot Be Broken*. Albl makes no mention of Theophilus of Antioch in his survey of prior research of testimonia in patristic writers. For a concise overview of the current state of testimonia studies, see Parsons, "Testimonia."

13. Albl, *And Scripture Cannot Be Broken*, 68–69.

14. Ibid., 66–67, 287. Albl describes over a dozen such methods for detecting use of testimony sources. The four most fruitful methods involve seeking common uses of conflations, common sequences of various quotations, common textual variants not

However, Stanley faults Albl for assuming Christian school traditions prior to the mid-second century.[15] For this reason, he asserts that the testimony hypothesis cannot be re-accepted by scholarly consensus without further work on the social context of first-century Christianity. While Albl fails to establish the existence of Christian school traditions prior to the second century, he holds that first-century Christians used testimonia in school settings because of analogous practices, as indicated by the Qumran discovery of *4QTestimonia* and *4QFlorigelium*, as well as common Greco-Roman use of anthologies in school settings. Stanley's critique of Albl threatens Albl's contention that testimonia studies are unduly neglected by students of first-century Christianity, but it does not threaten the relevance of testimonia studies for work in the second century. They are certainly relevant to studies of Theophilus. While he did not use testimony sources nearly as much as some second-century writers, we shall see that he used some.

A NEW COMPUTATIONAL APPROACH

In testimonia scholarship, the most important indications of plausible use of a testimony source are: (1) common sequences of biblical quotations and allusions; (2) common conflations of Scripture quotations; (3) false attributions, which could indicate that a writer was unaware of the true author of a passage because the passage was not accessed in a biblical manuscript; and (4) textual variations not traceable to any known biblical manuscript. In order to comprehensively and consistently identify quotation conflations and traditional sequences (#1 and 2) in *Ad Autolycum*, I use a new, automated approach denoted by the acronym "ACTS" (Application for Computerized Testimonia Searches). It involves searching a massive database of indexes of Scripture usage in almost all of the extant Jewish and Christian works written prior to *Ad Autolycum*.[16] Custom software intelligently and

---

traceable to any known biblical manuscripts, and false attributions which could indicate that a writer was unaware of the true author of a passage because the passage was not accessed in a biblical manuscript.

15. Stanley, Review of *And Scripture Cannot Be Broken*.

16. Index entries are generally gleaned from *Biblia Patristica*. For *Ad Autolycum*, index entries are included only if both Grant's and Marcovich's critical edition indexes include them, thus drawing from a measure of scholarly consensus as to whether Theophilus used a biblical passage. For extant works not included in *Biblia Patristica*, indexes of critical editions listed in the bibliography are used. While loss of funding forced the original *Biblia Patristica* team to disband after publishing seven volumes, its work has been resurrected with free online access by the Institut des Sources Chrétiennes. See www.biblindex.mom.fr. For a list of the Jewish and Christian treatises used by ACTS, see the appendix section, "List of Treatises Searched by the Application for

automatically issues repeated queries to this massive database in order to discover combinations of Scripture quotations or allusions in extant works of predecessors which are identical or close to those combinations in *Ad Autolycum*. This allows a truly exhaustive search, not otherwise possible in a practical sense, for all uses in *Ad Autolycum* of testimony sources. This method has uncovered previously unknown exegetical traditions behind *Ad Autolycum*. It even checks for "near matches" of biblical allusion or quotation sequences, widening the range of possibilities to plus or minus two verses for each element of each combination of verses in each patristic text. C. H. Dodd shows that such near matches, which are typically ignored in scholarly literature, can also indicate the existence of testimony sources.[17] Especially as a consequence of considering not only exact matches but also near matches of biblical allusion or quotation sequences as well as all possible subsets and combinations of those sequences, there is simply a massive number of possible biblical allusion or quotation sequences to examine in over four hundred extant texts of Theophilus's predecessors and which must not be ignored, hence the value of this new computational approach. So as to search for possible testimony sources not only among writings of all of Theophilus's extra-biblical Christian contemporaries and predecessors but also some biblical and Jewish predecessors, the database also includes biblical index information from the Greek New Testament (ref. OT use in the NT), the Old Testament Pseudepigrapha, the writings of Philo of Alexandria, Dead Sea Scrolls biblical anthologies (4QTestimonium, 4QFlorilegium), the *Mishnah*, and the *Seder Olam*.[18]

The ACTS approach consists of using a custom software application, written in the VisualBasic computer language, in concert with a massive relational database of Scripture use in most of the surviving Christian and Jewish texts contemporary or prior to a given writer, in this instance, the late-second-century Christian apologist, Theophilus of Antioch. The ACTS

Computerized Testimonia Searches (ACTS)."

17. Dodd, *According to the Scriptures*, 57–59.

18. The biblical index database was populated using the indexes or footnotes of biblical quotations, allusions, and verbal parallels in the following editions: Grant, *Ad Autolycum*; Marcovich, *Theophili Antiocheni*; Otto, "Gebrauch neutestamentlicher Schriften bei Theophilus," 617–22, which has no formal index but contains an insightful survey of biblical allusions; Delamarter, *Scripture Index to Charlesworth's Old Testament Pseudepigrapha*; "4Q174" (4QFlorilegium) and "4Q175" (4QTestimonium) in Charlesworth et al., *Dead Sea Scrolls*, 251–61, 313–17; Allenbach, *Supplément, Philon*; Aland et al., *Greek New Testament*; Allenbach, *Des origines*; Guggenheimer, *Seder Olam*; Neusner, *Mishnah*, which is used instead of Blackman's critical edition because Blackman's expansive pagination does not accord well with the type of pagination assumed in the ACTS application.

software performs a complex series of queries into the database, using the SQL database query language, in order to rapidly identify those uses of Scripture most likely involving biblical anthologies and other testimony sources. It harnesses the power of automation in order to identify combinations of Scripture uses hitherto unrecognized. It unearths these biblical combinations with a speed and efficiency orders of magnitude greater than traditional manual methods, akin to a jazz pianist who finds pleasing chords instantaneously and instinctively, producing hundreds of them in the time that a beginning pianist takes to work through an unfamiliar composition.

The massive ACTS database includes a number of tables that can be linked in various ways using the relational quality of the database. This database contains the following tables having the following table indexes and fields.

> scrref table—scripture reference table, where each record documents one use of a biblical passage in a particular ancient treatise.
>
> indexes:
>
> > idxBibvs1—consists of the bibbook & bibchap & bibvs1 fields. Since multiple records of the database will have the same such combination, this index is neither primary or unique.[19]
> >
> > idxBibvs2—consists of the bibbook & bibchap fields. Since multiple records of the database will have the same such combination, this index is neither primary or unique.
> >
> > treatise—The treatise field.
>
> fields:
>
> > bibbook—biblical book, 3 characters. Required field. Entry uses biblical book abbreviations used in biblical indexes such as Biblia patristica, but in lowercase.
> >
> > bibchap—biblical chapter, integer. If the value is zero, the entire book is denoted.
> >
> > bibvs1—biblical verse, or starting biblical verse of a range of verses, integer. If the value is zero, the entire chapter is denoted.
> >
> > bibvs2—ending biblical verse of a range of verses, integer. Use zero if no range is denoted.

---

19. For "primary," "normal form," and other relational database-related terms, see a standard treatment of relational database theory such as Date, *Database*.

vers—Boolean. Default value: false. This data indicates whether the biblical reference only is found in some versions of the text. Consult Biblia patristica or other scriptural indexes for the critical edition used for the scriptural index. The critical edition should indicate variant versions in the critical apparatus, and thus show the biblical reference in one of the variants.

treatise—Patristic, NT, or Jewish treatise in which the biblical reference occurs. Integer. Required field. The value corresponds to the primary key of the treatise table. The treatise table includes the author along with the treatise title.

book—Book of treatise. Byte. Default value: zero. If the value is zero, the treatise is a single volume work.

chapter—Chapter of treatise. Integer. Default value: zero.

section—Paragraph or section of treatise. Integer. Default value: zero.

pg—Page of treatise in the critical edition used in the biblical index volume used to supply data for the table. Integer. Default value: zero. In the various ACTS database tables for this kind of data, we must use "pg" instead of "page" since that term is a Visual Basic reserved word.

ln—Line of treatise in the critical edition used in the biblical index volume used to supply data for the table. Integer. Default value: zero. In the various ACTS database tables for this kind of data, we must use "ln" instead of "line" since that term is a Visual Basic reserved word.

idx_ed—Index edition used to supply information for the current table record. Required field. Byte. The value corresponds to the primary key of the index edition table (table name: idx_ed).

treatise table—author and treatise containing biblical references

indexes:
treatise_num. Integer. Indexed as a unique, primary key. Referenced as a foreign key in the scrref table.
treatise_name.

fields:
treatise_num—integer. Required.

treatise_name—50 characters, text. Abbreviated author & treatise, separated by a "$." For treatises referenced in Biblia patristica, use its abbreviations. For example, the Sibylline Oracles would appear as "ANON$OR.SIB."

crit_ed—name of critical edition. Use editor name or otherwise denote. 50 characters, text. Abbreviate information since the full bibliographic information will be kept in an Endnote bibliographic database (a non-SQL, proprietary database).

idx_ed table—This table contains the edition information for all indexes of biblical references in various collections of works (Jewish, NT, patristic, etc.)

indexes:
idx_ed. This is indexed as a unique, primary key and referenced as a foreign key in the scrref table.

fields:
idx_ed—byte, 0–255. Required.
edition_info—name of edition of index volume. Abbreviate title and editor, if necessary. 50 characters, text. Abbreviate information since the full bibliographic information will be kept in an Endnote bibliographic database (a non-SQL, proprietary database).

poss_verses table—This table contains all other uses of verses used by those authors using the input verse in the same section of their writings where they use the input verse.[20]

indexes: none.
fields:
bibbook—biblical book, 3 characters. Required field. Entry uses biblical book definitions used in Biblia patristica.
bibchap—biblical chapter, integer. If the value is zero, the entire book is denoted.
bibvs1—biblical verse, or starting biblical verse of a range of verses, integer. If the value is zero, the entire chapter is denoted.

---

20. For "input verse," see the following flowchart.

bibvs2—ending biblical verse of a range of verses, integer. Use zero if no range is denoted

treatise—Patristic, NT, or Jewish treatise in which the biblical reference occurs. Integer. Required field. The value corresponds to the primary key of the treatise table. The treatise table includes the author along with the treatise title.

book—Book of treatise. Byte, 0–255. Default value: zero. If the value is zero, the treatise is a single volume work.

chapter—Chapter of treatise. Integer. Default value: zero.

section—Paragraph or section of treatise. Integer. Default value: zero.

pg—Page of treatise in the critical edition used in the biblical index volume used to supply data for the table. Integer. Use this data when the book, chapter, and section are zero.

ln—Line of treatise in the critical edition used in the biblical index volume used to supply data for the table. Integer. Use this data when the book, chapter, and section are zero.

poss_treatises table—This table contains all treatise sections using the input verse. These are also possible candidates for use of testimony sources.

indexes: none

fields:

treatise—integer

book—Book of treatise. Byte, 0–255. Default value: zero. If the value is zero, the treatise is a single volume work.

chapter—Chapter of treatise. Integer. Default value: zero.

section—Paragraph or section of treatise. Integer. Default value: zero.

pg—Page of treatise in the critical edition used in the biblical index volume used to supply data for the table. Integer. Use this data when the book, chapter, and section are zero.

ln—Line of treatise in the critical edition used in the biblical index volume used to supply data for the table. Integer. Use this data when the book, chapter, and section are zero.

poss_verses2 table—This table is the same as the poss_verses table, except that it contains only records where the verse occurs more than once in the poss_verses table

The ACTS database is truly massive, containing data about roughly 50,000 uses of Scripture in the ancient treatises including quotations, allusions, and reminiscences. If this information were manually entered into the ACTS database from the biblical indexes of the various ancient treatises, populating the database would require months of data entry effort and the resulting database would surely be fraught with data entry errors. These difficulties were avoided by automating the task of populating the database. Individual pages of scholarly index volumes and index pages of ancient treatise critical editions were carefully scanned into digital image files. Then, optical character recognition software was used to produce files containing the index data in machine-readable character format. Then, custom software was developed that could take account of the various layouts and formats of the index pages, convert character-based numeric data into numeric format, and finally add each Scripture usage data element to the database. No manual database entry was required.

The high-level design of the ACTS software is visually represented in the following flow-chart. Note that this flow-chart is simplified, omitting for instance "maintenance" type operations such as emptying working database tables after iterations of the main processing loop. While this simplified flow-chart may not reflect such, nonetheless the ACTS design takes account of certain special situations:

1) verse overlap: As discussed above, C. H. Dodd has shown that near matches are important, since ancient biblical anthologies often included blocks of biblical text more than one verse in length. One writer may have used a verse from the top of the first two elements of a given biblical anthology while another writer may have used a verse from the bottom of those same two biblical anthology elements. So as to account for such near matches, the ACTS software uses a "VerseOverlap" factor which specifies how wide an overlap in verse numbers to consider when looking for uses of the same biblical texts.

2) treatise page overlap: Since treatise section numbers postdate the treatises themselves, treatise section boundaries are arbitrary, although useful nonetheless. Since use of a testimonia collection in a given writer might well begin near the end of one treatise section and overflow into the next treatise section, it is important to consider such situations. Therefore, the ACTS software uses a PageOverlap factor, which

is typically one in value, to consider overlaps of (typically) one page of treatise critical edition, so that it handles Scripture sequences which overflow the boundaries of a treatise section into the preceding or following treatise section.

3) Entire biblical chapters or books: Biblical indexes of critical patristic editions sometimes include entries for entire biblical chapters or books. The ACTS software is able to consider such when it queries the database for similar patterns of Scripture use by various ancient writers.

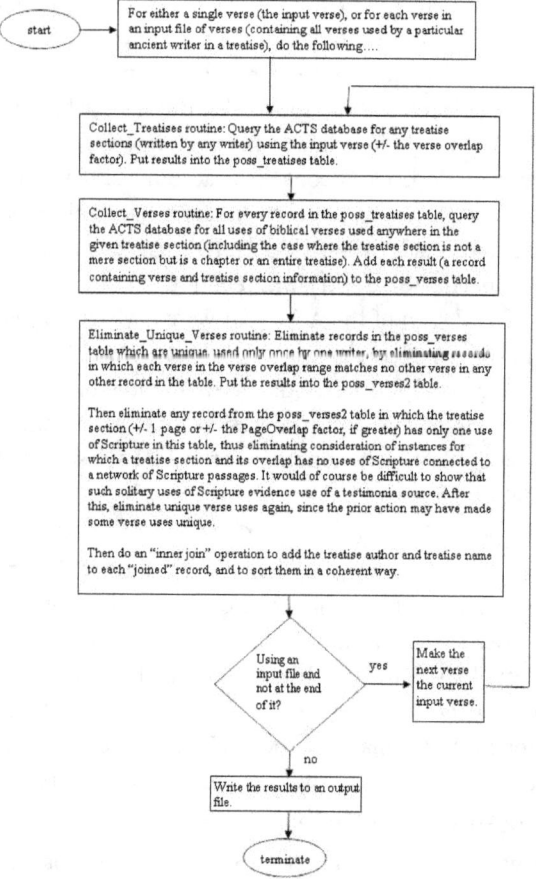

The accuracy of ACTS was demonstrated early on, when it successfully and accurately identified evidence of the same testimony sources behind Justin Martyr's writings as those which Skarsaune discovered. Additional verification of the accuracy of ACTS emerged when every one of the testimony sources ACTS discovered in connection with Theophilus accurately showed the precise biblical passages for all relevant treatises, as compared with the biblical indexes in the given print critical editions.

This electronic methodology proves valuable not only when it produces positive results. One illustration of its value in producing negative results is its strengthening of Grant's conclusion that the alleged commentary by Theophilus quoted in Jerome, *Ep.* 121 is not genuine. Grant disputes the authenticity of this commentary fragment in part by noting that this exposition identifies the unjust steward as Paul of Tarsus. Grant holds that this negative depiction of Paul is at odds with the free and positive use of Pauline texts in *Ad Autolycum*.[21] A comprehensive search using ACTS for all mathematically-possible common uses of Scripture networks, and even taking into account near-matches, shows that there are absolutely no Scripture conflations or quotation/allusion sequences common to the commentary fragment and to *Ad Autolycum*. This particular investigation is no trivial affair, since the letter contains 100 uses of the Hebrew Scriptures and 306 uses of New Testament writings. And since it is thus extremely unlikely that any common testimony sources lie behind Jerome's letter and *Ad Autolycum*, even though we shall see that there is plausible evidence for use of testimony sources in *Ad Autolycum*, there is less likelihood that the two writings have the same author than there would be otherwise. This ACTS finding strengthens Grant's conclusion that the alleged Theophilus commentary quoted in the letter is actually not from Theophilus's hand.

EVIDENCE OF TESTIMONY SOURCES BEHIND AD AUTOLYCUM

Has Theophilus used testimony sources? There is evidence that he did. In what follows, I will discuss the strength of evidence indicating possible or likely use of testimony sources, or at least previously-unknown exegetical traditions in play during his days.

Autol. 1.7

A possible use of a testimony source appears in *Autol.* 1.7 with his quotation of 1 Cor 15:53. In both *Autol.* 1.7 and *Epistula Apostolorum* 21 we find a use of this verse introduced by an exhortation to believe. The *Epistula Apostolorum* exhorted readers to believe in the future resurrection of those whom the Lord

---

21. Grant, "Studies in Theophilus," 25.

saves, and immediately after the exhortation used 1 Cor 15:53 to encourage such faith. Theophilus likewise urged Autolycus to believe. Likewise immediately following, he alluded to 1 Cor 15:53–54 and claimed that a reward of such faith is immortality. But it is striking that there is no explicit exhortation to believe in 1 Corinthians 15 anywhere near verse 53. Since *Autol.* 1.7 does not mimic the wording of *Epistula Apostolorum* 21, behind both writings there may lie a common testimony source, although we cannot be certain since the Greek original of the *Epistula Apostolorum* has been lost.

The possible use by Theophilus of this oral[22] or written testimony source, or at least of an exegetical tradition exhibiting these features, suggests that it may have become traditional in some quarters to use the "put on imperishability" language of 1 Cor 15:53–54 in early Christian protreptic appeals. This would have harmonized well with the philosophical coinage of the age.

Autol. 1.10

Evidence of Theophilus's using another testimony source appears several portions further into the first letter, in his discussion of demons and pagan gods. After an extended critique of Greco-Roman gods in *Autol.* 1.9 and the first part of *Autol.* 1.10, he declared that the pagan gods are unclean demons. In so doing, he alluded to Ps 95:5. Similarly, Justin Martyr used Ps 95:5 several times in order to make the same point.[23] However, what is truly telling about Theophilus's use of the verse is that he tightly conflated it with Ps 113:12 and 16. But this conflation is not unique to Theophilus. It represents a Christian exegetical tradition, for a conflation of Ps 95:5 with Ps 113:12 is also found in Rev 9:20.[24] Therefore, he has not simply referred to a manuscript of the Psalms, but most likely to a testimony source which is no longer extant. The source is not likely Rev 9:20 itself, because he also quotes Ps 113:16, but Rev 9:20 merely alludes to it.

With this conflation, there is also a striking echo of vv. 10–11 of Ps 113, which Theophilus did not quote, even though he sowed *Autol.* 1.1–10 with uses of Ps 113:12–16. In *Autol.* 1.2–3, he acknowledged Autolycus' request to show him the Christian God and to describe his form. Theophilus answered these requests throughout the remainder of *Ad Autolycum* 1, including *Autol.* 1.1 and 1.10, where citations and quotations of Ps 113:12–16

---

22. See the above discussion of Dodd's and Lindars's contributions to oral testimonia scholarship.

23. Justin, *Dialogue* 55, 73, 79, 83; cf. 1 *Apologiae* 41.

24. This conflation is not found in Justin.

are found. That he answered this question throughout *Ad Autolycum* 1 is indicated by his posing this question at the beginning of the letter and then again in its last line. The demands from the mouth of Autolycus to see God recalled the echoed but unquoted Ps 113:10, where the pagan nations mock by asking where is the true God. This echo carried force precisely because it jarred the ears of Theophilus's audience, as they suddenly recognized that the ancient pagan derision recited by the psalmist was now restated in their own world by Autolycus. Autolycus and modern readers unfamiliar with the Psalm would miss the echo. But the second-century Christian and Jewish readers of *Ad Autolycum* who were very familiar with the Psalm would hear the echo, and realize anew that the concerns of the psalmist were not irrelevant simply because he lived in a prior age.[25] They would be struck by the irony that the very same derisive question that pagan nations voiced in the days of the psalmist, "where is your God?" was yet again being voiced by pagans among them in their own day.

Theophilus used this source not only to declare that the many Greco-Roman gods are mere idols and unclean demons, but also to denigrate their value to their devotees. To this end, he proclaimed that those who trust in idols and demons should become like them.[26] His use of the source fits comfortably in his larger argument about the folly of false gods.

Autol. 1.14

In the epilogue of the first letter, we find evidence of Theophilus using a testimony source linking Rom 2:6 and 1 Cor 2:9. ACTS analysis shows that *Ad Autolycum*, *2 Clement*, and the *Martyrdom of Polycarp* all use Rom 2:6 and then quote 1 Cor 2:9.[27] There are additional parallels. *2 Clem.* 11:6-7 and *Autol.* 1.14 both introduce the uses of 1 Cor 2:9 and Rom 2:6 with exhortations to both believe and obey the words of the prophets. There are also parallels between *Mart. Pol.* 2.3 and *Autol.* 1.14. Both texts introduce the usages of 1 Cor 2:9 and Rom 2:6 with references to eternal punishment. Not only so, the martyrdom account uses the phrase, "eyes of the heart" (as

---

25. As discussed in chapter 3, Skarsaune shows that whereas gentile converts to Christianity in the early and mid-second century often possessed a rudimentary understanding of the Hebrew Scriptures, by the end of the second century, Christians coming out of a gentile background often developed a profound understanding of these texts. Christians having a Jewish heritage would naturally also possess this profound understanding. It is not improbable that Antiochene Christians at the end of the second century knew Psalm 113 well. See Skarsaune, "From Books to Testimonies."

26. Here Grant sees an allusion to Ps 134:18.

27. *Autol.* 1.14; *2 Clem.* 11:6-7; *Mart. Pol.* 2.3.

a dative phrase: τοῖς τῆς καρδίας ὀφθαλμοῖς),[28] similar to phrases used earlier in *Ad Autolycum*: "the eyes of your soul, and the ears of your heart" (τοὺς ὀφθαλμοὺς τῆς ψυχῆς σου, καὶ τὰ ὦτα τῆς καρδίας σου),[29] and "the blinding of your soul and blindness of your heart" (τὴν τύφλωσιν τῆς ψυχῆς καὶ πήρωσιν τῆς καρδίας σου).[30]

But there are also differences. The *Martyrdom of Polycarp* text does not use Rom 2:7–9 at all, while the passage in 2 *Clement* only recalls Rom 2:9a by its use of the word θλίψις. By contrast, *Autol.* 1.14 recalls Rom 2:7 and quotes Rom 2:8b–9a exactly. Furthermore, the quotation of 1 Cor 2:9 in *Ad Autolycum* matches extant manuscripts of 1 Corinthians, while the quotations of the verse in both 2 *Clement* and *Martyrdom of Polycarp* follow the word order of Isa 64:3 rather than 1 Cor 2:9. There are no 1 Corinthians manuscript variants to explain the transposition.

In light of these textual parallels and differences, it is safest to conclude that neither 2 *Clem.* 11:6–7 nor *Mart. Pol.* 2.3 was a testimony source for Theophilus. They and *Autol.* 1.14 likely used a common testimony source containing Rom 2:6 and 1 Cor 2:9.

The exegetical traditions represented in this testimony source supported well Theophilus's protreptic appeal as he concluded his letter with a flourish by exhorting Autolycus to believe and obey the prophets, and reminding him of the abundance of good benefits for those who do so.

Autol. 2.10

In the second letter, it is likely that Theophilus used a testimony source in his discussion of God as Creator in *Autol.* 2.10. Evidence of his use of the source is imbedded in a web of exegetical traditions including a seemingly curious identification of God's Logos with his Spirit, with the "First Cause" (ἀρχή), with God's Sophia, and with the Power of the Most High (δύναμις ὑψίστου). This identification is simply a remnant of a Hellenistic Jewish exegetical tradition associated with passages such as Gen 1:1 and Prov 8:22. Hellenistic Jews identified God's Logos with his law (νόμος) and with his Spirit, in much the same way that Theophilus identified these above-mentioned figures.[31] These Hellenistic Jews felt the need to apply their religion to issues that

---

28. The martyrdom account here recalls Eph 1:18.

29. *Autol.* 1.2.

30. Ibid., 1.7.

31. Grant marks δύναμις ὑψίστου in his edition of *Ad Autolycum* as a use of Luke 1:35. If so, this is an instance of Theophilus "christianizing" a Hellenistic Jewish exegetical tradition.

were important in their Greco-Roman culture, including its metaphysical concerns. Therefore, it is no surprise that the Hellenistic Jewish writer of the Wisdom of Solomon, writing a few decades before the advent of Christ, incorporated Stoic and Platonic ideas.[32] He used the Stoic idea that νόμος is "a manifestation or aspect of the Logos."[33] This is not too much different from the writer of *Sirach*, who more or less identified the Logos and the Sophia. The writer of the Wisdom of Solomon spoke of God's σοφία in Stoic ways. Sophia is a "pure emanation of the power of the Almighty. . .."[34] The writer regarded Wisdom not as a literary personification, but as a cosmic agent.

The identification of Logos with Pneuma, which we see in these Hellenistic Jewish exegetical traditions, aided apologetic efforts for both Christians and Jews in a Greco-Roman culture. In Stoic theory, the Logos is a rational principle which provides order in the universe. The Stoics, however, sometimes called the Logos by other names, depending on the context. Distinctions between various materials were explained by way of the Logos, denoted in *this* regard as the pneuma permeating materials, and establishing their consistencies according to its differing vibrations.[35] Accordingly, Theophilus's identification of God's Logos with his Pneuma and his Sophia, odd to modern eyes, would have appeared reasonable to Autolycus. Bentivegna rightly observes that while Theophilus opposed Stoic views, he described the Logos in Stoic terms.[36]

It is important to consider the specific meaning of ἀρχή, a word appearing in both Gen 1:1 and Prov 8:22, in order to understand how Theophilus used these passages. Pierre Nautin argues that Theophilus interpreted ἀρχή in Prov 8:22 not as "beginning" but as "chief."[37] Rick Rogers takes a similar line with Gen 1:1. His argument that Theophilus understood ἐν ἀρχῇ in Genesis 1:1 to mean "by the beginning" rather than "in the beginning" helps explain the linking of Gen 1:1 and Prov 8:22. Rogers notes that Theophilus explicitly called the Logos the ἀρχή of Gen 1:1[38] and he understood from

---

32. Goodenough, *Justin*, 43.

33. Ibid., 42.

34. *Wisdom* 7.25–26. For Sophia in Sirach and the Wisdom of Solomon, see Goodenough, *Justin*, 42–43, ref. Sirach Prologue and 24.22ff.

35. Stead, *Philosophy in Christian Antiquity*, 47. Cf. Rist, *Stoic Philosophy*, 86–87.

36. Bentivegna, "A Christianity without Christ," 118.

37. Nautin, "Genèse 1,1–2, de Justin à Origène," 61–94. A fine overview of early Christian interpretation of the phrase "ἐν ἀρχῇ" in Gen 1:1 is given in Winden, "Der Anfang," 3–48.

38. *Autol.* 2.10.

Proverbs 8 that the ἀρχή was a divine agent at the Creation. Furthermore, ἐν can mean "by" just as much as "in."[39]

Philo substantiates these observations about the meaning of ἀρχή. Philo and Theophilus both associated Prov 8:22 with similar strings of divine names.[40] Philo, who considered the Logos akin to the ruler and eldest of the angels, named him as "Beginning/Chief" (ἀρχή), "God's Name" (ὄνομα θεοῦ), "Word" (λόγος), "the Man after [God's] image" (ὁ κατ' εἰκόνα), "the Seeing One" (ὁ ὁρῶν), and "Israel" (Ισραήλ). Theophilus, who understood the Logos to be God's own imminent reason from eternity past, but also to be his expressed Word who along with God's Sophia was generated prior to the creation in order to assist with it, named the Logos as ἀρχή. He then explained this name, upholding not only the "Beginning" nuance of ἀρχή through his prior point that the Logos was generated forth from God prior to the creation of all things, but also upholding the "Chief" nuance of ἀρχή by asserting that the Logos dominates all of creation. Theophilus next enumerated a string of titles for the Logos: "Spirit of God" (πνεῦμα θεοῦ), "Beginning/Chief" (ἀρχή), "Wisdom" (σοφία), "Power of the Most High" (δύναμις ὑψίστου). Behind both writers' similar use of Prov 8:22 together with strings of divine names lies the similar theological pre-understanding that that ἀρχή mentioned in the proverb is indeed God's own Logos who goes forth from him in order to assist him with his divine operations in his created realm.

Theophilus not only followed Hellenistic Jewish exegetical traditions associated with Gen 1:1 and Prov 8:22, but also Christian development of them.[41] His sequence of titles (Beginning, Spirit of God, Beginning, Sophia, Power of the Most High) is similar to one in Justin's *Dialogue with Trypho* (Beginning, Holy Spirit, Glory of the Lord, Son, Sophia, Angel, God, Lord, Logos, Captain).[42] Following this sequence, Justin explained that the Logos both went out from the Father by the Father's will, and simultaneously remained united with the Father. We find the same idea near Theophilus's

---

39. Rogers, *Theophilus*, 97, 116n57. Zeegers, "Les trois cultures," 140–41, declares that while the Greek ἐν ἀρχῇ does not carry the sense of "by the agency of" since ἐν is not used to specify "by a personal agent," and ἀρχῇ is not used to specify a person. However, she goes on the say that the Hebrew "bereshit" actually does carry this sense since "be" often carries the sense of "by the agency of" and "reshit" can carry the sense of a person. She notes that this meaning is also attested in rabbinic interpretations of Gen 1:1. However, contra Zeeger's points here, ἐν is sometimes used in the sense of "with the help of." Ref. BAGD, 260 (definition III.b).

40. *Autol.* 2.10; Philo of Alexandria, *De confusione linguarum* 146.

41. ACTS analysis is especially helpful in identifying the exegetical traditions discussed below.

42. Justin, *Dialogue* 61.

sequence.⁴³ Both Justin and Theophilus discuss the begetting of the Logos in close proximity to a use of Prov 8:22.

A suspicion that Theophilus drew from Justin for his Logos doctrine gains support from their similar ideas about the activity of the Logos among the prophets. Theophilus explicitly claimed here that the Logos spoke through the prophets. We find the same assertion in Justin.⁴⁴ Here is a second-century view that the Logos inspired the prophets, yet one with a certain fluidity: at various times, either the Logos or the Spirit were said to have inspired the prophets.

But it is in additional Christian exegetical traditions where we uncover evidence of the testimony source. A few lines before the use of Gen 1:1–2 and Prov 8:22–23 in *Autol.* 2.10 we also find an allusion to John 1:3. This is almost the same as the sequences of John 1:2 and Prov 8:22 in Athenagoras, and John 1:1 and Prov 8:22 in the *Odes of Solomon* (where Prov 8:23, 25 are added).⁴⁵ In Athenagoras, the uses of John 1:1 and Prov 8:22 are not as close as in the *Odes of Solomon* and in Theophilus, being separated by several lines of text. The sequences in the *Odes* are especially intriguing because these *Odes* are now generally considered to be Christian hymns which likely been composed in Syriac either in Antioch itself or in the surrounding region.⁴⁶ Theophilus was the only known ancient writer to link Gen 1:1–2 along with John 1:1 and Prov 8:22 in such a tight sequence. Uses of Gen 1:1 together with John 1:3 are found in *Autol.* 2.10 and in a fragment of *Kerygma Petri*.⁴⁷ While both the *Kerygma Petri* and Theophilus also claimed that God the Creator needed nothing, the idea was a commonplace and does not necessarily derive from the *Kerygma Petri*. In both treatises these parallels all occur within a few lines, indeed a mere three words apart in *Autol.* 2.10. This suggests that the *Kerygma Petri* was a testimony source behind Theophilus's use of Gen 1:1 and John 1:3 here.⁴⁸ Otherwise, some work drawing on the

---

43. *Autol.* 2.10. He expressed this idea also in *Autol.* 2.22.

44. Ibid., 2.10; Justin, *Apologiae* 1.36. But Justin also claimed in 1.38–39 that prophets are inspired by the Spirit.

45. Athenagoras, *Supplicatio* 10; *Odes Sol.* 7, 41.

46. For the provenance of the *Odes* and their original language, see Charlesworth, "Odes of Solomon," in Charlesworth, *Old Testament Pseudepigrapha*, 2:726–27.

47. The fragment is preserved in Clement of Alexandria, *Stromata* 4.5.39–41. If Theophilus drew either directly or indirectly from the *Kerygma Petri*, he borrowed not only the parallels noted in this paragraph, but also Jewish apologetic themes. The incorporation of Jewish apologetic with Christian missionary preaching in *Kerygma Petri* is discussed in Fiedrowicz, *Apologie im frühen Christentum: Die Kontroverse um den christlichen Wahrheitsanspruch in den ersten Jahrunderten*, 30–31.

48. It is not possible to determine how many ancient texts draw from the *Kerygma Petri*, especially given that the majority of it is lost. It must have been fairly influential.

Kerygma Petri could have been the testimony source, since his use of the *Kerygma Petri* has been questioned, despite similarities between it and *Ad Autolycum*.[49] He also may have followed Melito. Both writers quoted Gen 1:1 and implied that Christ made heaven and earth.[50] Melito added that God created humanity "through the Chief" (διὰ τῆς ἀρχῆς).

Nautin argues that here in his discussion of Gen 1:1-2, Theophilus opposed the teachings of Hermogenes (who taught that God created the world out of pre-existent matter).[51] Theophilus claimed explicitly that God created matter, and argues on the basis of an implied chronology in Gen 1:1-2. But as helpful as Nautin's exposition is, there could have been another motivation for Theophilus's use of this biblical text: Plato's implication that matter is eternally existent would have been just as odious to Theophilus as Hermogenes'. Moreover, it would have been natural for Theophilus to oppose *both* Plato's and Hermogenes' creation theories, since he wrote *Ad Autolycum* 2 to demonstrate the inferiority of Greco-Roman religion.[52]

Autol. 2.13

We unearth evidence of Theophilus possibly using another testimony source or at least a hitherto unknown exegetical tradition in *Autol.* 2.13, where he strengthened his apologetic argument that the prophets provide the true history, but the poets and philosophers do not. In this portion, he explained specifically primeval history. Theophilus cited or quoted Isa 40:22; Gen 1:5, 6, and 9. ACTS analysis reveals that these *very same passages* were used also in another ancient text, a Hellenistic synagogal prayer, probably slightly christianized. Plausibly, this ancient prayer was used regularly by Greek-speaking Christians in Theophilus's very own region.[53]

Fragments of it remain in Clement of Alexandria's *Stromata*. Schneemelcher, "Kerygma Petri," 34, notes that the early Christian apology of Aristides appears to use the *Kerygma Petri*. Skarsaune, *Proof from Prophecy*, 228-34, presents evidence that Justin Martyr used the *Kerygma Petri* as a testimony source for many of his non-LXX biblical quotations.

49. Similarities especially lie in *Autol.* 1.10, 14; 2.2 and 2.10. Concerning doubt about Theophilus's use of the treatise, see Paulsen, "Kerygma Petri und die urchristliche Apologetik," 1-37, esp. 12-13. See also Schneemelcher, "Kerygma Petri," 34.

50. *Autol.* 2.10; Melito, *Peri Pascha* 104.

51. Nautin, "Genèse 1,1-2, de Justin à Origène," 73-74. Nautin notes that this same exegetical argument against Hermogenes would later be reused by Tertullian in *Adversus Hermogenem* 26.

52. *Autol.* 2.1.

53. While this prayer fragment, preserved in *Canones ecclesiastici apostolorum* 7.34.1-8, may have been composed in the late fourth century, it is not implausible that

Scriptural Anthologies and Testimonia (Excursus)   145

These identical sequences in *Ad Autolycum* and in the prayer might at first glance seem to be a false match, since both *Autol.* 2.13 and *Apostolic Constitutions* 7.34.1–8 where the prayer is preserved concern the creation of the universe. So both texts would naturally be expected to show abundant use of Genesis 1 and Isa 40:22, with its language about God stretching out the heavens like a tent. However, closer examination indicates at least a genuine exegetical tradition, if not a use of a lost testimony source. We find in each writing in especially close proximity the same set of biblical verses: Gen 1:1, 5, 6, 9 along with Isa 40:22. The only other uses of passages from Genesis 1 are 1:14–19 for the Hellenistic synagogal prayer, and 1:2–3, 11–12 for *Autol.* 2.13. *No other* extant Greek treatise from any Jewish or Christian contemporary or predecessor shows such a close match between these specific biblical quotation/allusion sequences or shows them packed together in such a tight grouping. While Theophilus used Gen 1:11–12 and the prayer used Gen 1:14–19, each writer likely used nearby selections taken out of the very same quotation block contained within the same testimony source (a practice that Dodd notes).[54]

If the prayer indeed had been appropriated by Christians in Syria, it would not be surprising that Theophilus, bishop of the church of the major Roman city in Syria, would be familiar with it. He may have used the prayer himself in congregational worship. If he learned to read the first chapter of Genesis in concert with Isa 40:22 because of this christianized synagogal prayer, then here is a case of liturgy pioneering the way forward and theology and exegesis following behind.

Some exegetical details of the prayer are striking. Allusions to Gen 1:6 appear twice, six lines apart, in the synagogal prayer. After the first, the redactor recalls Gen 1:2, asserting that God put a living spirit into the waters.[55] Philo of Alexandria likewise alluded to such a vivifying spirit. He wrote concerning the earth, that it is preserved from decay in part "by a spirit" (πνεύματος).[56] Tatian of Syria also had a similar concept of a vivifying spirit. Tatian distinguished between the spirit resident in matter and the "more divine" (τοῦ θειοτέρου) Spirit.[57]

These interpretations of Gen 1:2 in the synagogal prayer, in Philo, and in Tatian all are close to Theophilus's assertion that the spirit over the water,

---

it was composed circa 150 CE. See Charlesworth, "Odes of Solomon," in Charlesworth, *Old Testament Pseudepigrapha*, 2:671–73.

54. Dodd, *According to the Scriptures*, 57–59.
55. *Canones ecclesiastici apostolorum* 7.34.1.
56. Philo of Alexandria, *De opificio mundi* 131.
57. Tatian, *Oratio ad Graecos* 4.4.

as depicted in Gen 1:2, gave life to creation by penetrating the water and then nourishing creation as the water penetrates throughout. As Simonetti and others observe, Theophilus's understanding of this spirit as a material and vivifying spirit but not the Holy Spirit himself derives from his indebtedness to Stoic physics.[58] Since Philo and certain other Jews, as well as Tatian read Gen 1:2 similarly, Theophilus's Stoic exegesis of Gen 1:2 was no innovation. Rather, it was a traditional Jewish and Christian interpretation.[59]

There may also be an additional intertext. Theophilus may have combined his use of Gen 1:6–9 with a recollection of 2 Pet 3:5. He used the phrase "by the Logos of God" (τῷ τοῦ θεου λόγῳ)[60] to explain how dry land emerged out of the waters. He described the appearance of dry land with a similar phrase, "God by his Logos" (ὁ θεὸς διὰ τοῦ λόγου αὐτοῦ). This parallel does not necessarily indicate a literary dependency between *Ad Autolycum* and 2 Peter. But it at least suggests that both writers understood that the God's Logos served as his agent in the formation of dry land.

Whether this evidence indicates use by Theophilus of the synagogal prayer itself, or only of an exegetical tradition at play in Antioch at this time, the evidence suggests a hint of Theophilus's liturgical world, hitherto unknown, since none of his writings except his three apologetic letters to Autolycus have survived. Additional research may lend further support to this suggestion of a link between Theophilus and the synagogal prayer. If such additional support can be found, we may indeed gain a true glimpse of Theophilus's lost liturgical life.

Autol. 2.35

Towards the end of his second letter to Autolycus, Theophilus discussed idolatry and the coming judgment. As he derided idolatry in his summary of the Ten Commandments, the Decalogue, he may have consulted a testimony source. His summary of the Decalogue is unique in several ways. First, he omitted the injunction to honor the Sabbath. Further, he integrated his exegetical discussion of the creation week with this omission. While he

---

58. Simonetti, "La sacra scrittura in Teofilo," 202. Similarly, Nautin, "Ciel, pneuma et lumière chez Théophile," 167.

59. Grant posits that Wis 7.23 lies behind the mention in *Autol.* 2.13 of the "delicate" or "fine" (λεπτός) nature of the spirit which penetrates the waters. See Grant, "Bible of Theophilus," 180. This is plausible since Wis 7.23–24; and 8.1 depicts Wisdom in Stoic terms, penetrating and ordering all things. Ferguson discusses the purpose of the *Wisdom of Solomon* of showing the coherence between Jewish wisdom teachings and Hellenistic philosohical ideas. See Ferguson, *Backgrounds of Early Christianity*, 444.

60. The phrase is a dative of means, hence "by."

devoted great exegetical effort to the first six days of the creation week in *Autol.* 2.9-19, he barely discussed the seventh day. Second, he paraphrased the prohibitions of Exod 20:13-15 against adultery, murder, and theft, rearranging the order as compared with Exod 20:13-15 and Deut 5:17-19. Third, he inserted a prohibition against fornication between those prohibiting murder and theft.[61] Regarding these second and third features of his summary, he was the only Greek writer in the period 3 B. C. E. to C. E. 3 to summarize the Decalogue in this way. He freely paraphrased the Decalogue rather than followed any traditional paraphrase.

Psalms of Solomon 17, a pseudepigraphical messianic psalm presenting Jewish reaction to the Roman conquest of Jerusalem, may explain a striking aspect of Theophilus's use of Ps 13:1+3 here. There is nothing in Psalm 13 itself to suggest that the evildoers mentioned were involved in idolatry. Yet Theophilus clearly applied a conflation of 13:1+3 to the problem of idolatry. This same application of Psalm 13 to the problem of idolatry appears in *Psalms of Solomon* 17, following a complaint probably spurred by Roman idolatry.[62] Since the wording in *Pss. Sol.* 17.15 is dissimilar from that of *Autol.* 2.35, and its writer used only Ps 13:3 rather than Theophilus's conflation of 13:1+3, Theophilus did not use *Psalm of Solomon* 17 itself as a testimony source. But we have here some evidence that the writer of *Psalm of Solomon* and Theophilus may have both used a common testimony source, now lost.[63]

---

61. Another early Christian text where additional sexual sins appear to have been added to the Decalogue is *Didache* 2.3. One of the additions is the same one that Theophilus added: fornication. The second additional sexual sin was that of sexually corrupting children.

62. *Pss. Sol.* 17.15. Wright presents evidence for the composition of the Psalms of Solomon in the first century BCE in Jerusalem after the conquest of the city by Roman general Pompey. See Wright, "Psalms of Solomon," in Charlesworth, *Old Testament Pseudepigrapha*, 2:640-41. It would not be surprising if Roman idolatry were in view in *Pss. Sol.* 17.15.

63. One might wonder whether he used Rom 3:10-12 as a testimony source for his conflated use of Ps 13:1-3. However, this suggestion must be rejected, since he presented a reminiscence of a portion of Ps 13:1 which is not present in Rom 3:10-12. His conflation can be explained simply by the presence of a common phrase in both verses, "there is not one doing [acts of] goodness, there is not even one" (οὐκ ἔστι ποιῶν χρηστότητα, οὐκ ἔστιν ἕως ἑνός).

Autol. 2.38

In light of Theophilus's use of an anthology for his Greco-Roman poetic citations in *Autol.* 2.37,[64] it would be reasonable to suspect that he likewise took the dense string of biblical citations in the adjoining portion, *Autol.* 2.38, from an anthology. But no evidence of this appears. ACTS methodology indicates no extant writing with a sequence of biblical citations, quotations, reminiscences, or allusions similar to any portion of the citation sequence in *Autol.* 2.38. It is not surprising that such a biblical anthology has not survived. However, if it had circulated, one might suspect some other works derived from it to survive. As they have not, the weight of evidence is against the idea that Theophilus used a biblical anthology in *Autol.* 2.38. This negative result indicates something positive about Theophilus and Scripture: he drew from a rich personal knowledge of Scripture to focus his reader on traditional early Christian apologetic motifs, just as we have seen in chapter 3.

Autol. 3.11

Did Theophilus use a traditional testimonia collection as the source of his repentance citations in *Autol.* 3.11? The suggestion is plausible since his citations are thematically-related, and half of them come from *distinct* biblical books, and the three that come from Isaiah are *neither proximate in Isaiah nor sequential*. However, ACTS analysis does not indicate any extant text containing a sequence of citations, quotations, allusions, or remembrances that is similar to the sequence here in *Autol.* 3.11. The sequence was apparently unique to Theophilus. These citations do not show evidence of being memory reminiscences.[65] Two of his citations, Isa 55:6–7 and Ezek 18:21–23, especially are too long and too close to extant biblical manuscripts to be memory reminiscences.[66] While he may have

---

64. Zeegers, *Citations des poètes grecs*, 125–26.

65. Criteria for detection of copying as opposed to memory recollection based on citation/quotation length and on closeness to the biblical manuscripts are presented in research by Skarsaune, McIver, and Carroll. Their research is discussed in chapter 3.

66. His only alteration not explained by any manuscript variant in Isa 55:6–7 is the addition of the phrase "τὸν θεὸν αὐτοῦ" ("his God"). The only alteration not explained by any manuscript variant in Ezek 18:21–23 is the omission of "πάσας" ("all") in the phrase "πάσας τὰς ἐντολάς μου" ("all My commandments"). His text of Isa 55:6–7 is closest to the LXX Sinaiticus manuscript. By contrast, his text of Ezek 18:21–23 is closest to the Alexandrinus manuscript. This confirms Grant's analysis showing that Theophilus's LXX text cannot be identified with any particular LXX text-type. See Grant, "Bible of Theophilus," 177.

used a no longer extant testimony source, it seems at least as likely that he consulted biblical manuscripts. However if this was the case, his use of biblical link words here could explain how he selected the passages.

Autol. 3.12

There appears in *Autol.* 3.12 evidence of using a lost testimonia collection. When Theophilus and Justin Martyr used Isa 1:16–17, they both diverged from the LXX by excluding a phrase or two in the center of the quotation. Furthermore, there are no variants in either the Hebrew or Greek texts of Isa 1:16–17, or in the works of Justin, or in *Ad Autolycum* to explain the excluded phrases. Neither do similar quotations with these same excluded phrases appear in the New Testament or in any Christian predecessors, or in Philo. Yet it is interesting that both Justin and Theophilus should exclude the *same phrase* from the middle of their quotations. It is also interesting that not only in *1 Apol.* 44.3 but *also* in *1 Apol.* 61.7 Justin gives this exact same variation from the LXX. However, it is evident that Theophilus did not copy from Justin, since he included a phrase which Justin always omitted. This indicates that for Isaiah 1, at least, Justin and Theophilus may have been reading from the same text. This text is lost to history, since no other extant Christian or Jewish source contains a quotation of the passage with the same excluded phrase as in Justin and Theophilus. The lost text may be an instructional text from Hellenistic Jewish synagogues.[67] As it does not deviate from the Septuagint toward the Hebrew, it is unlikely to be a post-Septuagint Greek translation from the Hebrew.[68] The following tables compare these quotations by Justin and Theophilus with the Septuagint.

---

67. Kraft, "Epistle of Barnabas," 102–7, 115–17, posits that Pseudo-Barnabas may have drawn from either an instructional text from Hellenistic Jewish synagogues or from a Jewish commentary for his network of biblical justice citations in *Barn.* 2.4—3.6. This citation network is similar to that of *Autol.* 3.12 in that both networks combine portions from each of three passages, Isa 1:11–16, Isa 58:6–8, and Zech 7:9–10.

68. Use of a lost post-LXX Greek translation is probable when alterations are made to bring the LXX closer to the underlying Hebrew. See Albl, *And Scripture Cannot Be Broken*, 100–101. Such is not the case here.

Septuagint trans., Isa 1:16-17	Septuagint, Isa 1:16-17
Wash you, be clean;	λούσασθε, καθαροὶ γένεσθε,
remove your iniquities from your souls before my eyes;	ἀφέλετε τὰς πονηρίας ἀπὸ τῶν ψυχῶν ὑμῶν ἀπέναντι τῶν ὀφθαλμῶν μου,
cease from your iniquities;	παύσασθε ἀπὸ τῶν πονηριῶν ὑμῶν,
learn to do well; diligently seek judgment, deliver him that is suffering wrong,	μάθετε καλὸν ποιεῖν, ἐκζητήσατέ κρίσιν, ῥύσασθε ἀδικούμενον,
plead for the orphan, and obtain justice for the widow	κρίνατε ὀρφανῷ καὶ δικαιώσατε χήραν

Septuagint, Isa 1:16-17	Justin, 1 Apol. 44.3; 61.7[A]	Justin, Dial. 18.2	Theophilus, Autol. 3.12
λούσασθε, καθαροὶ γένεσθε,	Λούσασθε, καθαροὶ γενεσθε,	Λούσασθε οὖν καὶ νῦν καθαροὶ γένεσθε καὶ ἀφέλεσθε τὰς πονηρίας ἀπὸ τῶν ψυχῶν ὑμῶν	Αφέλετε
ἀφέλετε τὰς πονηρίας ἀπὸ τῶν ψυχῶν ὑμῶν	ἀφέλετε τὰς πονηρίας ἀπὸ τῶν ψυχῶν ὑμῶν,		τὰς πονηρίας ἀπὸ τῶν ψυχῶν ὑμῶν,
ἀπέναντι τῶν ὀφθαλμῶν μου, παύσασθε ἀπὸ τῶν πονηριῶν ὑμῶν,			
μάθετε καλὸν ποιεῖν, ἐκζητήσατέ κρίσιν, ῥύσασθε ἀδικούμενον,	μάθετε καλον ποιεῖν,		μάθετε καλὸν ποιεῖν, ἐκζητήσατε κρίσιν, ῥύσασθε ἀδικούμενον,
κρίνατε ὀρφανῷ καὶ δικαιώσατε χήραν	κρίνατε ὀρφανῷ καὶ δικαιώσατε χήραν		κρίνατε ὀρφανῷ καὶ δικαιώσατε χήραν

[A]. Justin also provided a one word allusion to Isa 1:16 in Dial. 12.3: "let him wash, and be clean" (λουσάσθω, καὶ καθαρός ἐστιν).

These details raise the suspicion that use of a testimonia collection lies behind *Autol.* 3.12. This suspicion grows when we consider common usage sequences. ACTS analysis reveals that there are a number of similar citation/quotation sequences shared among *Ad Autolycum* and texts of predecessors. The most striking sequences are found in *Barn.* 2.5—3.3; *2 Enoch* 9, 42; and especially Justin, *1 Apol.* 37.5, and *Dialogue* 14-15. Other sequences could be listed, but these are the most tightly packed in terms of the verbal distance between pairings of passages.[69] These sequences are the following:

Theophilus, *Autol.* 3.12:	Isa 1:16-17	Isa 58:6-8	Zech 7:9-10
2 Enoch 9:	Isa 1:17	Isa 58:7	
2 Enoch 42:	Isa 1:17		Zech 7:9, 10
Barn. 2.5—3.3:	Isa 1:11-13	Isa 58:4-5, 6-10	
Justin, *1 Apology* 37:	Isa 1:11-15	Isa 58:6-7	
Justin, *Dialogue* 14-15:	Isa 1:16	Isa 58:1-11	
Justin, *Dialogue* 27:	Isa 1:15	Isa 58:13-14	

It is important to remember that *exact matches* are not required to indicate use of a common anthology or testimony source, because various writers may have borrowed from differing portions of biblical quotation blocks contained in a particular anthology or testimony source.

Theophilus's use of Isa 1:16 near a use of Isa 58:6-8 corresponds to the similar pairing of these passages in Justin, *Dialogue* 14. *Dialogue* 14 cites the call to cease doing evil in Isa 1:16b, an emphasis similar to that of Theophilus. Significantly, Justin quoted Isa 58:1-11 in close proximity to this citation of Isa 1:16 in *Dialogue* 15, supporting his discussion of true fasting.

These similar sequences of the same verse from diverse portions of the Hebrew Scriptures, and the evidence concerning Isa 1:16-17 which shows Justin and Theophilus both using a written text, but not any extant LXX text, all constitute strong evidence for use of a testimony source. This is also an independent confirmation of Skarsaune's identification of Justin's use of a testimony source involving roughly the same biblical passages and of Kraft's

---

69. There is evidence of another exegetical tradition here in *Autol.* 3.12. Second Enoch 42.9, preserved in Slavonic manuscripts, depicts, in both the longer and shorter recensions, Enoch in paradise pronouncing blessings on those following the ethics of Zech 7:9-10 and Isa 1:17. Theophilus also used these two texts together, but *2 Enoch* also used a number of biblical texts which Theophilus did not use. Similarly, *2 Enoch* 9.1 alluded to both Isa 1:17 and 58:7, but also to other biblical texts not used in *Autol.* 3.12. If *2 Enoch* 9.1 and 42.9 were not testimony sources for Theophilus, we can conclude at least that he drew from a similar exegetical tradition.

identification of Pseudo-Barnabas using a testimony source having roughly the same biblical passages also.[70]

Was this testimony source transmitted orally? It is not likely. Theophilus's use of Isa 58:6–8 indicates that he used a written source for the passage rather than recalling the passage from memory. He quoted Isa 58:6–8 exactly except for some minor variants from the extant LXX manuscripts. He transposed the verbs διάλυε and λύε, and he used περίβαλλε in place of περίβαλε, and ὑπερόψῃ in place of ὑπερόψει. That these are the only variants as compared with 54 other words which *exactly* match the passage in extant LXX manuscripts means that he must have cited from a written source but *not* from memory. This lost testimony source may have been that same Hellenized synagogal teaching tract or Jewish biblical commentary which Kraft posited that Pseudo-Barnabas used in *Barn.* 2.5—3.3.

Theophilus's use of this lost testimony source served his argument admirably. He wanted to show Autolycus that while the poets and philosophers cannot supply legitimate ethics, the biblical prophets can. The lost testimony source supplied an example of it.

Autol. 3.13

Theophilus continued to emphasize the early Christian apologetic motif of the superiority of Christian ethics over those of pagan religionists, as he turned from the theme of justice to that of chastity in *Autol.* 3.13. Athenagoras of Athens provided a clue to why Theophilus added chapters (*Autol.* 3.13–14) concerning chastity after *Autol.* 3.12, his discussion of justice. Since justice was a prominent Greek virtue, any discussion of ethics would have been expected to include it, along with piety. Theophilus met this expectation apologetically. He added *Autol.* 3.13 to address chastity as a response to the false charges that Christians engage in incest and orgasmic meetings. His biblical reply to the false charge was not unique. Athenagoras asserted that the accusers are given "to create tales" (λογοποιεῖν) about Christian sexual scandals.[71] He then used the same passage that Theophilus did, Matt 5:28, to refute this and prove that Christians do not even harbor unchaste thoughts. Theophilus conflated Matt 5:32 with 5:28 to bring in a second aspect of Christian sexual ethics, which is their high standard regarding divorce. Athenagoras did the same, using Matt 5:28 in the very next portion of *Legatio*, although not conflating it with Matt 5:32. Athenagoras referred to a prohibition against second marriage, even

---

70. Kraft, "Epistle of Barnabas," 102–7, 115–17; Skarsaune, *Proof from Prophecy*, 168–69.

71. Athenagoras, *Leg.* 32.

when a man's first wife has died, alluding to Gen 1:27; 5:2; Matt 19:4; and Mark 10:6. Theophilus and Athenagoras used both Matt 5:28 and 5:32 to the same ends. The passages evidently had become standard proof texts for answering charges against the Christian love feast.

Theophilus also cited Prov 4:25–26 in his discussion of chastity. He took the language of making straight paths for one's feet to be an idiom for sexual purity. Thus, he sounded an echo of a neighboring passage, Prov 5:2–23. This passage warns the reader against fornication with a loose woman, whose feet lead to the grave (Prov 5:5), and who does not walk on the paths (ὁδούς) of life (Prov 5:6), and whose ways (τροχιαί) are slippery. Rather, one must make one's way (ὁκόν) far away from her (Prov 5:8), for one's ways (ὁδοί) are open before the eyes of God (Prov 5:21) who looks on all his paths (τροχιάς, Prov 5:21). Clearly, the passage is rife with feet and path imagery. Theophilus had warrant for hearing an echo of it in Prov 4:25–26. His deep familiarity with the Scriptures enabled him to hear the echo.

Theophilus was not the only one to interpret "straight paths" language in Prov 4:25–26 as being idiomatic of sexual purity. The writer of the *Testament of Simeon* exhorted the reader to have a virtuous heart and "make straight your paths" (εὐθύνατε τὰς ὁδούς ὑμῶν).[72] He immediately added an admonition about sexual ethics, "Therefore, guard yourselves from fornication" (Φυλάξασθε ουν ἀπὸ τῆς πορνείας).[73] Typically, Theophilus followed Hellenistic Jewish exegetical tradition.

Theophilus likely used a testimony source here. There are interesting parallels between *Autol.* 3.13–14 and Justin, *1 Apology* 15. First, both writers introduced their discussion with similar introduction formulas, in *Autol.* 3.13: "concerning solemnity" or "concerning chastity" as Grant renders it, appropriately so in light of the context of *Autol.* 3.13 (περὶ σεμνότητος), and in *1 Apology* 15: "concerning chastity" (περὶ . . . σωφροσύνης). Second, both writers used Matt 5:23, 32, 44, and 46. Theophilus used only one Matthean verse, 6:3, which was not used in *1 Apology* 15. But Theophilus cannot have used *1 Apology* 15 as a testimony source because of textual differences, such as the quotation from Matt 5:46b: "even plunderers and tax collectors do this" (τοῦτο καὶ οἱ λησταὶ καὶ οἱ τελῶναι ποιοῦσιν) for Theophilus; "For even fornicators do this" (Καὶ γὰρ οἱ πόρνοι τουτο ποιοῦσιν) for Justin. Nevertheless, that similar proof-texts appear in portions addressed to the same topics attests to a common Christian ethical tradition from which Justin and Theophilus both drew. In light of the above discussion concerning use of a testimonia collection in

---

72. *T. Sim.* 5.2.

73. The Greek text of the *Testament of Simeon* is from Charles, *Greek Versions of the Testaments of the Twelve Patriarchs*.

Autol. 3.12, involving *1 Apology* 14–15, the same testimonia likely at play in *Autol.* 3.12 was probably also used here in *Autol.* 3.13.

Autol. 3.14: After discussing justice and chastity in prior portions of his letter, Theophilus added another layer to his ethical portrait by considering beneficence, the doing of good works, in *Autol.* 3.14. We have evidence that he relied on a testimony source here as well.

Justin, *Dialoue* 85 is the only extant writing that preserves the same sequence of Isa 66:5 and Matt 5:44 found in *Autol.* 3.14. Theophilus cited Isa 66:5 to support his claim that the prophets and the gospels alike teach loving one's enemies, this part of a consistent and superior Christian ethic. He cited Matt 5:44 immediately after Isa 66:5 also to deflect criticism leveled against Christians that they only do good to their own. Justin responded to Jewish notice of his own benevolence by paraphrasing Matt 5:44 and then immediately citing Isa 66:5–11. Since Justin paraphrased Matt 5:44 where Theophilus did not, Theophilus did not use *Dialogue* 85 as his testimony source. However, he may have used Justin's source, or at the very least have followed an oral tradition of grouping Matt 5:44 with Isa 66:5–11.

Just as Athenagoras and Theophilus had used both Matt 5:28 and 5:32 to the same ends and in the same contexts, as discussed above in regard to *Autol.* 3.12–13, so also they both used Matt 5:44 similarly.[74] Athenagoras, after using Matt 5:28 and 5:32 to refute charges of sexual immorality then used Matt 5:44 to show that Christians do not cause evil, but treat well those who do them evil. Likewise, Theophilus added *Autol.* 3.14 as an entire chapter answering this charge similarly. However, he cannot have used the *Legatio* as a testimony source, since he quoted Matt 5:44 and conflated it with 5:46, while Athenagoras only alluded to 5:44.

However, Athenagoras did quote Matt 5:44 in *Leg.* 11 and Matt 5:46 in *Leg.* 12, where he made the same points made by Theophilus does in *Autol.* 3.14, that Christians are not evil doers, but even answer evil with good. Therefore, it may be that Theophilus used *Leg.* 11–12 as inspiration for his conflation of Matt 5:44+46 in *Autol.* 3.14. Nevertheless, he cannot have used it as a testimony source since he quoted Matt 5:46b, which Athenagoras did not quote.

Whether or not Theophilus used the *Legatio* as inspiration for his conflation, his use here of 5:44+46 shows that he was not totally unique regarding his treatment of non-retaliation. This should be no surprise. The apologists typically used the statements of Jesus about loving enemies and about repaying evil with good as a basis for refuting slanders.[75]

---

74. *Autol.* 3.14; *Leg.* 34.
75. Ferguson, "Love of Enemies," 85–92.

Scriptural Anthologies and Testimonia (Excursus) 155

The protreptic ethical appeal in *Autol.* 3.12–14 was attractive in light of his age's hunger for virtue. This appeal appeared as Theophilus moved from explicitly discussing justice (*Autol.* 3.12) and chastity (*Autol.* 3.13) to beneficence (*Autol.* 3.14). These portions served protreptic ends by confronting pagans with insightful discussion of ethics which they might well have appreciated hearing or reading. And furthermore, these portions further served protreptic ends by emphasizing how fitting it is that there is a coming judgment at the end of time, as the prophets consistently testified. Thus, these portions and the testimony sources used in them all support Theophilus's explicit goal for his third letter of showing that the prophets convey true history while the poets and philosophers do not.

In the treatment of testimonia scholarship near the beginning of this chapter, I mentioned that testimonia scholars cannot locate use of testimonia and testimony sources with absolute certainty. Nevertheless, they can detect use of these with good plausibility by utilizing the standard criteria of testimonia scholarship which I have discussed. I have shown in this chapter evidence, using these same standard criteria, that Theophilus used some testimony sources not only in *Autol.* 3.12–14 but also in his first two letters. Thus, we have seen how Theophilus accessed Scripture and harnessed its power and riches in a variety of ways: through use of biblical manuscripts, through memory recollection entailing potent mental dynamics, and even through biblical anthologies and testimony sources.

However, we have also seen that Theophilus's use of scriptural anthologies or testimony sources is relatively sparse compared with their rich use in early- and mid-second-century writers such as Pseudo-Barnabas and Justin.[76] This result is exactly what one would expect for an apologist living just after the close of the "age of testimonies," and confirms the results displayed in chapter 3 about Theophilus's memory retrieval of Scripture.[77] Put simply, while testimony sources and scriptural anthologies were favored tools of the immediately-prior generations, by Theophilus's day, there was no longer much need of them. Just as a flailing non-swimmer who upon nearing shore discovers that she can touch bottom with her feet casts away the flotsam upon which she previously had clung so tightly and begins to walk through the water with a new confidence and speed, so also Christians at the end of the second century had increasingly cast away those testimonia collections upon which they previously had clung so tightly. They no longer needed them, because by this time even Gentile Christians had gained deep expertise in Israel's Scriptures.

76. For details of this rich use, see the studies by Prigent, Kraft, and Skarsaune referenced earlier in this chapter.

77. For the "age of testimonies," that great age of Christian testimony sources, see the discussion in chapter 3.

Epilogue

I have argued here, against prior research, that when we look behind anachronistic views of genre, literacy, and rhetoric, we discover a hidden Theophilus and a forgotten exegesis of Scripture unique to his age, albeit one of several important exegetical streams running through the second century. Protreptic approaches, abundant memory recall of Scripture in a highly-oral culture, and use of Scripture tightly integrated with Greco-Roman judicial rhetoric distinguish the second-century world of the early Christian apologists from the modern, highly-literate Western Christian world. These dynamics came quite naturally to Theophilus and others of his age, even if they appear foreign and unfamiliar to us moderns.

Since the only writing by Theophilus which survives is *Ad Autolycum*, and since no writing by Autolycus survives and we know virtually nothing about him, I have proceeded by analyzing *Ad Autolycum* in light of its historical and cultural setting.

Like any skilled advocate of his day, Theophilus used the standard Greco-Roman rhetorical device of recapitulation (ἀνακεφαλαίωσις) to remind his audience of his argument's essential points. It is fitting then, to conclude this study as he would have, by recapitulating essential points.

INTENT

Against a prevailing tendency in Theophilus studies I have argued that *Ad Autolycum* was not intended to convey a soteriology but rather, as a collection of protreptic letters, it was only meant to draw outsiders towards Christianity as the first step in their spiritual progression. Indeed, Theophilus would have been horrified at the thought of presenting a soteriology to outsiders who were not yet ready to receive such. In his mind, if he had presented advanced knowledge to them while they were not yet ready for it, he would have induced in them the foolish mistake of taking advanced knowledge that simply cannot be received by someone who is not ready for it, akin to Adam's eating from the Tree of Knowledge food for which he was not yet ready.[1] Then it is not surprising that Theophilus's letters to Autolycus exactly meet ancient expectations concerning protreptic literature, writings designed for outsiders not yet ready for advanced knowledge. Among these expectations is a threefold structure of attack on a competing philosophy or way of life, then promotion of the preferred one, and finally, concluding appeal to embrace the preferred philosophy or way of life. We have seen this threefold protreptic structure in all three individual letters as well as across the entire collection of all the letters to Autolycus. Attempts to derive Theophilus's soteriology from *Ad Autolycum* can only fail from the very onset, precisely because of this protreptic nature of the letters. Even when scholarship has recognized the protreptic nature of *Ad Autolycum*, it has tended to acknowledge such in preliminary remarks but then forget this reality while making rash and anachronistic theological assessments. But Theophilus is severely misunderstood unless the protreptic nature of *Ad Autolycum* is truly recognized and kept foremost. Thus, in no way do I call for any sort of theological renovation of *Ad Autolycum*. Rather, I champion a more historically-sensitive "agnostic" approach concerning Theophilus's soteriology, one that consistently takes the ancient protreptic nature of the treatise seriously. Future studies of Theophilus and other second-century apologists who appealed to Greco-Roman religionists ought to follow this lead.

Ad Autolycum exhibits a protreptic likeness to early Christian apologetic speeches presented before Greco-Roman pagan audiences such as those recorded in the book of Acts. Theophilus spoke to pagan Gentiles in much the same way that Paul of Tarsus spoke to Felix or to the philosophers of Athens.[2] In these cases, Paul did not say much about the person of Jesus himself or atonement provided on the Cross, but he spoke a great deal about monotheism, repentance, divine judgment, righteousness, and self-control. He knew that his particular audiences in these instances were not yet ready for Christology and the details of atonement. And it is also significant that Theophilus followed the pedagogic model of Jesus himself. Matthew describes a rich young man who asked Jesus how he could be saved.[3] But Jesus withheld his disclosure of soteriology for a pedagogic and protreptic purpose. The rich young man was not yet ready to hear the entire answer to his question. He first needed to be rattled from his overconfidence in his

---

1. *Autol.* 2.25.
2. Acts 17, 24.
3. Matt 19:16–26.

own piety and possessions. Similarly, Theophilus withheld his own disclosure of soteriology because he knew that Autolycus also had to be rattled from his overconfidence in his pious but foolish devotion to the traditional Greco-Roman gods. This insight helps settle the controversy concerning the supposed presence of soteriology in *Ad Autolycum*. And even if modern scholars sometimes dismiss Theophilus for appearing to know little about the Cross or Christology, we have seen that these dismissals can only be anachronistic. Theophilus's protreptic approach fully explains that appearance. Scholarship sometimes pays lip-service to the protreptic nature of his letters but has yet to grapple seriously with this reality.

Heb 5:12—6:2 informed Theophilus's apologetic strategy. He reflected a traditional Christian concern based on its contents. He incorporated this concern into his concept of spiritual advancement.

ORALITY AND RECOLLECTION

We have seen that the dynamics of memory-recall, allusion and literary echo added potency to *Ad Autolycum* for its original audience. These pervaded the mainly-illiterate culture of the second century. These dynamics were both expected and appreciated by both the literate and illiterate alike. While highly-literate cultures such as our own automatically and unthinkingly focus mainly on full- and partial-quotation, highly-illiterate cultures appreciate the value of allusions and of mere reminiscences of texts which do not even provide a partial quotation. The importance of allusions in *Ad Autolycum* is indicated partly by their great frequency as compared to quotations. Nearly 70 percent of all uses of Scripture in *Ad Autolycum* are either allusions or reminiscences. Scholarship that attends only to citations and quotations has been blinded by modern prejudices, and misses most of the picture. The inspired texts had become so a part of Theophilus's language that he could hardly write a paragraph without echoing numerous biblical passages, often doing so unconsciously. He used most of his biblical allusions and reminiscences compositionally as he constructed his protreptic appeal.

He harnessed formidable rhetorical power through his literary echoes to the inspired texts. This rhetorical power came through two separate dynamics. First, when he applied a biblical passage to his own second-century context, he brought to mind the original literary context of the given biblical passage, even though frequently he neither explicitly mentioned the details of that original context nor quoted from it. In so doing, he achieved a striking sense of irony by means of the literary echo. His Christian and biblically-attuned audience became struck by his ironic re-application of a biblical passage which appeared at first rather odd, because their own historical setting in Antioch in the late second century differed from the original historical setting of the biblical passage itself. However, as they reflected a bit further, it would have become clear to them that, in a surprising way, the re-application of the given inspired passage to their own world indeed truly *was* appropriate. The irony both seized their attention and also entertained.

The second dynamic owed to the non-explicit nature of literary echo. For instance, Theophilus did not explicitly use Ps 113:11 in *Autol.* 1.1–2. Nevertheless, his illiterate yet biblically-attuned hearers themselves would have easily recalled Ps 113:11 after they first recognized use of Ps 113:12–14 and then recognized its immediate context. Then, once they perceived that the mocking question of the second-century pagan Autolycus almost exactly matched the mocking question of those more ancient pagans quoted by the psalmist in Ps 113:11, they would suddenly have been able to grasp the ironic relevance of Ps 113:12–14 for their own context. All of this would have required sophisticated and detailed mental engagement on their part, even if it was both automatic and subconscious. It is this very necessity that they be mentally engaged, plus the sense of personal accomplishment they would naturally feel once they understood the connections joining the original and contemporary settings, that enhance rhetorical force and made *Ad Autolycum* truly intriguing to them. Theophilus did not "spoon feed" these connections to them. They themselves would have had to recall literary contexts and then draw contextual parallels. Thus, Theophilus used Scripture in a dynamic way to force his mostly-illiterate audience to engage with his sophisticated arguments and to entertain them in the process, much the way that "brain-teasers" entertain us today.

We have also seen that the forms of his uses of Scripture indicate that a significant portion of those uses did not involve his copying them from biblical manuscripts. Rather, he recalled many biblical passages from memory. I have demonstrated this in my analysis of *Ad Autolycum* in the discussion of Skarsaune's evidence, and by recourse to McIver and Carroll's various objective criteria for detecting memory access of Scripture. Theophilus could abundantly harness powerful memory-based dynamics common to largely-illiterate cultures. Likewise, his Christian audience, much of which would have been illiterate, could similarly benefit from that potent dynamic precisely because they also held within themselves large stocks of memorized Scripture. In our highly-literate modern culture, we are largely ignorant of the great memory abilities of illiterate cultures and the potent memory dynamics common to them. *Ad Autolycum* opens a window for us, revealing the life of Scripture in the mostly-illiterate world of the second century.

We have also seen examples of how biblical allusions and reminiscences functioned in Theophilus's world in ways that biblical quotations could not. The capstone of these examples was a comprehensive treatment of the Book of Job in Theophilus's extant works. It provided us a programmatic example of how one can take orality and memory seriously in studies of the Scripture in early Christian apologetic texts.

The dynamics of allusion and literary echo which added such potency to Theophilus's apology explain many of his uses of Scripture, uses which may appear odd or careless to modern eyes with our modern presuppositions. We must take more seriously orality and ancient illiteracy. For example, we must go beyond the mere five partial quotations of Job listed in our biblical indexes of *Ad Autolycum* and open our eyes to the scores of unquoted reminiscences of Job which greatly shaped the logic of the argument from creation in *Autol*. 1.6–8. We must notice and reject the modern prejudice of our own highly-literate world which assumes that without a *written* passage of Scripture, nothing much happens.

SCRIPTURE'S ROLE IN THE COHERENCE OF THEOPHILUS'S THOUGHT

Theophilus's use of Scripture cannot even begin to be understood apart from his use of an ancient judicial rhetoric of witness interrogation. I have shown that his judicial rhetoric allows us to see that the organization of *Ad Autolycum* is anything but haphazard or confused, despite claims of prior scholarship. Rather, second-century minds would have clearly recognized and appreciated *Ad Autolycum* as a highly coherent, and carefully constructed rhetorical saber capable of persuasively-devastating effect.

Theophilus's explicit theory of inspiration added credibility to his rhetorical moves.[4] His judicial rhetoric so often relied on the consistent testimony of the biblical writers who functioned as friendly witnesses in the court of opinion. Lest his audience assume that his consistency claims worked merely by guile, he provided a theory of inspiration that explained how his witnesses could be so thoroughly consistent.

Patristic scholarship is increasingly recognizing that ancient rhetorical standards for structuring an argument provide essential keys for understanding the content of patristic texts. This is a very positive development, since patristic scholarship lags behind NT scholarship in its attention to

---

4. *Autol*. 3.12, cf. *Autol*. 3.17.

ancient rhetorical expectations. Studies attending to these ancient rhetorical expectations may be familiar and unexceptional in the eyes of NT scholars, but for present-day patrologists, they are fresh and exciting. I have shown how ancient judicial rhetoric operates at a detailed level, and surfaces throughout virtually every one of the many portions of *Ad Autolycum*. I have also shown that this judicial rhetoric also operates above the level of details, because each of the three letters was organized in conformity to a standard judicial rhetorical structure. Attention to ancient rhetorical expectations has allowed the role of the inspired texts used in *Ad Autolycum* to be explained with more historical accuracy than would be possible using modern categories alone. Theophilus used the inspired texts throughout *Ad Autolycum* as friendly textual witnesses, and the writings of the pagan poets and philosophers as hostile ones. It is therefore not at all surprising that he used conventional ancient judicial rhetorical τόποι in conjunction with his uses of the inspired texts, and with his citations of the poets and philosophers. Specifically, he employed τόποι of discoursing on the authority of friendly witnesses,[5] on their virtuous lives,[6] and the consistency of their testimony.[7] When citing hostile textual witnesses, he used the conventional τόποι of discoursing on their foul lives,[8] on their inconsistent testimony,[9] of showing that they testify about what they could not have known,[10] of showing how what they testify concerning could not have happened,[11] or that these things indeed did not happen.[12] His general practice was to undercut the testimony of hostile textual witnesses at the start of an argument, so as to place them on the defensive if it were possible, before introducing testimonies of friendly textual witnesses. This pattern is exactly what would have been expected in Greco-Roman protreptic literature. The mass of standard ancient rhetorical devices pervading *Ad Autolycum* tends not to move modern readers. But Theophilus's second-century audience was accustomed to hearing these very same rhetorical devices, and even expected them. His audience would have been deeply disappointed had it not seen these devices in *Ad Autolycum*. Indeed, they would have grasped and followed his argument easily *at every turn*, even if they disagreed. Friend and foe alike would

5. Ibid., 1.14; 2.9, 12, 18–22, 28, 30, 32–33, 35; 3.17, 20–23, and 26–27.
6. Ibid., 1.14; 2.9, 14–16; 3.9–10, and 12–13.
7. Ibid., 1.14; 2.9–10, 13, 22, 29–31, 33, 35–38; 3.11–14, and 17.
8. Ibid., 1.1–2, 7, 9–10; 3.3, 6–8, 12, 15, and 30.
9. Ibid., 1.8–10, 13; 2.4–8, 37; 3.7–8, 16, 26, and 30.
10. Ibid., 1.2, 5, 7; 2.5, 12, 32–33; 3.2, 16, and 30.
11. Ibid., 2.3.
12. Ibid., 2.3, 12.

have respected it. The organization and force of *Ad Autolycum*, far from being haphazard or poorly-constructed as frequently depicted in our scholarship, would actually have appeared brilliant to second-century eyes. And amid this rhetorical brilliance, Scripture, supplying a chorus of trustworthy witnesses, drove the protreptic argument.

ANCIENT WITNESS INTERROGATION RHETORIC AND THE NEW PORTRAIT OF PATRISTIC EXEGESIS

I have argued that Theophilus cast Scripture in his protreptic letters to play a powerful, very central and indispensable role in his classic rhetoric of witness interrogation. The ancients believed that the most trustworthy witness testimony came from the dead, whose testimony was fixed and therefore absolutely incorruptible. This helps explain why the ancients eagerly recited portions of trusted classic works in their disputations. Since Theophilus did not write his letters to Autolycus primarily to contend with other Christians about biblical interpretations, he would not have used judicial rhetorical devices that treated Scripture as *written* evidence and challenged certain interpretations of it. Rather, he labored in a context of inter-religious dialogue to demonstrate *whose* testimony was trustworthy: that of the prophets and Christian inspired writers, or that of the pagan poets and philosophers. Therefore, Theophilus's selection of those rhetorical devices which were *specifically intended for use in witness interrogation* was entirely appropriate.

The skillful selection of these specific witness interrogation devices by Theophilus and allied second-century Christian apologists who also dialogued with Greco-Roman religionists, including those who trained for rhetorical battle by hearing or reading *Ad Autolycum*, is what set their distinctive exegesis apart from exegetical habits of other apologists. Since some apologists fought on dissimilar rhetorical fronts, they used differing exegetical strategies and tactics. These include the proof-text exegetical habits displayed in Justin's *Dialogue with Trypho the Jew*, and the anti-dualistic exegetical traditions evidenced in Irenaeus's and Tertullian's various arguments against gnostic teachers. I in no way claim that the distinctive mode of exegesis described herein, that exegesis used by Theophilus and the other apologists who faced Greco-Roman religionists, was uniformly employed by all second-century apologists in some monolithic sense. However, even if this exegesis was only one of several in the great apologetic age, it was prominent and indispensable nevertheless. This had to be so, given the protreptic, oral, and rhetorical realities of that age, and also given the unavoidable pressures from Greco-Roman religionists.

These insights connected to ancient witness-interrogation rhetoric can help fill in an area of the emerging new portrait of patristic exegesis and patristic use of Scripture. This new portrait has been partially drawn by Young with her rhetorically-oriented reading strategies, by Mitchell, who shows how epideictic rhetoric and judicial rhetoric involving conventions for handling *written* evidence informed patristic exegesis, and by Dawson, who shows how dynamic inter-play between mimetic and anti-mimetic rhetoric informs it. A further region of this new portrait is drawn by this present study, suggesting that in apologetic writings directed to Gentile audiences (whereby Christian writers appealed to Scripture but their pagan opponents did not), classic rhetorical τόποι intended for use in witness interrogation were used with superb effect to play up the trustworthiness of biblical writers and to challenge the trustworthiness of pagan ones.

TESTIMONY SOURCES AND A NEW ERA IN BIBLICAL TESTIMONIA STUDIES

Theophilus performed creative exegesis, but also followed select exegetical traditions when they served his traditional early Christian apologetic goals. This tendency is typified by his use of testimony sources. He likely used testimony sources in *Autol.* 1.7; in *Autol.* 1.10 in the discussion of idols; in *Autol.* 1.14 involving Rom 2:6 and 1 Cor 2:9; in *Autol.* 2.10 concerning the Logos; in *Autol.* 2.13 where a christianized synagogal prayer likely was the testimony source; in *Autol.* 2.35 for prophetic citations dealing with monotheism; and in *Autol.* 3.12–14 in the discourses on justice, chastity, and beneficence. This suggests that not every sequence of inspired texts in *Ad Autolycum* derives from Theophilus's own creative grouping.

However, his use of scriptural anthologies and testimony sources is fairly sparse compared to rich uses of such by Pseudo-Barnabas and Justin. This is exactly what we would expect for an apologist living just at the end of the gradually-closing "age of testimonies."[13] Theophilus's elders may have frequently used these tools, but by his day, they had fallen largely into disuse. The few evidences of their use in his writings confirms not only Skarsuane's conclusion that use of testimony sources died out in the late second century, but also the evidence discussed in chapter 3 that Theophilus was able to access much OT Scripture by memory rather than from written manuscripts or written testimony sources. He was of a new age, when

---

13. The phrase is coined by Skarsaune. This is that great age of testimonia use discussed in chapter 3.

even Gentile Christians could frequently and easily access the words of the Hebrew prophets by memory rather than by reading.

As to the methods of testimonia research, we have never before seen the sort of truly comprehensive searches for testimony sources as those produced by the ACTS software with its intelligent automatic searches of a massive database of biblical indexes. It facilitates discovery of less obvious testimony sources. Exhaustively searching for sequences of citations, quotations, allusions, or reminiscences reoccurring among the hundreds of extant Jewish and Christian writings, and the dozens of thousands of treatise sections they contain, from the second century or prior is a practically impossible task if done manually. The testimonia searches that I have discussed were accomplished by examining Scripture indexes of over four hundred extant ancient treatises for multitudes of Scripture combinations located within certain proximities. When examining combinations of three or more passages, rather than combinations of merely two passages, the task is so much the harder. Dodd has shown that one cannot only deal with exact matches when seeking testimony sources. Often ancient biblical anthologies include sequences not of single verses, but rather sequences made up of blocks, each containing multiple verses from a biblical passage, often a half dozen verses in each block of biblical text. There is no reason that a writer had to use every verse in a given block of text contained in an ancient anthology. Rather, the top of one block, the bottom of another, and the middle of a third block in a given biblical anthology or testimony source might be used. A second writer, even one picking from the same textual blocks of the very same anthology, might use a similar but *not* identical selection of biblical verses taken from the anthology. He might even use them in a different order than that of the first writer. Therefore when searching for possible uses of testimonia, biblical anthologies and other testimony sources, it is necessary to seek both exact and near matches of Scripture combinations. It is also necessary in such searches to consider various orderings of Scripture combinations. In practical terms, manual methods are simply inadequate for truly *comprehensive* searches for testimony sources. In the end, hundreds of millions of examinations for use of a particular grouping of biblical passages must be performed. The practical limitations of manual searches are insurmountable if one wants to be comprehensive. But electronic methods such as ACTS are capable in real-life practical terms of handling such complexity. ACTS pioneers this electronic approach for *truly* comprehensive searches for possible use of testimony sources. A new era in biblical testimonia studies has dawned.

CODA: THE APOLOGETIC FUNCTION OF SCRIPTURE

In short, we have seen some significant but forgotten realities about the second-century and one of its distinctive apologetic exegetical traditions. First, while specialists may acknowledge in passing the protreptic genre of various early Christian writings, they often fail to take seriously ancient expectations about protreptic appeals. As a result, they levy anachronistic and misleading theological criticisms that ignore or misunderstand the very purpose of ancient protreptic writings. Accordingly, they also fail to discover the biblical justifications that early Christians constructed for their protreptic efforts. Second, the function and richness of Scripture in the apologetic age remains mostly hidden if we ignore the pervasive illiteracy of late antiquity and the great memory abilities of highly-illiterate cultures.[14] Present-day patristic scholarship has not yet adequately dealt with the orality of second-century Christianity, because this scholarship is the product of our own highly-literate modern age. We often tend to presume a *written* text behind every biblical quotation and allusion. This tendency fits well in our own world of high literacy and readily-obtainable texts but not with that of the early Christian apologists. Third, although Theophilus has been described by various prominent scholars as being a disorganized writer who did not understand very much of Christian teaching, this stereotypical view of him is actually the very opposite of historical reality. Actually, a masterful coherence runs throughout *every* section of *Ad Autolycum*, upon a stage of ancient judicial witness-interrogation rhetoric, whereupon Scripture performed an absolutely central and essential role. We simply *must* look beyond our anachronistic ideas about genre, literacy, and rhetoric in order to recover this prominent yet forgotten stream of exegesis of the second-century. These conclusions bring us back to where we began when we reflected on Robert Louis Wilken's conviction about the transformational power of Scripture in the early Christian period. How exceedingly rich was that power in the age of the second-century Christian apologists.

---

14. While chapter 3 focuses on this reality, the sparse use of testimony sources discussed in chapter 5 partially confirms it.

Appendix 1

Methodological Notes

SPECIFIC METHODOLOGIES REFERENCED IN the various chapters are discussed in detail in those chapters. Some readers may be curious about other methodological details. These are discussed below.

QUOTATION AND ALLUSION CRITERIA

For the "usage database analysis" of chapter 3, and the scripture usage tables in the following appendix, I follow the computational approach of Ernest, who categorizes uses of inspired texts as citations, quotations, reminiscences, or allusions.[1] Since this approach applies the same numerical criteria to *every* use of an inspired text, it is both consistent and comprehensive.[2] Its main utility for the present study is to provide a consistent initial

---

1. Ernest, "Uses of Scripture in the Writings of Athanasius." For an updated version, see Ernest, *The Bible in Athanasius*. In the present study, *citations* are distinguished by formulas which signal to the reader that reference is being made to a biblical text. Such formulas may include phrases that explicitly alert the reader that a quotation is coming, or as Ernest notes, something as subtle as the definite article τό. *Allusions* are mentions of biblical writers, books, events, characters, or features in the content of biblical texts, but that do not match or mimic any biblical text itself. *Quotations, reminiscences*, and *locutions* are references to Scripture via language that is close to that of a biblical text. These three types are distinguished according to how closely they match a biblical text. Quotations match or almost match a biblical text. Reminiscences match specific biblical texts, but not as closely as quotations. Finally, locutions so loosely match biblical language that it is not possible to determine exactly which biblical text is the referent.

2. The numerical criteria are explained in the "Terminology in Tables" in appendix 2.

categorization of every use of an inspired text. Modern categories such as "citation," "quotation," "reminiscence," or "allusion" only provide a starting point for understanding how Theophilus uses the inspired texts. Therefore, the focus in this present study upon ancient rhetoric allows us to transcend the limitations of modern categories and to understand Theophilus' use of inspired texts historically, according to the conventions of his own day.

However, usage database analysis also provides further benefit. It can reveal distribution variations of biblical citations, quotations, allusions, and reminiscences across the various portions of *Ad Autolycum*.[3] It can also show how uses of individual inspired books vary across the various portions of *Ad Autolycum*. These variations are indicated in the Scripture distribution tables in appendix 2.

"Database usage analysis" involves populating a database with Scripture usage word counts, *Ad Autolycum* word counts, and Scripture introduction formulas.[4] Reports were generated out of it to show consistently and comprehensively how the types of Scripture usage and selected biblical books differ in each chapter of *Ad Autolycum*.

RABBINICA

As Timothy J. Horner aptly points out, it is questionable in second-century studies to look to late rabbinic writings for evidence of second-century rabbinic exegetical traditions.[5] Accordingly, I follow his call for caution by restricting testimony source analysis only to a few early Tannaic writings. These are the *Mishnah*, a codification of rabbinic oral teaching from the early third century; and because it provides the early rabbinic perspective on biblical chronology, a topic central to the third letter of *Ad Autolycum*, the *Seder 'Olam Rabbah*, portions of which at least were composed in the second century.[6] Later rabbinic writings which are excluded include the Palestinian and Babylonian Talmuds, composed in the fifth and sixth centuries respectively, the medieval Amoraic Midrashim, and also Tannaic Midrashim composed no earlier than the late fourth century, such as the

---

3. Since I rely on a sort of scholarly consensus by considering *only* those uses of Scripture which appear in *both* Biblia Patristica's and Marcovich's biblical indexes of *Ad Autolycum*, locutions do not appear in any part of the present study.

4. Refer to the "Terminology in Tables" in appendix 2 for the formulas used in this analysis and for the specific types of word counts which factor into these formulas.

5. Horner, Review of *Justin Martyr*.

6. Blackman, *Mishnayoth*; Neusner, *Mishnah*; Guggenheimer, *Seder Olam*.

Mekilta, the *Sipra*, and the *Sipre* on Numbers and Deuteronomy.[7] I also exclude the *Tosefta*, the commentary on the *Mishnah* which was composed in the third and fourth centuries C. E. While the *Tosefta* likely contains some material in use prior to 200 C. E., there is not very much.[8] Even for material in the *Tosefta* which was in use prior to 200 C.E., it is likely that little of this usage occurred in Antioch. Major rabbinic academies were never established in Antioch as they had in other cities, even though Antioch was by far the most prominent Eastern Roman city.[9] Erring on the side of caution in regard to Horner's above-mentioned critique, I set aside the *Tosefta*.

Oskar Skarsaune aptly notes that patristic specialists who are less than fully trained in rabbinic literature must enter that field hesitantly. At the same time, he felt it necessary to do so in his masterful study on Justin's proof-text tradition.[10] I share this attitude of hesitancy about entering into the complexities of rabbinica coupled with the sense that at least some entrance is advantageous.

A re-engagement with rabbinica that endeavors to isolate and reconsider exegesis in early portions of some excluded rabbinic works such as the *Tosefta* could be a worthy extension of the present study. However, such an extension is beyond the scope of the present study, which is already occupied with several hundred Hellenistic Jewish and Christian sources in addition to those few rabbinic sources which can confidently be dated prior to the third century.

MISCELLANEOUS METHODOLOGICAL DETAILS

Unless noted, all English translations of ancient and modern quoted material are my own. Hebrew Scripture verse numeration follows that of the LXX, as per Grant and Marcovich's biblical indexes of *Ad Autolycum*. Greek texts are those editions used in the *Thesaurus Linguae Graecae* (TLG), unless noted.[11] Source titles are abbreviated and capitalization is implemented according to the *SBL Handbook of Style*. In general, I give the English names

---

7. For dating of rabbinic materials, see Evans, *Noncanonical Writings*, 114–48.
8. Neusner, "Preface," in *Mishnah*, xi.
9. Brooten, "Jews of Ancient Antioch," 36. For the prominence of Antioch in the Eastern region of the empire, see Kondoleon, "The City of Antioch," 4.
10. Skarsaune, *Proof from Prophecy*, 248–49.
11. TLG is copyrighted by the TLG Project, located at University of California/Irvine, and by the Regents of the University of California. Some of these texts are accessed in their original print form while others are accessed through TLG. Bibliographical details for these texts are provided below in the bibliography.

of works in the text and their Greek or Latin names in notes, except in the case of *Ad Autolycum*. Categories in the scripture usage tables, "prophetic books," "gospels," and "inspired writings," are translations of the ancient categories Theophilus himself used.

LIST OF TREATISES SEARCHED BY THE APPLICATION FOR COMPUTERIZED TESTIMONIA SEARCHES (ACTS)

The ACTS software searches the biblical indexes of 418 ancient Jewish and Christian treatises, these composing the great majority of surviving Greek "exegetical" works that may be safely dated as contemporaneous with or prior to Theophilus, as well as some additional treatises in some other languages, for patterns that may indicate testimonia collections used by Theophilus.

First- and Second-Century Works included in Biblia patristica, vol. 1 (224 treatises)

These are listed in the order of the treatise list in *Biblia patristica*, vol. 1. Refer to it for the bibliographic information for the critical edition of each treatise.

Anonyma, Apophasis megale

Anonyma, Canon Muratorianus

Anonyma, Didache

Anonyma, Epistula ad Diognetum

Anonyma, Papyrus Egerton 3

Anonyma, Liber Eichasai

Anonyma, Epistula Valentinianorum

Anonyma, De hypostasi archontium

Anonyma, Interpretatio animae

Anonyma, Liber authenticus (CG 6,3)

Anonyma, Aduersus Miltiadem

Anonyma, De origine mundi (CG 2,5)

Anonyma, Oracula Sibyllina

Anonyma, Ad Rheginum de resurrectione

Anonyma, De sensu Potestatis magnae (CG 6,4)

Anonyma, Sententiae Sexti

Anonyma apocrypha, Acta Andreae (Lipsius and Bonnet ed.)

Anonyma apocrypha, Acta Andreae (Hornschuh ed.)

Anonyma apocrypha, Acta Ioannis 1 (Lipsius and Bonnet ed.)

Anonyma apocrypha, Acta Ioannis 1 (Wessely ed.)

Anonyma apocrypha, Acta Ioannis 1 (in Anonyma Apocrypha, Epistula Titi)

Anonyma apocrypha, Acta Ioannis 2 (Lipsius and Bonnet ed.)

Anonyma apocrypha, Acta Pauli (Vouaux ed.)

Anonyma apocrypha, Acta Pauli (Schmidt ed.)

Anonyma apocrypha, Acta Pauli (Kasser ed.)

Anonyma apocrypha, Acta Pauli (Testuz ed.)

Anonyma apocrypha, Acta Petri graeca

Anonyma apocrypha, Acta Petri coptica (BG 8502,4)

Anonyma apocrypha, Acta Petri coptica (CG 6,1)

Anonyma apocrypha, Apocalypsis Iacobi prima

Anonyma apocrypha, Apocalypsis Iacobi secunda

Anonyma apocrypha, Apocalypsis Pauli coptica

Anonyma apocrypha, Apocalypsis Petri graeca (Maurer and Duensing ed.)

Anonyma apocrypha, Apocalypsis Petri graeca (Klostermann ed.)

Anonyma apocrypha, Apocalypsis Petri coptica

Anonyma apocrypha, Apocryphon Iacobi

Anonyma apocrypha, Apocryphon Ioannis (Kasser ed.)

Anonyma apocrypha, Papyri Argentoratenses coptici 5 et 6

Anonyma apocrypha, Ascensio Isaiae (Tisserant ed.)

Anonyma apocrypha, Ascensio Isaiae (Charles ed.)

Anonyma apocrypha, Papyrus Der El-Balizeh gnosticus

Anonyma apocrypha, Epistula Barnabae

Anonyma apocrypha, Papyrus Cairensis 10735

Anonyma apocrypha, Papyrus Egerton 2

Anonyma apocrypha, Epistula Apostolorum

Anonyma apocrypha, Euangelium Aegyptiorum graecum

Anonyma apocrypha, Euangelium Aegyptiorum copticum

Anonyma apocrypha, Euangelium Ebionitarum

Anonyma apocrypha, Euangelium Euae

Anonyma apocrypha, Euangelium Hebraeorum (in Clemens Alexandrinus, Stromata)

Anonyma apocrypha, Euangelium Hebraeorum (in Hieronymus, Commentarii in Isaiam)

Anonyma apocrypha, Euangelium Hebraeorum (in Origenes, Commentarii in Ioannem)

Anonyma apocrypha, Euangelium Hebraeorum (in Hieronymus, Commentarius in Ephesios)

Anonyma apocrypha, Euangelium Hebraeorum (in Hieronymus, Commentarii in Ezechielem)

Anonyma apocrypha, Euangelium Hebraeorum (in Hieronymus, De uiris illustribus)

Anonyma apocrypha, Euangelium Mariae (Till ed.)

Anonyma apocrypha, Euangelium Mariae (Pugliese Carratelli and Till ed.)

Anonyma apocrypha, Euangelium Nazarenorum (in Hieronymus, Conunentarii in Mattheum)

Anonyma apocrypha, Euangelium Nazarenorum (in Hieronymus, De uiris illustribus)

Anonyma apocrypha, Euangelium Nazarenorum (in Hieronymus, Dialogus contra Pelagianos)

Anonyma apocrypha, Euangelium Nazarenorum (in Origenes, In Mattheum)

Anonyma apocrypha, Euangelium Nazarenorum (in Eusebius Caesariensis, Theophania)

Anonyma apocrypha, Euangelium Nazarenorum (in Eusebius Caesariensis, Theophania syriaca)

Anonyma apocrypha, Euangelium Petri

Anonyma apocrypha, Euangelium Thomae graecum (Michel and Peeters ed.)

Anonyma apocrypha, Euangelium Thomae graecum (Tischendorf ed.)

Anonyma apocrypha, Euangelium Thomae copticum (Guillaumont ed.)

Anonyma apocrypha, Euangelium Thomae copticum (Wessely ed.)

Anonyma apocrypha, Euangelium Thomae copticum (Santos Otero ed.)

Anonyma apocrypha, Euangeliuni ueritatis (Malinine, Puech, and Quispel ed.)

Anonyma apocrypha, Euangelium ueritatis (Malinine, Puech, Quispel, and Till ed.)

Anonyma apocrypha, Papyrus Fayumensis

Anonyma apocrypha, Genus Mariae

Anonyma apocrypha, Kerygma Petri

Anonyma apocrypha, Liber secundus Seth Magni

Anonyma apocrypha, Odae Salomonis (Harris and Mingana ed.)

Anonyma apocrypha, Odae Salomonis (Testuz ed.)

Anonyma apocrypha, Oratio Ioseph (in Origenes, In Ioannem)

Anonyma apocrypha, Oratio Ioseph (in Origenes, Philocalia)

Anonyma apocrypha, Papyrus Oxyrhynchus 840

Anonyma apocrypha, Papyrus Oxyrhynchus 1224

Anonyma apocrypha, Proteuangelium Iacobi

Anonyma apocrypha, Sophia Iesu Christi (Till ed.)

Anonyma apocrypha, Sophia Iesu Christi (Wessely ed.)

Anonyma apocrypha, Liber Thomae Athletae

Anonyma Hagiographica, Acta Scillitanorum

Anonyma Hagiographica, Epistula ecclesiarum Lugdunensis et Viennensis

Anonyma Hagiographica, Martyrium Polycarpi

Anonyma Hagiographica, Passio Apollonii Romani

Anonyma Hagiographica, Passio Carpi, Papyii et Agathonicae

Anonyma Hagiographica, Passio Iustini et sociorura

Anonyma Hagiographica, Passio Perpetuae et Felicitatis

Anonyma Hagiographica, Passio Pionii

Anonyma Liturgica, Papyrus Bodmer 12

Anonyma Liturgica, Psalmus Naassenorum

Apelles, Fragmenta uaria (in Ambrosius, De paradise)

Apelles, Fragmenta uaria (in Origenes, Homiliae in Genesim)

Apelles, Fragmenta uaria (in Epiphanius, Panarion)

Apollonius Antimontanista, Aduersus Cataphrygas

Apollinarius Hierapolitanus, De pascha

Aristides Atheniensis, Apologia

Aristo Pellaeus, Altercatio

Asterius Urbanus, Fragmenta uaria

Athenagoras Atheniensis, Supplicatio

Athenagoras Atheniensis ?, De resurrectione mortuorum

Basilides Gnosticus, Explanationes

Basilides Gnosticus, Fragmenta uaria

Clemens Alexandrinus, Canon ecclesiasticus

Clemens Alexandrinus, Quis diues saluetur

Clemens Alexandrinus, Eclogae ex scripturis propheticis

Clemens Alexandrinus, Excerpta ex scriptis Theodoti

Clemens Alexandrinus, Fragmenta uaria (Staehlin, Fruechtel, and Treu ed.)

Clemens Alexandrinus, Fragmenta uaria (Fleisch ed.)

Clemens Alexandrinus, Hypotyposeis

Clemens Alexandrinus, Paedagogus

Clemens Alexandrinus, De pascha

Clemens Alexandrinus, Protrepticus

Clemens Alexandrinus, Stromata

Clemens Alexandrinus ?, Cohortatio de perseuerantia

Clemens Alexandrinus ?, De prouidentia

Clemens Romanus, Epistula ad Corinthios prima

Clemens Romanus Pseudo, Epistula ad Corinthios secunda
Dionysius Corinthius, Ad Soterem
Epiphanius Gnosticus, De iustitia
Gaius Presbyter, Fragmenta uaria
Gaius Presbyter, Aduersus Proculum
Hegesippus, Memorabilia
Heracleon Gnosticus, Fragmenta uaria
Heracleon Gnosticus, In Ioannem
Hermias Philosophus, Irrisio gentilium philosopher urn
Hermas Romanus, Pastor
Ignatius Antiochenus, Epistula ad Ephesios
Ignatius Antiochenus, Epistula ad Magnesios
Ignatius Antiochenus, Epistula ad Philadelphenos
Ignatius Antiochenus, Epistula ad Polycarpum
Ignatius Antiochenus, Epistula ad Romanes
Ignatius Antiochenus, Epistula ad Smyrnaeos
Ignatius Antiochenus, Epistula ad Trallianos
Irenaeus Lugdunensis, Demonstratio
Irenaeus Lugdunensis, Ad Florinum
Irenaeus Lugdunensis, Fragmenta uaria (Harvey ed.)
Irenaeus Lugdunensis, Fragmenta uaria (Jordan ed.)
Irenaeus Lugdunensis, Fragments uaria (in Ioannes Damascenus)
Irenaeus Lugdunensis, Fragmenta uaria (Devreesse ed.)
Irenaeus Lugdunensis, Aduersus haereses
Irenaeus Lugdunensis ?, Fragmenta uaria (Harvey ed.)
Irenaeus Lugdunensis ?, Fragmenta uaria (Jordan ed.)
Irenaeus Lugdunensis Pseudo, Fragmenta uaria (Harvey ed.)
Isidorus Gnosticus, Explanationes prophetae Parchor
Iulius Cassianus, De continentia
Iulius Cassianus, Fragmenta uaria
Iustinus Gnosticus, Liber Baruch

Iustinus Martyr, Apologiae
Iustinus Martyr, Dialogus cum Tryphone
Iustinus Martyr, Aduersus Marcionem
Iustinus Martyr ? Fragmenta uaria
Iustinus Martyr ?, Aduersus Iudaeos
Iustinus Martyr ?, De resurrectione
Melito Sardianus, Apologia
Melito Sardianus, De baptismo
Melito Sardianus, De die dominica
Melito Sardianus, Eclogae
Melito Sardianus, Fragmenta uaria (in Origenes, Selecta in Psalmos)
Melito Sardianus, Fragmenta uaria (Pitra ed.)
Melito Sardianus, De incarnatione Christ
Melito Sardianus, Homilia de pascha
Melito Sardianus ?, De anima et corpore
Melito Sardianus ?, De cruce
Melito Sardianus ?, De fide
Melito Sardianus Pseudo, Apologia
Minucius Felix, Octavius
Papias Hierapolitanus, Explanationes uerborum dominicorum
Polycrates Ephesius, Epistula ad Victorem et ad Romanos
Polycarpus Smyrnaeus, Epistula ad Philippenses
Ptolemaeus Gnosticus, Epistula ad Floram
Serapion Antoichenus, De Euangelio Petri
Tatianus Syrus, Fragmenta uaria
Tatianus Syrus, Oratio ad Graecos
Tatianus Syrus, De perfectione secundum Saluatoris praecepta
Tertullianus, De anima
Tertullianus, Apologeticum
Tertullianus, De baptismo
Tertullianus, De carne Christi

Tertullianus, De exhortatione castitatis
Tertullianus, De corona
Tertullianus, De cuitu feminarum
Tertullianus, Fragmenta uaria
Tertullianus, De fuga in persecutione
Tertullianus, Aduersus Hermogenem
Tertullianus, De idololatria
Tertullianus, De ieiunio aduersus psychicos
Tertullianus, Aduersus Iudaeos
Tertullianus, Aduersus Marcionem
Tertullianus, Ad martyras
Tertullianus, De monogamia
Tertullianus, Ad nationes
Tertullianus, De oratione
Tertullianus, De paenitentia
Tertullianus, De pallio
Tertullianus, De patientia
Tertullianus, De praescriptione haereticorum
Tertullianus, Aduersus Praxean
Tertullianus, De pudicitia
Tertullianus, De resurrectione mortuorum
Tertullianus, Ad Scapulam
Tertullianus, Scorpiace
Tertullianus, De spectaculis
Tertullianus, De testimonio animae
Tertullianus, Aduersus Valentinianos
Tertullianus, De uirginibus uelandis
Tertullianus, Ad uxorem
Theodotus Coriarius, Fragments uaria (in Epiphanius, Panarion)
Theodotus Gnosticus, Fragmenta uaria (in Clemens Alexandrinus, Excerpta ex scriptis Theodoti)

Theophilus Antiochenus, *Ad Autolycum*

Theophilus Antiochenus, Fragmenta uaria (in Hieronymus, Epistula 121)

Valentinus Gnosticus, De amicis

Valentinus Gnosticus, Fragmenta uaria (Voelker ed.)

Hellenistic Jewish and Early Rabbinic Jewish Works (105 treatises)

Especially because of their nature as testimonia collections, two works from the Dead Sea Scrolls (DSS) are included. See the Philo Supplement volume of Biblia patristica for bibliographic information for the Philo treatises. For critical editions of the other treatises, see the bibliography.

Babylonian Talmud (Socino), Aboth.

Babylonian Talmud (Socino), 'Arakin.

Babylonian Talmud (Socino), 'Abodah Zarah.

Babylonian Talmud (Socino), Baba Bathra.

Babylonian Talmud (Socino), Bekoroth.

Babylonian Talmud (Socino), Berakoth.

Babylonian Talmud (Socino), Bezah.

Babylonian Talmud (Socino), Bikkurim.

Babylonian Talmud (Socino), Baba Kamma.

Babylonian Talmud (Socino), Baba Mezi'a.

Babylonian Talmud (Socino), Demai.

Babylonian Talmud (Socino), 'Eduyyoth.

Babylonian Talmud (Socino), 'Erubin.

Babylonian Talmud (Socino), Gittin.

Babylonian Talmud (Socino), Hagigah.

Babylonian Talmud (Socino), Hallah.

Babylonian Talmud (Socino), Horayoth.

Babylonian Talmud (Socino), Hullin.

Babylonian Talmud (Socino), Kelim.

Babylonian Talmud (Socino), Kerithoth.

Babylonian Talmud (Socino), Kethuboth.
Babylonian Talmud (Socino), Kiddushin.
Babylonian Talmud (Socino), Kil'ayim.
Babylonian Talmud (Socino), Kinnin.
Babylonian Talmud (Socino), Ma'asroth.
Babylonian Talmud (Socino), Ma'aser Sheni.
Babylonian Talmud (Socino), Makkoth.
Babylonian Talmud (Socino), Maksirin.
Babylonian Talmud (Socino), Megillah.
Babylonian Talmud (Socino), Me'ilah.
Babylonian Talmud (Socino), Menahoth.
Babylonian Talmud (Socino), Middoth.
Babylonian Talmud (Socino), Mikwa'oth.
Babylonian Talmud (Socino), Mo'ed Katan.
Babylonian Talmud (Socino), Ma'aser Sheni.
Babylonian Talmud (Socino), Nazir.
Babylonian Talmud (Socino), Nedarim.
Babylonian Talmud (Socino), Naga'im.
Babylonian Talmud (Socino), Niddah.
Babylonian Talmud (Socino), Oholoth.
Babylonian Talmud (Socino), 'Orlah.
Babylonian Talmud (Socino), Parah.
Babylonian Talmud (Socino), Pesahim.
Babylonian Talmud (Socino), Rosh Hashanah.
Babylonian Talmud (Socino), Sanhedrin.
Babylonian Talmud (Socino), Shabbath.
Babylonian Talmud (Socino), Shebi'ith.
Babylonian Talmud (Socino), Shebu'oth.
Babylonian Talmud (Socino), Shekalim.
Babylonian Talmud (Socino), Sotah.
Babylonian Talmud (Socino), Sukkah.

Babylonian Talmud (Socino), Ta'anith.
Babylonian Talmud (Socino), Tamid.
Babylonian Talmud (Socino), Temurah.
Babylonian Talmud (Socino), Terumoth.
Babylonian Talmud (Socino), Tohoroth.
Babylonian Talmud (Socino), v. Toh.
Babylonian Talmud (Socino), Tebul Yom.
Babylonian Talmud (Socino), 'Ukzin.
Babylonian Talmud (Socino), Yebamoth.
Babylonian Talmud (Socino), Yoma.
Babylonian Talmud (Socino), Zabim.
Babylonian Talmud (Socino), Zebahim.
Dead Sea Scroll 4Q175 (4QTestimonia, Charlesworth ed.)
Dead Sea Scroll 4Q174 (4QFlorilegium, Charlesworth ed.)
Mishnah (Neusner ed.)
Philo of Alexandria, De Abrahamo.
Philo of Alexandria, De aeternitate mundi.
Philo of Alexandria, De agricultura.
Philo of Alexandria, De animalibus (Alexander).
Philo of Alexandria, De Cherubim.
Philo of Alexandria, De confusione linguarum.
Philo of Alexandria, De congressu eruditionis gratia.
Philo of Alexandria, De decalogo.
Philo of Alexandria, De Deo.
Philo of Alexandria, De ebrietate.
Philo of Alexandria, De fuga et inuentione.
Philo of Alexandria, De gigantibus.
Philo of Alexandria, De Iosepho.
Philo of Alexandria, De migratione Abrahami.
Philo of Alexandria, De mutatione nominum.
Philo of Alexandria, De opificio mundi.

Philo of Alexandria, De plantatione.

Philo of Alexandria, De posteritate Caini.

Philo of Alexandria, De praemiis et poenis, de exsecrationibus.

Philo of Alexandria, De Prouidentia.

Philo of Alexandria, De sacrificiis Abelis et Caini.

Philo of Alexandria, De sobrietate.

Philo of Alexandria, De somniis.

Philo of Alexandria, De specialibus legibus.

Philo of Alexandria, De uirtutibus.

Philo of Alexandria, De uita contemplatiua.

Philo of Alexandria, De uita Mosis.

Philo of Alexandria, Fragmenta uaria.

Philo of Alexandria, Hypothetica.

Philo of Alexandria, In Flaccum.

Philo of Alexandria, Legatio ad Caium.

Philo of Alexandria, Legum allegoriae.

Philo of Alexandria, Quaestiones in Exodum.

Philo of Alexandria, Quaestiones in Genesim.

Philo of Alexandria, Quis rerum diuinarum heres sit.

Philo of Alexandria, Quod deterius potiori insidiari soleat.

Philo of Alexandria, Quod Deus sit immutabilis.

Philo of Alexandria, Quod omnis probus liber sit.

Seder Olam (Guggenheimer ed.)

New Testament (27 books)

The biblical indexes of quotations, allusions, and verbal parallels of OT passages in the 1983 United Bible Societies edition of the New Testament, edited by Kurt Aland, et. al., is used to populate the ACTS database for the NT books. See the bibliography for full bibliographic information.

OT Pseudepigrapha (62 treatises)

The biblical indexes of James A. Charlesworth's 1983 edition of the OT Pseudepigrapha is used to populate the ACTS database for these treatises. See the bibliography for full bibliographic information.

APPENDIX 2

Scripture Usage Tables[1]

TABLE 1: USES OF SCRIPTURE AND INSPIRED WRITINGS IN *AD AUTOLYCUM*

Ad Autolycum	1	2	3
Total words in the letter	3089	11550	6963
Instances of use of Scripture or inspired writings	45	105	129
Totals words identified as Scripture or inspired writing	284	3096	1187
Words of Scripture or inspired writing per 1000 words of the letter	92	268	170
Number of citations	3	32	31
Words in citations	27	2061	653
Words in citations per 1000 words in the letter	9	178	93
Number of quotations	16	22	4
Words in quotations	114	275	30
Words in quotations per 1000 words in the letter	37	24	4
Number of reminiscences	14	17	41
Words in reminiscences	61	257	73
Words in reminiscences per 1000 words in the letter	20	22	10

1. For details on the computer-based generation of these tables, see the discussion of quotation and allusion terminology in chapter 3 and in the prior appendix.

Number of allusions	12	34	53
Words in allusions	82	503	431
Words in allusions per 1000 words in the letter	27	44	62

Note: In this table and in the following tables, following the practice of Ernest in his similar tables, blank entries are used to represent zero values, so that non-zero values can more easily be located.

TABLE 2: USES OF SCRIPTURE AND INSPIRED WRITINGS IN *AD AUTOLYCUM* 1

	Ad Autolycum 1	1–5: The True God	6–8: God as Creator and Ruler	9–10: Folly of False Gods	11–13: Objections Answered	14: Conclusion
Total words in text	3089	1058	731	424	594	282
Instances of use of Scripture or inspired writings	45	5	16	3	11	10
Totals words identified as Scripture or inspired writing	284	35	100	10	53	86
Words of Scripture or inspired writing per 1000 words of text	92	33	137	24	89	305
Number of citations	3		1	1	1	
Words in citations	27		9	4	14	
Words in citations per 1000 words in text	9		12	9	24	
Number of quotations	16	2	7	1	2	4
Words in quotations	114	16	60	5	7	26
Words in quotations per 1000 words in text	37	15	82	12	12	92
Number of reminiscences	14	1	6		3	4
Words in reminiscences	61	5	15		11	30
Words in reminiscences per 1000 words in text	20	5	20		18	106
Number of allusions	12	2	2	1	5	2
Words in allusions	82	14	16	1	21	30
Words in allusions per 1000 words in text	27	13	22	2	35	106

TABLE 3: USES OF SCRIPTURE AND INSPIRED WRITINGS IN *AD AUTOLYCUM* 2

	Ad Autolycum 2	1: Introduction	2–8: Origin of the Gods and of the Cosmos	9–19: Genesis and Creation	20–33: Genesis and Early Generations	34–38: Idolatry and the Coming Judgment
Total words in text	11550	115	2143	3334	4113	1845
Instances of use of Scripture or inspired writings	105	1		34	52	18
Totals words identified as Scripture or inspired writing	3096	4		1196	1658	238
Words of Scripture or inspired writing per 1000 words of text	268	35		359	403	129
Number of citations	32			11	6	15
Words in citations	2061			940	902	219
Words in citations per 1000 words in text	178			282	219	119
Number of quotations	22			8	14	
Words in quotations	275			47	228	
Words in quotations per 1000 words in text	24			14	55	
Number of reminiscences	17	1		4	11	1
Words in reminiscences	257	4		35	213	5
Words in reminiscences per 1000 words in text	22	35		10	52	3
Number of allusions	34			11	21	2
Words in allusions	503			174	315	14
Words in allusions per 1000 words in text	44			52	77	8

TABLE 4: USES OF SCRIPTURE AND INSPIRED WRITINGS IN *AD AUTOLYCUM* 3

	Ad Autolycum 3	1–8: Philosophy	9–15: Ethics	16–30: Chronology
Total words in text	6963	1619	1413	3931
Instances of use of Scripture or inspired writings	129	1	33	95
Totals words identified as Scripture or inspired writing	1187	4	661	522
Words of Scripture or inspired writing per 1000 words of text	170	2	468	133
Number of citations	31		30	1
Words in citations	653		644	9
Words in citations per 1000 words in text	93		456	2
Number of quotations	4		2	2
Words in quotations	30		11	19
Words in quotations per 1000 words in text	4		8	5
Number of reminiscences	41	1	1	39
Words in reminiscences	73	4	6	63
Words in reminiscences per 1000 words in text	10	2	4	16
Number of allusions	53			53
Words in allusions	431			431
Words in allusions per 1000 words in text	62			110

TABLE 5: INDIVIDUAL USES OF SCRIPTURE AND INSPIRED WRITINGS, WITH CITATION FORMULAS, IN *AD AUTOLYCUM* 1

Sect.	Scripture/Inspired Text	Type	Words	Citation Formula and Notes
Autol. 1.1: προοίμιον				
1	Ps 113:13–14	A	8	
1	Ps 113:12	R	5	
Autol. 1.2–5: The True God				
2	2 Cor 7:1	Q	5	
4	Gen 1:26	A	6	
4	Gen 1:14	Q	11	
Autol. 1.6–8: God as Creator and Ruler				
6	Job 9:9	R	3	
6	Ps 18:4	R	3	
6	Eph 3:10	Q	5	
6	Ps 146:4	R	3	
6	Ps 32:7	R	2	
6	Job 9:9	R	2	
6	Ps 32:7	R	2	
6	Jer 10:12–13	Q	12	
7	Job 9:8	Q	5	
7	Job 38:18	Q	5	
7	Ps 88:10	Q	9	
7	Ps 23:2	A	7	
7	Job 34:14–15	A	9	
7	Ps 32:6	Q	9	
7	Prov 3:19–20	Q	19	
7	1 Cor 15:53	Q	5	
Autol. 1.9–10: Folly of False Gods				
10	Ps 113:12	C	4	καθὸς προειρήκαμεν
10	Ps 95:5	A	1	
10	Ps 113:16	Q	5	

Scripture Usage Tables

Autol. 1.11–13: Objections Answered				
11	1 Pet 2:13	A	3	
11	Rom 13:1	A	3	
11	Rom 13:1	Q	3	
11	1 Pet 2:17	R	3	
11	Rom 13:1	R	1	
11	1 Tim 2:2	A	3	
11	1 Pet 2:15	Q	4	
11	Prov 24:21–22	C	14	λέγει γὰρ ὁ νόμος ὁ τοῦ θεοῦ·
12	2 Cor 1:21	A	2	
13	John 12:24	A	10	
13	1 Cor 15:37	R	7	
Autol. 1.14: ἐπίλογος				
14	John 20:27	Q	4	
14	John 20:27	Q	3	
14	Ps 93:9	A	11	
14	Exod 4:11	A	19	
14	Rom 2:6	R	4	
14	Rom 2:7	R	10	
14	1 Cor 2:9	Q	12	
14	Rom 2:8–9	R	14	
14	Rom 2:8–9	Q	6	
14	4 Macc 12:12	R	2	

Note: In tables five through seven, the usage types are: C=citations; Q=quotations; R=reminiscences; A=allusions.

TABLE 6: INDIVIDUAL USES OF SCRIPTURE AND INSPIRED WRITINGS, WITH CITATION FORMULAS, IN *AD AUTOLYCUM* 2

Sect.	Scripture/Inspired Text	Type	Words	Citation Formula and Notes
Autol. 2.1: προοίμιον					
1	1 Cor 1:18	R	4	
Autol. 2.2–8: Origin of the Gods and of the Cosmos					
Autol. 2.9–19: Genesis and Creation					
9	2 Pet 1:21	A	18	
10	Prov 8:22–23	A	1	
10	John 1:3	R	3	
10	Gen 1:1	R	1	
10	Prov 8:22	A	1	
10	Prov 8:29–30	C	12	διὰ Σολομῶνος προφήτου οὕτως λέγει· Prov 8:30 is not indicated in Biblia patristica but is clearly quoted in *Autol.* 2.10.
10	Prov 8:27	C	6	διὰ Σολομῶνος προφήτου οὕτως λέγει·
10	Gen 1:1	C	10	Μωσῆς δὲ ὁ καὶ Σολομῶνος πρὸ πολλῶν ἐτῶν γενόμενος μᾶλλον δὲ ὁ λόγος ὁ τοῦ θεοῦ ὡς δι' ὀργάνου δι' αὐτοῦ φησιν
10	Gen 1:1	C	10	ἔφη
10	Gen 1:2	C	19	δηλοῖ ἡμῖν
11	Gen 1:3—2:3	C	771	διὸ λέγει Theophilus adds only a four word commentary to his quotation, the comment on Gen 1:4, "that is to say, made good for man (δηλονότι καλὸν ἀνθρώπῳ γενονός)." His extensive quotation is taken from an unknown LXX manuscript, since there are minor varients not explainable by any known variant of either the LXX or of *Ad Autolycum*.
13	Luke 18:27	C	8	γάρ
13	Gen 1:1	C	7	λέγων
13	Gen 1:3	Q	5	
13	Isa 40:22	C	11	ἕτερος προφήτης ὀνόματι Ἡσαΐας λέγων·

13	Gen 1:5	Q	14	The *Autol.* 1.13 location in Marcovich's index should be *Autol.* 2.13.
13	Gen 1:6	A	40	
13	Gen 1:9	R	5	
13	Gen 1:11–12	A	33	
16	Eph 3:10	Q	5	
16	Gen 1:22	A	9	
16	Titus 3:5	Q	2	
16	Luke 24:47	Q	4	
16	Gen 1:22	A	4	
16	Gen 1:22	A	13	
17	Gen 1:31	Q	2	
17	Gen 1:28	A	1	
18	Gen 1:26	Q	8	
18	Gen 1:26	Q	7	
18	Gen 1:26	A	19	
18	Gen 1:28–29	A	35	
19	Gen 2:1–2	R	26	
19	Gen 2:4–5	C	48	ἀνακεφαλαιοῦταί λέγουσα ἡ ἁγία γραφή·
19	Gen 2:6–7	C	38	διδάσκει ἡμᾶς ἡ γραφὴ λέγουσα·
Autol. 2.20-33: Genesis and Early Generations				
20	Gen 2:8—3:19	C	832	Τὰ δὲ ῥητὰ τῆς ἱστορίας τῆς ἱερᾶς ἡ γραφὴ οὕτως περιέχει·
22	Luke 1:35	R	1	
22	Gen 3:10	A	6	αὐτὴ ἡ θεία γραφὴ διδάσκει ἡμᾶς
22	Col 1:15	Q	3	
22	John 1:1	C	12	Ἰωάννης λέγει
22	John 1:1	C	5	λέγει
22	John 1:3	C	9	λέγει
23	John 16:21	A	22	
23	Gen 1:28	Q	3	
23	Gen 3:14	A	18	
24	Gen 2:9	Q	16	
24	Gen 1:12	A	33	

24	Gen 1:11	A	33	
24	Gen 2:9	A	17	
24	Gen 2:8–9	C	31	ἡ γραφὴ λέγει·
24	Gen 2:10	C	13	σεσήμακεν
24	Gen 2:13	A	19	σεσήμακεν
24	Gen 2:11	A	19	σεσήμακεν
24	Gen 2:14	A	5	σεσήμακεν
24	Gen 2:15–17	Q	41	
25	Heb 5:12	A	14	
25	Gen 2:17	A	6	
25	Heb 12:9	A	16	
26	Gen 3:23	A	5	
26	Gen 2:8–15	A	19	
26	Gen 3:9	R	8	
27	Rom 5:17	A	8	
27	1 Cor 15:50	Q	3	
28	Gen 4:1	Q	5	
28	Gen 3:5	Q	3	
28	Gen 2:21–22	A	10	
28	Gen 2:23	Q	15	
28	Gen 2:24	Q	23	
29	Gen 4:1–2	R	28	
29	Gen 4:4–5	A	15	
29	Gen 4:8	A	7	
29	Gen 4:9–11	Q	50	
29	Gen 4:12	Q	7	
30	Gen 4:17	R	15	
30	Gen 4:18–22	R	47	
30	Gen 4:25	A	18	
31	Gen 10:9–14	R	58	
31	Gen 11:1	R	6	
31	Gen 11:4	Q	14	
31	Gen 11:4	Q	11	
31	Gen 11:7–8	A	20	

31	Gen 14:1	R	12	
31	Gen 14:2	R	24	
31	Gen 14:4	R	11	
31	Gen 14:5–6	Q	34	
31	Gen 20:2	R	3	
31	Gen 26:1	A	5	
Autol. 2.34–37: Idolatry and the Coming Judgment				
34	1 Pet 1:18	A	8	
34	Exod 20:13–17	A	6	ἐδίδαξαν
35	Deut 4:19	R	5	
35	Exod 20:13–17	C	15	φησιν ὁ ἅγιος νόμος·
35	Prov 4:25	C	11	Σολομὼν μὲν οὖν καὶ τὸ δἰ ἐννεύματος μὴ ἁμαρτάνειν διδάσκει ἡμᾶς λέγων·
35	Isa 42:5	C	30	Ἠσαΐας δὲ καὶ αὐτός φησιν·
35	Isa 45:12	C	14	καὶ πάλιν δἰ αὐτοῦ
35	Isa 40:28	C	18	ἐν ἑτέρῳ κεφαλαίῳ
35	Jer 10:12–13	C	41	ὁμοίως καὶ Ἰερεμίας
35	Ps 13:1	C	13	ὁ Δαυὶδ λέγει·
35	Ps 13:3	C	4	ὁ Δαυὶδ λέγει·
35	Hab 2:18–19	C	18	ὁμοίως καὶ Ἀββακούμ·
Autol. 2.38: ἐπίλογος				
38	Mal 3:19	C	10	προείρηκεν
38	Isa 30:30	C	6	καὶ Ἠσαΐας·
38	Isa 30:28	C	3	καὶ Ἠσαΐας·
38	Prov 3:8	C	8	καὶ τῶν μὲν προφητῶν Σολομὼν περὶ τῶν τεθνηκότων εἶπεν·
38	Ps 50:10	C	3	τὸ δ' αὐτὸ καὶ Δαυίδ·
38	Hos 14:10	C	25	καὶ γάρ τις εἶπεν προφήτης ὢν προεγράψαμεν ὀνόματι Ὡσηέ·

TABLE 7: INDIVIDUAL USES OF SCRIPTURE AND INSPIRED WRITINGS, WITH CITATION FORMULAS, IN *AD AUTOLYCUM* 3

Sect.	Scripture/Inspired Text	Type	Words	Citation Formula
Autol. 3.2–8: Philosophy				
4	1 Cor 1:18	R	4	
Autol. 3.9–15: Ethics				
9	Exod 20:3–5	C	47	λέγει
9	Exod 20:12	C	25	ἔφη
9	Exod 20:13–17	C	55	Ἔτι περὶ δικαιοσύνης·
9	Deut 5:17–20	C	14	Ἔτι περὶ δικαιοσύνης·
9	Exod 23:6–8	C	35	Ἔτι περὶ δικαιοσύνης·
9	Exod 14:31	Q	4	
10	Exod 12:40	R	6	
10	Exod 23:9	C	18	λέγων
11	Deut 18:18	Q	7	
11	Isa 55:6–7	C	41	Περὶ μὲν οὖν τῆς μετανοίας Ἠσαΐας ὁ προφήτης κοινῶς μὲν πρὸς πάντας διαρρήδην δὲ πρὸς τὸν λαὸν λέγει·
11	Ezek 18:21–23	C	56	καὶ ἕτερος προφήτης Ἐζεχιὴλ φησιν·
11	Isa 31:6	C	8	πάλιν ὁ Ἠσαΐας·
11	Isa 45:22	C	1	πάλιν ὁ Ἠσαΐας·
11	Jer 6:9	C	7	καὶ ἕτερος Ἰερεμίας·
12	Isa 1:16	C	7	Ἠσαΐας οὕτως ἔφη·
12	Isa 1:17	C	12	Ἠσαΐας οὕτως ἔφη·
12	Isa 58:6–8	C	58	ἔτι ὁ οὐτός·
12	Jer 6:16	C	24	ὁμοίως καὶ ἕτερος Ἰερεμίας·
12	Hos 13:4	C	11	Ὡσηὲ λέγει·
12	Joel 2:16	C	31	ἔφη

Scripture Usage Tables

12	Joel 1:14	C	6	ἔφη When Theophilus adds τὸν θεὸν ὑμῶν after κύριον, he adds the θεὸν ὑμῶν from 1:14b after the phrase in 1:14c. I consider this is a reordering of two words from the verse, with the addition of τὸν, rather than an addition of three words to the quotation.
12	Zech 7:9–10	C	35	ὁμοίως καὶ ἕτερος Ζαχαρίας·
13	Matt 5:28	C	2	διδάσκει ἡμᾶς ὁ ἅγιος λόγος
13	Prov 4:25–26	C	16	Σολομὼν μὲν οὖν ὁ βασιλεὺς καὶ προφήτης γενόμενος ἔφη· Prov 4:26 is not indicated in Biblia patristica but indeed is quoted.
13	Matt 5:28	C	14	λέγουσα
13	Matt 5:32	C	15	φησιν
13	Prov 6:27–29	C	30	ὁ Σολομὼν φησιν·
14	Isa 66:5	C	19	Ἡσαΐας ὁ προφήτης ἔφη·
14	Matt 5:44	C	10	τὸ δὲ εὐαγγέλιον
14	Matt 5:46	C	8	
14	Matt 6:3	C	10	φησιν
14	1 Tim 2:1–2	C	6	κελεύει ἡμᾶς ὁ θεῖος λόγος
14	Rom 13:7–8	C	23	διδάσκει
Autol. 3.16–27: Chronology				
19	1 Pet 3:20	A	11	
19	Gen 7:20	C	9	ἐσήμανεν ὁ Μωσῆς
20	Exod 1:11	Q	13	
21	Exod 14:28	A	11	
23	Zech 1:1	A	13	
24	Gen 5:3	A	13	
24	Gen 5:6	A	7	
24	Gen 5:9	A	7	
24	Gen 5:12	A	4	
24	Gen 5:18	A	7	
24	Gen 5:15	A	7	
24	Gen 5:25	A	7	
24	Gen 5:21	A	7	

24	Gen 5:32	A	8	
24	Gen 5:28	A	3	
24	Gen 7:6	R	6	
24	Gen 11:10	Q	6	
24	Gen 11:12–13	A	7	
24	Gen 11:14	A	11	
24	Gen 11:16	A	8	
24	Gen 11:18	A	8	
24	Gen 11:20	A	8	
24	Gen 11:22	A	8	
24	Gen 11:24	A	8	
24	Gen 11:26	A	8	
24	Gen 21:5	R	6	
24	Gen 25:26	R	5	
24	Exod 12:40	A	10	
24	Exod 16:35	A	7	
24	Judg 3:8	R	5	
24	Judg 3:30	A	9	
24	Judg 3:11	A	3	
24	Judg 3:14	A	3	
24	Judg 4:3	A	4	
24	Judg 5:31	A	5	
24	Judg 6:1	A	5	
24	Judg 9:22	A	3	
24	Judg 8:28	A	5	
24	Judg 12:7	R	5	
24	Judg 10:8	A	7	
24	Judg 10:3	A	3	
24	Judg 10:2	A	3	
24	Judg 12:14	A	3	
24	Judg 12:11	A	3	
24	Judg 12:9	A	3	
24	Judg 13:1	A	5	
24	Judg 16:31	A	5	

24	Judg 3:31	A	5	
24	1 Sam 4:18	A	3	
25	1 Kgs 2:11	A	6	
25	1 Kgs 11:42	A	5	
25	1 Kgs 15:2	R	1	
25	1 Kgs 14:21	A	6	
25	2 Chr 13:2	R	1	
25	2 Chr 12:13	R	1	
25	1 Kgs 15:10	R	1	
25	2 Chr 20:31	R	1	
25	2 Kgs 8:17	R	1	
25	2 Chr 21:5	R	1	
25	2 Kgs 8:26	R	2	
25	2 Chr 22:2	R	1	
25	2 Chr 24:1	R	1	
25	2 Kgs 12:1	R	1	
25	2 Chr 22:12	R	2	
25	2 Chr 25:1	R	1	
25	2 Chr 26:3	R	1	
25	2 Kgs 14:2	R	1	
25	2 Kgs 15:2	R	1	
25	2 Kgs 15:33	R	1	
25	2 Chr 28:1	R	1	
25	2 Chr 29:1	R	1	
25	2 Kgs 18:2	R	1	
25	2 Kgs 16:2	R	1	
25	2 Chr 33:1	R	1	
25	2 Kgs 21:19	R	1	
25	2 Chr 33:21	R	1	
25	2 Kgs 21:1	R	1	
25	2 Kgs 22:1	R	1	
25	2 Kgs 23:31	R	1	
25	2 Chr 36:2	R	1	
25	2 Kgs 24:8	R	1	

25	2 Chr 34:1	R	1	
25	2 Kgs 24:18	R	1	
25	2 Chr 36:9	R	1	
25	2 Chr 36:11	R	1	
25	Jer 6:22	A	11	
25	2 Chr 36:21	A	3	
25	2 Chr 36:17	A	16	
25	2 Kgs 25:9	A	6	
25	2 Kgs 25:2	A	33	
25	2 Chr 36:19	A	6	
25	Jer 25:12	A	2	
25	1 Esdr 2:1–7	A	37	
25	1 Esdr 2:10–11	A	35	
26	2 Kgs 23:36	R	1	

TABLE 8: DISTRIBUTION OF USES OF SCRIPTURE AND INSPIRED WRITINGS IN *AD AUTOLYCUM* 1

Category/Book	Citations	Quotations	Reminiscences	Allusions	Unchanged Words	Modified Words	Reordered Words	Close Cognate Words
Prophets	3 (100%)	7 (43.8%)	8 (57.1%)	7 (58.3%)	160 (65%)	10 (38.5%)	3 (60%)	3 (42.9%)
Gen		1 (6.3%)		1 (8.3%)	17 (6.9%)			
Exod				1 (8.3%)	19 (7.7%)			
Lev								
Num								
Deut								
Josh								
Judg								
Ruth								
1 Sam								
2 Sam								
1 Kgs								
2 Kgs								
1 Chr								
2 Chr								
Ezra								
Neh								
Esth								
Job		2 (12.5%)	2 (14.3%)	1 (8.3%)	23 (9.3%)	1 (3.8%)		
Ps	2 (66.7%)	2 (12.5%)	5 (35.7%)	4 (33.3%)	59 (24%)	7 (26.9%)	2 (40%)	1 (14.3%)
Prov	1 (33.3%)	1 (6.3%)			30 (12.2%)		1 (20%)	2 (28.6%)
Eccl								
Song								
Isa								

Jer		1 (6.3%)			11 (4.5%)	1 (3.8%)		
Lam								
Ezek								
Dan								
Hos								
Joel								
Amos								
Obad								
Jonah								
Mic								
Nah								
Hab								
Zeph								
Hag								
Zech								
Mal								
Tob								
Jdt								
1 Macc								
2 Macc								
4 Macc			1 (7.1%)		1 (0.4%)	1 (3.8%)		
Wis								
Sir								
Bar								
Gospel		2 (12.5%)		1 (8.3%)	13 (5.3%)	4 (15.4%)		1 (14.3%)
Matt								
Mark								
Luke								
John		2 (12.5%)		1 (8.3%)	13 (5.3%)	4 (15.4%)		1 (14.3%)
Inspired Writings		7 (43.8%)	6 (42.9%)	4 (33.3%)	73 (29.7%)	12 (46.2%)	2 (40%)	3 (42.9%)
Acts								

Scripture Usage Tables   201

Rom		2 (12.5%)	4 (28.6%)	1 (8.3%)	33 (13.4%)	7 (26.9%)	1 (20%)	
1 Cor		2 (12.5%)	1 (7.1%)		17 (6.9%)	3 (11.5%)	1 (20%)	3 (42.9%)
2 Cor		1 (6.3%)		1 (8.3%)	6 (2.4%)	1 (3.8%)		
Gal								
Eph		1 (6.3%)			5 (2%)			
Phil								
Col								
1 Thess								
2 Thess								
1 Tim				1 (8.3%)	3 (1.2%)			
2 Tim								
Titus								
Phlm								
Heb								
Jas								
1 Pet		1 (6.3%)	1 (7.1%)	1 (8.3%)	9 (3.7%)	1 (3.8%)		
2 Pet								
1 John								
2 John								
3 John								
Jude								
Rev								
Totals	3 (100%)	16 (100%)	14 (100%)	12 (100%)	246 (100%)	26 (100%)	5 (100%)	7 (100%)

Notes:

1. In tables eight through ten, table conventions follow the practice of Ernest in his similar tables: blank entries are used to represent zero values, so that non-zero values can more easily be located; category and grand totals are provided; and percentages of grand totals are calculated.

2. Tables eight through ten indicate only those categories that Theophilus himself uses: "prophets," "gospel," and "inspired writings."

TABLE 9: DISTRIBUTION OF USES OF SCRIPTURE AND INSPIRED WRITINGS IN *AD AUTOLYCUM 2*

Category/Book	Citations	Quotations	Reminiscences	Allusions	Unchanged Words	Modified Words	Reordered Words	Close Cognate Words
Prophets	28 (87.5%)	17 (77.3%)	14 (82.4%)	28 (82.4%)	2834 (95.4%)	54 (90%)	35 (92.1%)	28 (100%)
Gen	10 (31.3%)	17 (77.3%)	13 (76.5%)	25 (73.5%)	2602 (87.6%)	43 (71.7%)	26 (68.4%)	19 (67.9%)
Exod	1 (3.1%)			1 (2.9%)	21 (0.7%)			
Lev								
Num								
Deut			1 (5.9%)			4 (6.7%)		1 (3.6%)
Josh								
Judg								
Ruth								
1 Sam								
2 Sam								
1 Kgs								
2 Kgs								
1 Chr								
2 Chr								
Ezra								
Neh								
Esth								
Job								
Ps	3 (9.4%)				18 (0.6%)	1 (1.7%)		1 (3.6%)
Prov	4 (12.5%)			2 (5.9%)	34 (1.1%)	3 (5%)	1 (2.6%)	1 (3.6%)
Eccl								
Song								
Isa	6 (18.8%)				75 (2.5%)		4 (10.5%)	3 (10.7%)

Jer	1 (3.1%)				41 (1.4%)			
Lam								
Ezek								
Dan								
Hos	1 (3.1%)				22 (0.7%)			3 (10.7%)
Joel								
Amos								
Obad								
Jonah								
Mic								
Nah								
Hab	1 (3.1%)				14 (0.5%)	2 (3.3%)	2 (5.3%)	
Zeph								
Hag								
Zech								
Mal	1 (3.1%)				7 (0.2%)	1 (1.7%)	2 (5.3%)	
Tob								
Jdt								
1 Macc								
2 Macc								
4 Macc								
Wis								
Sir								
Bar								
Gospel	4 (14.5%)	1 (4.5%)	2 (11.8%)	1 (2.9%)	61 (2%)		3 (7.9%)	
Matt								
Mark								
Luke	1 (3.1%)	1 (4.5%)	1 (5.9%)		11 (0.4%)		2 (5.3%)	
John	3 (9.4%)		1 (5.9%)	1 (2.9%)	50 (1.7%)		1 (2.6%)	

In-spired Writ-ings		4 (18.2%)	1 (5.9%)	5 (14.7%)	75 (2.5%)	6 (10%)		
Acts								
Rom				1 (2.9%)	8 (0.3%)			
1 Cor		1 (4.5%)	1 (5.9%)		2 (0.1%)	5 (8.3%)		
2 Cor								
Gal								
Eph		1 (4.5%)			5 (0.2%)			
Phil								
Col		1 (4.5%)			2 (0.1%)	1 (1.7%)		
1 Thess								
2 Thess								
1 Tim								
2 Tim								
Titus		1 (4.5%)			2 (0.1%)			
Phlm								
Heb				2 (5.9%)	30 (1%)			
Jas								
1 Pet				1 (2.9%)	8 (0.3%)			
2 Pet				1 (2.9%)	18 (0.6%)			
1 John								
2 John								
3 John								
Jude								
Rev								
Totals	32 (100%)	22 (100%)	17 (100%)	34 (100%)	2970 (100%)	60 (100%)	38 (100%)	28 (100%)

TABLE 10: DISTRIBUTION OF USES OF SCRIPTURE AND INSPIRED WRITINGS IN *AD AUTOLYCUM* 3

Category/Book	Citations	Quotations	Reminiscences	Allusions	Unchanged Words	Modified Words	Reordered Words	Close Cognate Words
Prophets	23 (76.7%)	4 (100%)	40 (95.2%)	52 (98.1%)	1004 (93.0%)	44 (80%)	19 (55.9%)	17 (94.4%)
Gen	1 (3.3%)	1 (25%)	3 (7.1%)	18 (34%)	148 (13.7%)	9 (16.4%)	5 (14.7%)	6 (33.3%)
Exod	5 (16.7%)	2 (50%)	1 (2.4%)	3 (5.7%)	214 (19.8%)	6 (10.9%)	5 (14.7%)	6 (33.3%)
Lev								
Num								
Deut	1 (3.3%)	1 (25%)			19 (1.8%)	1 (1.8%)		1 (5.6%)
Josh								
Judg			2 (4.8%)	17 (32.1%)	78 (7.2%)	4 (7.3%)	1 (2.9%)	1 (5.6%)
Ruth								
1 Sam				1 (1.9%)	3 (0.3%)			
2 Sam								
1 Kgs			2 (4.8%)	3 (5.7%)	18 (1.7%)	1 (1.8%)		
2 Kgs			15 (35.7%)	2 (3.8%)	49 (4.5%)	6 (10.9%)		
1 Chr								
2 Chr			17 (40.5%)	3 (5.7%)	37 (3.4%)	6 (10.9%)		
Ezra				2 (3.8%)	72 (6.7%)			
Neh								
Esth								
Job								
Ps								
Prov	2 (6.7%)				43 (4%)		1 (2.9%)	2 (11.1%)
Eccl								

Song								
Isa	7 (23.3%)				144 (13.3%)		2 (5.9%)	
Jer	2 (6.7%)			2 (3.8%)	41 (3.8%)	2 (3.6%)	1 (2.9%)	
Lam								
Ezek	1 (3.3%)				53 (4.9%)	1 (1.8%)	1 (2.9%)	1 (5.6%)
Dan								
Hos	1 (3.3%)				6 (0.6%)	5 (9.1%)		
Joel	2 (6.7%)				35 (3.2%)	1 (1.8%)	1 (2.9%)	
Amos								
Obad								
Jonah								
Mic								
Nah								
Hab								
Zeph								
Hag								
Zech	1 (3.3%)			1 (1.9%)	44 (4.1%)	2 (3.6%)	2 (5.9%)	
Mal								
Tob								
Jdt								
1 Macc								
2 Macc								
4 Macc								
Wis								
Sir								
Bar								
Gospel	5 (16.7%)		1 (2.4%)		50 (4.6%)	4 (7.3%)	5 (14.7%)	
Matt	5 (16.7%)		1 (2.4%)		50 (4.6%)	4 (7.3%)	5 (14.7%)	
Mark								

Luke								
John								
Inspired Writings	2 (6.7%)		1 (2.4%)	1 (1.9%)	26 (2.4%)	7 (12.7%)	10 (29.4%)	1 (5.6%)
Acts								
Rom	1 (3.3%)				10 (0.9%)	3 (5.5%)	10 (29.4%)	
1 Cor			1 (2.4%)			4 (7.3%)		
2 Cor								
Gal								
Eph								
Phil								
Col								
1 Thess								
2 Thess								
1 Tim	1 (3.3%)				5 (0.5%)			1 (5.6%)
2 Tim								
Titus								
Phlm								
Heb								
Jas								
1 Pet				1 (1.9%)	11 (1%)			
2 Pet								
1 John								
2 John								
3 John								
Jude								
Rev								
Totals	30 (100%)	4 (100%)	42 (100%)	53 (100%)	1080 (100%)	55 (100%)	34 (100%)	18 (100%)

TERMINOLOGY IN TABLES

Allusion	Allusions are mentions of biblical writers, books, events, characters, or features in the content of biblical texts, but which do not match or mimic any biblical text itself.
Citation	Citations are distinguished by formulas which signal to the reader that reference is being made to a biblical text.
Close cognates	Close cognates are words which are very close substitutes for a biblical word, in a semantic sense.
Interpolated	Interpolated words are words in a use of Scripture or inspired writing which do not correspond to any words in the given biblical text, and which appear between the first and last words which do correspond to words in the given biblical text.[2]
Locution	Locutions are uses of Scripture for which it is impossible to determine exactly which verse is being used. Some locutions are uses of Scripture which so loosely match biblical language that it is not possible to determine exactly which biblical text is the referent. Other locutions closely match biblical texts which appear in more than one place in biblical writings. Since I rely on a sort of scholarly consensus by considering *only* those uses of Scripture which appear in *both* Biblia patristica's and Marcovich's biblical indexes of *Ad Autolycum*, locutions do not appear in any part of the present study.
Quotation	A use of a biblical text that is not a citation and matches or nearly matches the text. The following formulas, adapted from those used by Ernest, are used to consistently determine whether the match is close enough to be considered a quotation. The value of quotation_quotient is equal to ((number of biblical words) + 0.75*((number of modified words)+(number of reordered words)+(number of close cognates)))/((number of biblical words)+(number of modified words)+(number of reordered words)+(number of close cognates)+(number of interpolated words)).[3] Quotation_density is the number of

---

2. Ernest, "Uses of Scripture in the Writings of Athanasius," 446–47, distinguishes between interpolated words and substituted words. I have chosen not to use the substituted words category since substituted words in *Ad Autolycum* can be categorized as "close cognates." Close cognates are words which are very close substitutes for a biblical word, in a semantic sense.

Theophilus is provided the benefit of doubt for counts of interpolated words. That is, if a word is present from any known biblical manuscript of a particular verse, even though it is not found in some manuscripts, it is not counted as being interpolated in *Ad Autolycum*.

3. The requirement from Ernest's formula that quotations occupy no more than two blocks of text is put aside because the presence of interpolated words are already taken into account in the formula indicating reminiscences. Indeed, sometimes quotations can be intentionally interspersed more than once by interpolated words, as in the

unchanged, modified, reordered, and close_cognate words divided by the sum of unchanged, modified, reordered, close_cognate and interpolated words. Quotation_compression is the number of unchanged, modified, reordered, and close_cognate words divided by the sum of the number of unchanged, modified, reordered, and close_cognate words and words in the quoted book which are missing in Theophilus' quotation.[4] On the basis of these formulas, quotations are uses of Scripture in which the text in *Ad Autolycum* closely matches a biblical text (quotation_density ≥ 0.75 and quotation_compression ≥ 0.75), and for which either quotation_quotient is ≥ 0.9, and sum of the numbers of biblical words, modified words, reordered words, and close cognates is two, and there are no interpolated words, or quotation_quotient is ≥ 0.8 and the sum of the numbers of biblical words, modified words, reordered words, and close cognates is three, or quotation_quotient is ≥ 0.7 and the sum of the numbers of biblical words, modified words, reordered words, and close cognates is ≥ four.[5]

---

continuous form of *pesher* exegesis in the Qumran commentaries on Habakkuk and Nahum. The Hebrew word *pesher* (and Aramaic cognate *peshar*) means "interpretation." The exegetical method is seen often in the Dead Sea Scrolls, and took a particular form, hence it's name: a biblical text was quoted, then followed an instance of *pesher*, interpretation, which explained the significance of the text for the life and concerns of the Qumran community. This sort of interpretation testified to the Qumran belief that the community was participating in eschatological events. *Pesher* interpretation was marked with a historical-eschatological pattern whereby it carried commentary on the historical setting of the Qumran community and on the eschatological hopes of the community. Three types of *pesharim* can be observed in the Dead Sea Scrolls. Continuous *pesher* took the form of a running commentary on a single biblical passage, as seen in the commentaries on Habakkuk or Nahum. Again, the interpretations made reference to people and events in the Qumran community. Thematic *pesher* is a collection of a variety of biblical passages that relate to a single theme, these interspersed by commentary, as seen in *4QFlorilegium*. Isolated *pesher* consists of quotation and accompanying commentary for one single biblical passage, placed into a treatise in order to support a given point. Examples include the *pesharim* on Zech 13:7 and Amos 5:26–27 in the Damascus Document. See "Pesher," in Green, *Dictionary of Judaism*, 476; and Aune, "Pesherim," in *Early Christian Literature*, 347–50.

4. Theophilus is provided the benefit of doubt for counts of missing words. That is, if a word is missing from a particular verse in any known biblical manuscript, even though it occurs in some manuscripts, it is not counted as being missing in *Ad Autolycum*.

5. This formula is a modification of that used in the quotation definition in Ernest, "Uses of Scripture in the Writings of Athanasius," 447: "This instance does not qualify as a citation, but the marked-up words are reasonably comparable both in Athanasius and in the biblical text (*Quot. dens.* > 75 and *Quot. cmprs.* > 75) and are not broken up into more than two discrete chunks (Blocks < 2); and in addition one of the following three statements applies. In these statements, 'QQuotient' represents the percentage that results when the number of unchanged words is added to three-fourths of the number of adapted words and the sum is divided by the total number of words

Reminiscence	Reminiscences match specific biblical texts, but not as closely enough to be identified as quotations.

---

unchanged, adapted, substituted, and interpolated. (1) The total number of unchanged and adapted words is 2, they are contiguous, and the QQuotient is at least 90; (2) the total number of unchanged and adapted words is 3, and the QQuotient is at least 80; (3) the total number of unchanged and adapted words is 4 or more, and the QQuotient is at least 70."

Bibliography

Aland, Kurt, et al., eds. *The Greek New Testament, United Bible Societies, Third Edition (Corrected)*. Stuttgart: United Bible Societies, 1983.

Albl, Martin C. *"And Scripture Cannot Be Broken": The Form and Function of the Early Christian Testimonia Collections*. Leiden: Brill, 1999.

Allenbach, J., and Centre d'analyse et de documentation patristique. *Biblia patristica: Index des citations et allusions bibliques dans la littérature patristique*. 7 vols. Paris: Éditions du Centre national de la recherche scientifique, 1975–2000.

———. *Biblia patristica: Supplément, Philon d'Alexandrie*. Paris: Éditions du Centre national de la recherche scientifique, 1982.

Andia, Ysabel de. "Modèles de l'unité des testaments selon Irénée de Lyon." In *Papers presented to the Tenth International Conference on Patristic Studies Held in Oxford 1987*, edited by Elizabeth A. Livingstone, 49–59. Studia Patristica 21. Leuven: Peeters, 1989.

Anonymous. "Correspondance apocryphe des Corinthiens et de l'apôtre Paul." In *Papyrus Bodmer X–XII*, edited by Michel Testuz, 7–45. Cologny-Genève: Bibliothèque Bodmer, 1959.

———. "Pesher." In *Dictionary of Judaism in the Biblical Period*, edited by William Scott Green et al., 476. New York: Simon & Schuster, 1996.

Armstrong, A. H. *An Introduction to Ancient Philosophy*. Totowa, NJ: Rowman and Allanheld, 1947.

Athenagoras. *Embassy for the Christians. The Resurrection of the Dead*. Translated by Joseph Hugh Crehan. Ancient Christian Writers 23. New York: Newman, 1955.

Bacq, Pierre. *De l'ancienne à la nouvelle alliance selon S. Irénée: unité du livre IV de l'adversus haereses*. Paris: Lethielleux, 1978.

Bammel, Caroline P. "Justin der Märtyrer." In *Tradition and Exegesis in Early Christian Writers*, 51–68. Brookfield, VT: Ashgate, 1995.

Bardy, Gustave, ed. *Théophile d'Antioche: Trois livres à Autolycus*. Translated by Jean Sender. Sources Chrétiennes 20. Paris: Cerf, 1948.

Barnard, L. W. "Justin, Martyr in Recent Study." *Scottish Journal of Theology* 22 (1969) 152–64.

Barnard, Leslie W. *Justin Martyr: His Life and Thought*. London: Cambridge University Press, 1967.

Barnard, Leslie W., ed. *S. Justin Martyr. The First and Second Apologies*. Ancient Christian Writers 56. New York: Paulist, 1997.

Bauer, Walter. *Orthodoxy and Heresy in Earliest Christianity*. Translated by Robert A. Kraft et al. Translation of 2nd German ed. Philadelphia: Fortress, 1971.

Behr, John. *On the Way to Nicaea. Formation of Christian Theology*. Crestwood, NY: St. Vladimir's Seminary Press, 2001.

Bellinzoni, Arthur J. *The Sayings of Jesus in the Writings of Justin Martyr*. Supplements to Novum Testamentum 17. Leiden: Brill, 1967.

Bentivegna, J. "A Christianity without Christ by Theophilus of Antioch." In *Papers presented to the Sixth International Conference on Patristic Studies held in Oxford, 1971*, ed. Elizabeth A. Livingstone, 107–30. Studia Patristica 13. Berlin: Akademie, 1975.

Bergjan, Silke-Petra. "How to Speak about Early Christian Apologetic Literatuare? Comments on the Recent Debate." In *Papers presented at the Thirteenth International Conference on Patristic Studies held in Oxford 1999*, edited by M. W. Wiles, E. J. Yarnold, and P. M. Parvis, 177–83. Studia Patristica 26. Leuven: Peeters, 2001.

Betz, Hans Dieter. *Galatians: A Commentary on Paul's Letter to the Churches in Galatia*. Hermeneia. Minneapolis: Fortress, 1989.

Bingham, D. Jeffrey. *Irenaeus' Use of Matthew's Gospel in Adversus Haereses*. Traditio Exegetica Graeca 7. Leuven: Peeters, 1998.

———. "Response to Margaret M. Mitchell." Paper presented at the Southwest Regional Meeting of the SBL, March 6, 2004, Dallas, Texas.

Blackman, P., ed. *Mishnayoth*. New York: Judaica, 1983.

Blas, Pedro de, ed. *Essential Dialogues of Plato*. Translated by Benjamin Jowett and Pedro de Blas. New York: Barnes & Noble, 2005.

Boeft, J., and D. T. Runia, eds. *Arche: A Collection of Patristic Studies by J. C. M. van Winden*. Leiden: Brill, 1997.

Botha, Pieter J. J. *Orality and Literacy in Early Christianity*. Performance Biblical Criticism 5. Eugene, OR: Wipf and Stock, 2012.

Bradshaw, Paul F. *The Search for the Origins of Christian Worship: Sources and Methods for the Study of Early Liturgy*. New York: Oxford University Press, 1992.

Bream, Howard N., ed. *The Apocryphon of John and Other Coptic Translations*. Translated by Howard N. Bream. Baltimore, MD: Halgo, 1987.

Brooten, Bernadette J. "The Jews of Ancient Antioch." In *Antioch: The Lost Ancient City*, edited by Christine Kondoleon, 26–37. Princeton, NJ: Princeton University Press, 2000.

Brox, Norbert. "Die biblische Hermeneutik des Irenäus." *Zeitschrift für Antikes Christentum* 2 (1998) 26–48.

Bullard, Roger Aubrey, ed. *The Hypostasis of the Archons*. Translated by Roger Aubrey Bullard. Patristische Texte und Studien 10. Berlin: de Gruyter, 1970.

Burnet, John. *Platonis Opera*. Oxford: Oxford University Press, 1903.

Bury, R. G., ed. *Plato Laws*. Loeb Classical Library. London: Heinemann, 1926.

———. *Plato: Timaeus, Critias, Cleitophon, Menexenus, Epistles*. Loeb Classical Library. London: Heinemann, 1929.

Butler, H. E., ed. *Quintilian. Institutio oratoria*. Translated by H. E. Butler. Loeb Classical Library. London: Heinemann, 1921.

Campenhausen, Hans von. "Tradition and Succession in the Second Century." In *Ecclesiastical Authority and Spiritual Power in the Church of the First Three Centuries*, 149–77. Stanford, CA: Stanford University Press, 1969.

Caplan, Harry, ed. *Cicero. Rhetorica ad Herennium*. Translated by Harry Caplan. Loeb Classical Library. London: Heinemann, 1981.
Charles, Robert Henry, ed. *The Greek Versions of the Testaments of the Twelve Patriarchs*. Oxford: Clarendon, 1960.
Charlesworth, James H., ed. *The Old Testament Pseudepigrapha*. Vol. 1, *Apocalyptic Literature and Testaments*. New York: Doubleday, 1983.
———. *The Old Testament Pseudepigrapha*. Vol. 2, *Expansions of the "Old Testament" and Legends, Wisdom and Philosophical Literature, Prayers, Psalms, and Odes, Fragments of Lost Judeo-Hellenistic Works*. New York: Doubleday, 1983.
Charlesworth, James H., et al., eds. *The Dead Sea Scrolls: Hebrew, Aramaic, and Greek Texts with English Translations*. Vol. 6B, *Pesharim, Other Commentaries, and Related Documents*. Princeton Theological Seminary Dead Sea Scrolls Project. Tübingen: Mohr/Siebeck, 2002.
Charry, Ellen T. *By the Renewing of Your Minds: The Pastoral Function of Christian Doctrine*. New York: Oxford University Press, 1997.
Ciholas, Paul. *The Omphalos and the Cross: Pagans and Christians in Search of a Divine Center*. Macon, GA: Mercer University Press, 2003.
Clark, Elizabeth A. *Reading Renunciation: Asceticism and Scripture in Early Christianity*. Princeton, NJ: Princeton University Press, 1999.
Collins, John J. *Between Athens and Jerusalem: Jewish Identity in the Hellenistic Diaspora*. Grand Rapids: Eerdmans, 2000.
Crouzel, Henri. "La distinction de la 'typologie' et de l'"allégorie."" *Bulletin de littérature ecclésiastique* 65, no. 3 (1964) 161–74.
Daniélou, Jean. *Études d'exégèse judéo-chrétienne (les Testimonia)*. Théologie historique 5. Paris: Beauchesne et ses fils, 1966.
———. *Gospel Message and Hellenistic Culture*. London: Darton Longman & Todd, 1973.
———. *The Theology of Jewish Christianity*. Translated and edited by John A. Baker. Vol. 1, *The Development of Christian Doctrine before the Council of Nicea*. London: Darton Longman & Todd, 1964.
Daube, David. *The New Testament and Rabbinic Judaism*. 1956. Reprint, Peabody, MA: Hendrickson, 1998.
Davids, Adelbert. "Hésiode et les prophètes chez Théophile d'Antioche (Ad Autol. II, 8–9)." In *Fides Sacramenti Sacramentum Fidei: Feistschrift for Pieter Smulders*, edited by H. J. Auf den Maur et al., 205–10. Assen: van Gorcum, 1981.
Davis, Janet B. "Teaching Violence in the Schools of Rhetoric." In *Violence in Late Antiquity: Perceptions and Practices*, edited by H. A. Drake, 197–204. Burlington, VT: Ashgate, 2006.
Delamarter, Steve. *A Scripture Index to Charlesworth's The Old Testament Pseudepigrapha*. London: Sheffield, 2002.
Desjardins, Michel. "Bauer and Beyond: On Recent Scholarly Discussions of Αἵρεσις in the Early Christian Era." *Second Century* 8, no. 2 (1991) 65–83.
Diels, H. and W. Kranz, eds. *Die Fragmente der Vorsokratiker*. Vol. 2. Berlin: Weidmann, 1952.
Dillistone, F. W. *Scripture and Tradition*. London: Lutterworth, 1955.
Dodd, C. H. *According to the Scriptures: The Substructure of New Testament Theology*. New York: Scribner's Sons, 1953.

Dörrie, Heinrich. "Der Prolog zur Evangelium nach Johannes im Verständnis der älteren Apologeten." In *Kergma und Logos: Festschrift für Carl Andresen*, ed. A. M. Ritter, 136–52. Göttingen: Vandenhoeck & Ruprecht, 1979.

Downey, Glanville. *A History of Antioch in Syria: From Seleucus to the Arab Conquest.* Princeton, NJ: Princeton University Press, 1961.

Dunn, James D. G. *New Perspective on Jesus: What the Quest for the Historical Jesus Missed.* Grand Rapids: Baker, 2005.

Edwards, Mark J. "Justin's Logos and the Word of God." *Journal of Early Christian Studies* 3, no. 3 (1995) 261–80.

Edwards, Mark, et al., eds. *Apologetics in the Roman Empire: Pagans, Jews, and Christians.* Oxford: Oxford University Press, 1999.

Epstein, I., ed. *The Babylonian Talmud (Soncino).* London, 1952.

Erbes, C. "Die Lebenszeit des Hippolytus nebst der des Theophilus von Antiochien." *Jarbücher für protestantische Theologie* 14 (1888) 611–56.

Ernest, James David. "Uses of Scripture in the Writings of Athanasius of Alexandria." PhD diss., Boston College, 2000.

Evans, Craig A. *Noncanonical Writings and New Testament Interpretation.* Peabody, MA: Hendrickson, 1992.

Farkasfalvy, Dennis. "Theology of Scripture in St. Irenaeus." *Revue bénédictine* 78 (1968) 319–33.

Ferguson, Everett. *Backgrounds of Early Christianity.* 3rd ed. Grand Rapids: Eerdmans, 2003.

———. "Introduction to Early Christianity and Judaism." In *Early Christianity and Judaism*, edited by Everett Ferguson, 11–14. New York: Garland, 1993.

———. "Love of Enemies and Nonretaliation in the Second Century." In *The Contentious Triangle: Church, State, and University. A Festschrift in Honor of Professor George Huntston Williams*, edited by Rodney L. Petersen and Clavin Augustine Pater, 81–96. Kirksville, MO: Thomas Jefferson University Press, 1999.

Ferlay, Philippe "Irénée de Lyon exegete du quatrième évangile." *La nouvelle revue théologique* 106 (1984) 222–34.

Fiedrowicz, Michael. *Apologie im frühen Christentum: Die Kontroverse um den christlichen Wahrheitsanspruch in den ersten Jarhunderten.* Zürich: Schöningh, 2000.

Flesseman-Van Leer, Ellen. *Tradition and Scripture in the Early Church.* Assen, Netherlands: van Gorcum, 1954.

Fontenrose, Joseph. *The Delphic Oracle: Its Responses and Operations with a Catalogue of Responses.* Berkeley: University of California Press, 1978.

Forster, E. S., trans. "De rhetorica ad Alexandrum." In *The Works of Aristotle*, edited by W. D. Ross, 231–316. Oxford: Oxford University Press, 1959.

Fowler, Harold North, ed. *Plato. Euthyphro, Apology, Crito, Phaedo, Phaedrus.* Loeb Classical Library. Cambridge, MA: Harvard University Press, 1914.

Freese, John Henry, trans. *Aristotle. Art of Rhetoric.* Loeb Classical Library. Cambridge, MA: Harvard University Press, 1926.

Frend, W. H. C. "Christianity in the Second Century: Orthodoxy and Diversity." *Journal of Ecclesiastical History* 48 (1997) 302–13.

Geffcken, Johannes, ed. *Die Oracula Sibyllina.* Die griechischen christlichen Schriftsteller, 8:1–226. Leipzig: Hinrichs, 1902.

———. *Zwei griechische Apologeten.* Leipzig: Teubner, 1907.

Good, Deirdre. "Rhetoric and Wisdom in Theophilus of Antioch." *Anglican Theological Review* 73, no. 3 (1991) 323–30.
Goodenough, Erwin Ramsdell. *The Theology of Justin Martyr.* Amsterdam: Philo, 1968.
Goodspeed, E. J., ed. *Die ältesten Apologeten. Texte mit kurzen Einleitungen.* Göttingen: Vandenhoeck und Ruprecht, 1984.
———. "Justinus Martyr. Apologia." In *Die ältesten Apologeten*, 26–77. Göttingen: Vandenhoeck und Ruprecht, 1915.
———. "Justinus Martyr. Apologia secunda." In *Die ältesten Apologeten*, 78–89. Göttingen: Vandenhoeck und Ruprecht, 1915.
———. "Justinus Martyr. Dialogus cum Tryphone." In *Die ältesten Apologeten*, 90–265. Göttingen: Vandenhoeck und Ruprecht, 1915.
Goodspeed, Edgar J., and Robert M. Grant. *A History of Early Christian Literature.* Rev. ed. Chicago: University of Chicago Press, 1966.
Grant, Robert M. *After the New Testament.* Philadelphia: Fortress, 1967.
———. "The Bible of Theophilus of Antioch." *Journal of Biblical Literature* 66 (1947) 173–96.
———. "Conflict in Christology at Antioch." In *Papers presented at the Ninth International Conference on Patristic Studies held in Oxford 1983*, edited by Elizabeth A. Livingstone, 141–50. Studia Patristica 18/1. Leuven: Peeters, 1989.
———. "The Decalogue in Early Christianity." *Harvard Theological Review* 40, no. 1 (1947) 1–17.
———. *Greek Apologists of the Second Century.* London: SCM, 1988.
———. *Jesus after the Gospels: The Christ of the Second Century.* Louisville: Westminster John Knox, 1990.
———. "Jewish Christianity at Antioch in the Second Century." *Recherches de sciences religieuse* 60 (1972) 97–108.
———. "Notes on the Text of Theophilus, Ad Autolycum III." *Vigiliae christianae* 12 (1958) 136–44.
———. "The Problem of Theophilus." *Harvard Theological Review* 43 (1950) 179–96.
———. Review of *Justin et l'Ancien Testament. L'argumentation scripturaire du traité de Justin contre toutes les hérésies comme source principale du Dialogue avec Tryphon et de la Première Apologie*, by Pierre Prigent. *Journal of Biblical Literature* 84 (1965) 440–43.
———. "Scripture, Rhetoric and Theology in Theophilus." *Vigiliae christianae* 13 (1959) 33–45.
———. "Studies in Theophilus of Antioch." PhD diss., Harvard University, 1944.
———. "The Textual Tradition of Theophilus of Antioch." *Vigiliae christianae* 6 (1952) 146–59.
Grant, Robert McQueen, ed. and trans. *Theophilus of Antioch. Ad Autolycum.* Oxford: Clarendon, 1970.
Greer, R. A. "The Christian Bible and Its Interpretation." In *Early Biblical Interpretation*, edited by J. L. Kugel and R. A. Greer, 107–99. Philadelphia: Westminster, 1986.
Greer, Rowan A., and Margaret Mary Mitchell. *The "Belly-Myther" of Endor: Interpretations of 1 Kingdoms 28 in the Early Church.* Leiden: Brill, 2007.
Guerra, Anthony J. "The Conversion of Marcus Aurelius and Justin Martyr: The Purpose, Genre, and Content of the First Apology." *Second Century* 9 (1992) 171–87.
Guggenheimer, Heinrich W., ed. *Seder Olam.* Northvale, NJ: Aronson, 1998.

Habinek, Thomas. *Ancient Rhetoric and Oratory*. Malden, MA: Blackwell, 2005.
Hagner, Donald A. "The Sayings of Jesus in the Apostolic Fathers and Justin Martyr." In *The Jesus Tradition Outside the Gospels*, ed. David Wenham, 233–68. Sheffield, UK: Journal for the Study of the Old Testament Press, 1985.
Hall, Stuart George, ed. and trans., *Melito of Sardis. On Pascha*. Oxford Early Christian Texts. Oxford: Clarendon, 1979.
Hanson, R. P. C. "Biblical Exegesis in the Early Church." In *The Cambridge History of the Bible: From the Beginnings to Jerome*, edited by P. R. Ackroyd and C. F. Evans, 412–53. Cambridge: Cambridge University Press, 1970.
Harnack, Adolf von. *History of Dogma*. Edited by A. B. Bruce. Vols. 1–2 translated by Neil Buchanan; vols. 3, 5 translated by James Millar; vol. 4 translated by E. B. Speers and James Millar; vols. 6–7 translated by William M'Gilchrist. Theological Translation Library. London: Williams & Norgate, 1894.
———. *History of Dogma*. Vol. 2. Translated by Neil Buchanan. London: Williams & Norgate, 1910.
———. *Das Neue Testament um das Jahr 200: Theodor Zahn's Geschichte des neutestamentlichen Kanons (1. Bd., 1 Hälfte)*. Freiburg: Mohr, 1889.
———. "Theophilus von Antiochien und das Neue Testament." *Zeitschrift für Kirchengeschichte* 11 (1890) 1–21.
———. *What is Christianity?* Translated by Thomas Bailey Saunders. 2nd rev. ed. New York: Putnam's Sons, 1903.
Harrington, Daniel J. "The Reception of Walter Bauer's *Orthodoxy and Heresy in Earliest Christianity* during the Last Decade." *Harvard Theological Review* 73, nos. 1–2 (1980) 289–98.
Harris, J. Rendel. *Testimonies*. 2 vols. Cambridge: Cambridge University Press, 1916–1920.
Harris, Rendel, and Alphonse Mingana, eds. *The Odes and Psalms of Solomon*. Vol. 1, *The Text with Facsimile Reproductions*. Manchester: Manchester University Press, 1916.
———. *The Odes and Psalms of Solomon*. Vol. 2, *The Translation with Introduction and Notes*. Manchester: Manchester University Press, 1920.
Hays, Richard B. *Echoes of Scripture in the Letters of Paul*. New Haven: Yale University Press, 1989.
———. "Reading Scripture in Light of the Resurrection." Paper presented at the 2003 annual meeting of the Evangelical Theological Society, November 19, 2003, Atlanta, GA.
Hicks, Richard. "Markan Discipleship according to Malachi: The Significance of μὴ ἀποστερήσῃς in the Story of the Rich Man (Mark 10:17–22)." *Journal of Biblical Literature* 132, no. 1 (2013) 179–99.
Hitchcock, F. R. Montgomery. "Loof's Theory of Theophilus of Antioch as a Source of Irenaeus." *Journal of Theological Studies* 38 (1937) 130–39; 255–66.
Hollander, John. *The Figure of Echo: A Mode of Allusion in Milton and After*. Berkeley: University of California Press, 1981.
Holmes, Michael W., ed. and trans. *The Apostolic Fathers: Greek Texts and English Translations*. Grand Rapids: Baker, 1999.
Horner, Timothy J. "Listening to Trypho: Uncovering the Subtext of Justin's *Dialogue*." In *Papers presented at the Thirteenth International Conference on Patristic Studies*

held in Oxford 1999, edited by M. W. Wiles, E. J. Yarnold, and P. M. Parvis, 249–55. Studia Patristica 36. Leuven: Peeters, 2001.

———. Review of *Justin Martyr, The First and Second Apologies*, by Leslie William Barnard. *Journal of Early Christian Studies* 5, no. 4 (1997) 602–3.

Hurtado, L. W. "Christ." In *Dictionary of Jesus and the Gospels*, edited by Joel B. Green and Scot McKnight, 106–17. Downers Grove, IL: InterVarsity, 1992.

Hurtado, Larry W. *At the Origins of Christian Worship: The Context and Character of Earliest Christian Devotion*. Grand Rapids: Eerdmans, 2000.

Ignace, d'Antioche. "Lettres." In *Ignace d'Antioche. Polycarpe de Smyrne. Lettres. Martyre de Polycarpe*, edited by P. T. Camelot, 56–154. Sources Chrétiennes 10. Paris: Cerf, 1969.

Isacson, Mikael. *To Each Their Own Letter: Stucture, Themes, and Rhetorical Strategies in the Letters of Ignatius of Antioch*. Stockholm: Ahmqvist & Wiksell, 2004.

Jaeger, Werner. *Paideia: the Ideals of Greek Culture*. Vol. 3, *The Conflict of Cultural Ideals in the Age of Plato*. Translated by Gilbert Highet. New York: Oxford University Press, 1944.

Jones, H. Stuart, and J. E. Powell, eds. *Thucydides Historiae*. 2 vols. Oxford: Oxford University Press, 1970.

Jourjoun, Maurice. "Irenaeus' Reading of the Bible." In *The Bible in Greek Christian Antiquity*, ed. Paul M. Blowers, 105–11. Notre Dame, IN: University of Notre Dame, 1997.

Kannengeisser, C. "The 'Speaking God' and Irenaeus' Interpretative Pattern: The Reception of Genesis." *Annai di storia dell' esegesi* 15, no. 2 (1998) 337–52.

Kannengiesser, Charles. *Handbook of Patristic Exegesis*. Bible in Ancient Christianity 1/1–2. Leiden: Brill, 2004.

Kasher, Rimon. "The Interpretation of Scripture in Rabbinic Literature." In *Mikra: Text, Translation, Reading and Interpretation of the Hebrew Bible in Ancient Judaism and Early Christianity*, edited by Martin Jan Mulder, 547–94. Assen, Netherlands: Van Gorcum, 1988.

Kelly, J. N. D. *Early Christian Doctrines*. Rev. ed. New York: HarperCollins, 1978.

Kennedy, George A. *Classical Rhetoric and Its Christian and Secular Tradition from Ancient to Modern Times*. Chapel Hill: University of North Carolina Press, 1980.

———. *New Testament Interpretation through Rhetorical Criticism*. Chapel Hill: University of North Carolina Press, 1984.

Kennedy, George A., trans. *Progymnasmata: Greek Textbooks of Prose Composition and Rhetoric*. Atlanta: Society of Biblical Literature, 2003.

Kennedy, George A., ed. and trans. *Aristotle. On Rhetoric: A Theory of Civic Discourse*. New York: Oxford University Press, 2007.

———. *Invention and Method: Two Rhetorical Treatises from the Hermogenic Corpus*. Atlanta: Society of Biblical Literature, 2005.

Kinzig, Wolfram. "Καινὴ διαθήκη: The Title of the New Testament in the Second and Third Centuries." *Journal of Theological Studies* NS, 45 (1994) 519–44.

Klauck, Hans-Josef. *The Religious Context of Early Christianity: A Guide to Graeco-Roman Religions*. Translated by Brian McNeil. Minneapolis: Fortress, 2003.

Klostermann, Erich, ed. *Apocrypha II: Evangelien*. Kleine Texte für Theologische und Philologische Vorlesungen und Übungen 8. Bonn: Marcus und Weber, 1910.

Koester, Helmut. *Ancient Christian Gospels: Their History and Development*. Philadelphia: Trinity, 1990.

Kondoleon, Christine. "The City of Antioch: An Introduction." In *Antioch: The Lost Ancient City*, edited by Christine Kondoleon, 3–11. Princeton, NJ: Princeton University Press, 2000.

Kraft, Richard Alan. "Barnabas' Isaiah Text and the 'Testimony Book' Hypothesis." *Journal of Biblical Literature* 79 (1960) 336–50.

———. "The Epistle of Barnabas: Its Quotations and their Sources." PhD diss., Harvard University, 1961.

Lake, Kirsopp, ed. and trans. *Eusebius. The Ecclesiastical History I*. Loeb Classical Library. London: Heinemann, 1926.

Layton, Bentley, ed. *Nag Hammadi Codex II,2–7 together with XIII,2*, Brit. Lib. Or.4926(1), and P.Oxy. 1, 654, 655 with Contributions by Many Scholars*. Nag Hammadi Studies. Leiden: Brill, 1989.

Layton, Bentley, ed. and trans. *The Gnostic Scriptures*. New York: Doubleday, 1987.

Liddell, Henry George, and Robert Scott, eds. *An Intermediate Greek-English Lexicon: Founded upon the Seventh Edition of Liddell and Scott's Greek-English Lexicon*. Oxford: Clarendon, 2002.

Lindars, Barnabas. *New Testament Apologetic: The Doctrinal Significance of the Old Testament Quotations*. Philadelphia: Westminster, 1961.

Litfin, Duane A. *St. Paul's Theology of Proclamation: 1 Corinthians 1–4 and Greco-Roman Rhetoric*. Cambridge: Cambridge University Press, 1994.

Long, Frederick J. *Ancient Rhetoric and Paul's Apology: The Compositional Unity of 2 Corinthians*. Cambridge: Cambridge University Press, 2008.

Loofs, Friedrich. *Theophilus von Antiochen Adversus Marcionem und die Anderen Theologischen Quellen bei Irenaeus, Texte und Untersuchungen zur Geschichte der altchristlichen Literatur* 46/2. Leipzig: Hinrichs, 1930.

MacDonald, Dennis Ronald. *Christianizing Homer: The Odyssey, Plato, and the Acts of Andrew*. New York: Oxford University Press, 1994.

MacDonald, Dennis Ronald, ed. *Mimesis and Intertextuality in Antiquity and Christianity*. Studies in Antiquity and Christianity. Harrisburg, PA: Trinity, 2001.

Mack, Burton L. *Rhetoric and the New Testament*. Guides to Biblical Scholarship, New Testament. Minneapolis: Ausburg Fortress, 1990.

Manns, Frederic. "L'exégèse de Justin dans le Dialogue avec Tryphon, témoin de l'exégèse juive ancienne." In *Essais sur le Judéo-Christianisme*, 130–52. Jerusalem: Franciscan, 1977.

Marcovich, Miroslav, ed. *Athenagoras Legatio Pro Christianis*. Berlin: de Gruyter, 1990.

———. *Iustini Martyris. Apologiae pro Christianis*. Patristische Texte und Studien 38. Berlin: de Gruyter, 1994.

———. *Tatiani Oratio Ad Graecos. Theophili Antiocheni Ad Autolycum*. Berlin: de Gruyter, 1995.

Marcus, Ralph, ed. and trans. *Philo*. Cambridge, MA: Harvard University Press, 1979.

Margerie, Bertrand de. *An Introduction to the History of Exegesis*. Vol. 1, *The Greek Fathers*. Petersham, MA: Saint Bede's, 1993.

———. "Saint Irenaeus, Ecclesial Exegete of Christocentric Recapitulation." In *The Greek Fathers*, 1:51–77. Petersham, MA: Saint Bede's, 1994.

Martens, Peter William. "Origen on the Reading of Scripture." PhD diss., University of Notre Dame, 2004.

———. "Revisiting the Allegory/Typology Distinction: The Case of Origen." *Journal of Early Christian Studies* 16, no. 3 (2008) 283–317.

Massaux, Édouard. *The Influence of the Gospel of Saint Matthew on Christian Literature before Saint Irenaeus.* Translated by Norman J. Beval and Suzanne Hecht. Edited by Arthur J. Bellinzoni. 3 vols. Macon, GA: Mercer University Press, 1990–1993.

McIver, Robert K. *Memory, Jesus, and the Synoptic Gospels.* Atlanta: Society of Biblical Literature, 2011.

McIver, Robert K., and Marie Carroll. "Experiments to Develop Criteria for Determining the Existence of Written Sources, and Their Potential Implications for the Synoptic Problem." *Journal of Biblical Literature* 121, no. 4 (2002) 667–87.

Meeks, Wayne A., and Robert L. Wilken. *Jews and Christians in Antioch in the First Four Centuries of the Common Era.* Missoula, MT: Scholars, 1978.

Metzger, Marcel, ed. *Les Constitutions Apostoliques.* Sources Chrétiennes, no. 336. Paris: Cerf, 1987.

Mitchell, Margaret M. "Biblical Interpretation as a Trial: Patristic Disputes about the 'Belly-Talker' of Endor (1 Sam 28)." Paper presented at the Southwest Regional Meeting of the SBL, March 6, 2004 in Dallas, Texas.

———. *Heavenly Trumpet: John Chrysostom and the Art of Pauline Interpretation.* Louisville:Westminster Knox, 2002.

———. *Paul and the Rhetoric of Reconciliation: An Exegetical Investigation of the Language and Composition of 1 Corinthians.* Louisville: Westminster John Knox, 1993.

Nahm, Charles. "The Debate on the «Platonism» of Justin Martyr." *Second Century* 9 (1992) 129–51.

Nautin, Pierre. "Ciel, pneuma et lumière chez Théophile d'Antioche (notes critiques sur *Ad Autol.* 2, 13)." *Vigiliae christianae* 27 (1973) 165–71.

———. "Genèse 1, 1–2 de Justin à Origène." In *In principio: interprétations des premiers versets de la Genèse,* edited by André Caquot et al., 61–94. Centre d'Études des Religions du Livre, CNRS 152. Paris: Études Augustiniennes, 1973.

Neusner, Jacob, ed. "The Hermeneutics of the Law in Rabbinic Judaism: Mishnah, Midrash, Talmuds." In *Hebrew Bible / Old Testament: The History of Interpretation.* Volume 1, *From the Beginnings to the Middle Ages (Until 1300),* ed. Magne Sæbø, 303–22. Göttingen: Vandenhoeck und Ruprecht, 1996.

———. *The Mishnah: A New Translation.* New Haven: Yale University Press, 1988.

Neymeyr, Ulrich. "Christliche Lehre im 2. Jahrhundert. Ihre Lehrtätigkeit, ihr Selbstverständnis und ihre Geschichte." In *Papers presented to the Tenth International Conference on Patristic Studies in Oxford 1987,* edited by Elizabeth A. Livingstone, 158–62. Studia Patristica 21. Leuven: Peeters, 1989.

Neyrey, Jerome. "The Forensic Defense Speech and Paul's Trial Speeches in Acts 22–26: Form and Function." In *Luke-Acts: New Perspectives from the Society of Biblical Literature Seminar,* edited by Charles H. Talbert, 210–24. New York: Crossroad, 1984.

Noormann, Rolf. *Irenäus als Paulusinterpret.* Wissenschaftliche Untersuchungen zum Neuen Testament 2/66. Tübingen: Mohr/Siebeck, 1994.

Norlin, George, ed., *Isocrates. Works.* Loeb Classical Library. London: Heinemann, 1928.

Norris, Richard A. "Irenaeus' Use of Paul in His Polemic Against the Gnostics." In *Paul and the Legacies of Paul,* edited by W. S. Babcock, 79–98, 337–40. Dallas: Southern Methodist University Press, 1990.

Osborn, Eric Francis. "Defense of Truth and Attack on Heresy." In *History of Theology: The Patristic Period*, edited by A. di Benardino and B. Studer, 119–44. Collegeville, MN: Liturgical, 1997.

———. "From Justin to Origen: The Pattern of Apologetic." *Prudentia* 4 (1972) 1–22.

———. *Justin Martyr*. Beiträge zur historischen Theologie 47. Tübingen: Mohr/Siebeck, 1973.

Otto, Johann C. Theodor von, ed. *Corpus Apologetarum Christianorum Saeculi Secundi*. Wiesbaden: Sändig, 1969–1971.

Otto, Karl. "Gebrauch neutestamentlicher Schriften bei Theophilus von Antiochien." *Zeitschrift für historische Theologie* 29 (1859) 617–22.

Oulton, J. E. L., and H. J. Lawlor, eds. and trans. *Eusebius. The Ecclesiastical History II*. Loeb Classical Library. London: Heinemann, 1932.

Parke, H. W. *Sibyls and Sibylline Prophecy in Classical Antiquity*. Edited by B. C. McGing. London: Routledge, 1988.

Parsons, Stuart E. "Coherence, Rhetoric, and Scripture in Theophilus of Antioch's *Ad Autolycum*." *Greek Orthodox Theological Review* 53, nos. 1–4 (2008) 155–222.

———. "Elementary Teaching according to Theophilus of Antioch." Paper presented at the Annual Meeting of the North American Patristics Society, May 25, 2001, Chicago, IL.

———. "Testimonia." In *Encyclopedia of Christian Civilization*, edited by George Thomas Kurian, 2340. Oxford: Wiley-Blackwell, 2012.

———. "Theophilus of Antioch." In *Encyclopedia of Christian Civilization*, edited by George Thomas Kurian, 2369. Oxford: Wiley-Blackwell, 2012.

Parsons, Stuart Edward. "'By One and the Same Spirit': Inspired Texts in Theophilus of Antioch's *Ad Autolycum*." PhD diss., Dallas Theological Seminary, 2005.

Paulsen, Henning. "Das Kerygma Petri und die urchristliche Apologetik." *Zeitschrift für Kirchengeschichte* 88 (1977) 1–37.

Perelman, Chaïm, and Lucie Olbrechts-Tyteca. *The New Rhetoric: A Treatise on Argumentation*. Translated by John Wilkinson and Purcell Weaver. Notre Dame, IN: University of Notre Dame Press, 1969.

Perendy, László. "Judging Philosophers: Theophilus of Antioch on Hellenic Inconsistency." *Folia theologica* 19 (2008) 185–217.

———. "The Outlines of Sytematic Theology in the *Ad Autolycum* of Theophilus of Antioch." *Folia theologica* 18 (2007) 171–78.

Perler, Othmar, ed. *Méliton de Sardes Sur la Pâque et Fragments*. Sources Chrétiennes 123. Paris: Cerf, 1966.

Piper, Otto. "The Nature of the Gospel according to Justin Martyr." *Journal of Religion* 41 (1961) 155–68.

Polhill, John B. *Paul and His Letters*. Nashville: Broadman & Holman, 1999.

Potterie, Ignace de la. "Le sens spirituel de l'Écriture." *Gregorianum* 78, no. 4 (1997) 627–45.

Price, Richard M. "'Hellenization' and Logos Doctrine in Justin Martyr." *Vigiliae christianae* 42 (1988) 18–23.

Prigent, Pierre. *Justin et L'Ancien Testament: L'argumentation scriptuaire du traité de Justin contre toutes les hérésies comme source principale du dialogue avec Tryphon et de la première apologie*. Paris: Gabalda, 1964.

———. *Les testimonia dans le christianisme primitif. L'Epître de Barnabé I–XVI et ses sources*. Paris: Gabalda, 1961.

Prostmeier, F. R. "Genesis 1–3 in Theophilos von Antiochia ‚An Autolykos': Beobachtungen zu Text und Textgeschichte der Septuagintagenesis." In *Textual History and the Reception of Scripture in Early Christianity: Textgeschichte und Schriftrezeption im frühen Christentum*, 359–94. Septuagint and Cognate Studies. Atlanta: Society of Biblical Literature, 2013.

Quasten, Johannes. *Patrology*. Vol. 1, *The Beginnings of Patristic Literature*. Westminster, MD: Newman, 1953.

Rahlfs, D. Alfred, ed. *Septuaginta: Id est Vetus Testamentum graece iuxta LXX interpretes, Duo volumina in uno*. Stuttgart: Deutsche Bibelgesellshaft, 1979.

Reventlow, Henning Graf. "Harmonie der Testamente: Irenäus von Lyon." In *Epochen der Bibelauslegung*. In *Vom Alten Testament bis Origenes*, 1:150–70. Münich: Beck, 1990.

Richard, Marcel. "Les fragments exégétiques de Théophile d'Alexandria et de Théophile d'Antioche." In *Opera minora II*, edited by Richard Marcel, 38. Turnhout: Brepols, 1978.

Rist, J. M. *Stoic Philosophy*. Cambridge: Cambridge University Press, 1969.

Roberts, Alexander, et al., eds. *The Ante-Nicene Fathers. Translations of the Writings of the Fathers Down to A.D. 325*. 1885. Reprint, Peabody, MA: Hendrickson, 1994.

Robinson, James M., ed. *The Nag Hammadi Library*. New York: HarperCollins, 1988.

Rodríguez, Rafael. *Oral Tradition and the New Testament*. London: Boomsbury, 2014.

Rogers, Rick. *Theophilus of Antioch: The Life and Thought of a Second-Century Bishop*. Lanham, MD: Lexington, 2000.

Rokéah, David. *Justin Martyr and the Jews*. Leiden: Brill, 2002.

Rousseau, Adelin. "Plan du livre v." In *Irenaeus. Contre les hérésies, livre 5*, edited by Adelin Rousseau, Louis Doutreleau, and Charles Mercier, 166–91. Sources Chrétiennes 152/1. Paris: Cerf, 1969.

Rudolph, Kurt. *Gnosis: The Nature and History of Gnosticism*. San Francisco: Harper & Row, 1983.

Runia, David. "Philo of Alexandria and the Greek *Hairesis*-Model." *Vigiliae christianae* 53, no. 2 (1999) 117–47.

Runia, David T. *Philo in Early Christian Literature: A Survey*. Minneapolis: Fortress, 1993.

Ruzer, Serge. "*The Cave of Treasures* on Swearing by Abel's Blood and Expulsion from Paradise: Two Exegetical Motifs in Context." *Journal of Early Christian Studies* 9, no. 2 (2001) 251–71.

Sailhamer, John. *Genesis Unbound: A Provocative New Look at the Creation Account*. Sisters, OR: Multnomah, 1996.

Sanchez, Sylvain Jean Gabriel. *Justin apologiste chrétien: travaux sur le Dialogue avec Tryphon de Justin Martyr*. Cahiers de la Revue biblique 50. Paris: Gabalda, 2000.

Savage, John J., ed. and trans. *Saint Ambrose Hexameron, Paradise, and Cain and Abel*. Fathers of the Church 42. New York: Fathers of the Church, 1961.

Schenkl, Carolus, ed. *Ambrossii Opera*. Corpus Scriptorum ecclesiasticorum latinorum 32/1. Prague: Timpsky, 1897.

Schneemelcher, Wilhelm, and R. McL. Wilson, eds. *New Testament Apocrypha*. Vol. 1, *Gospels and Related Writings*. Louisville: Westminster John Knox, 1991.

———. *New Testament Apocrypha*. Vol. 2, *Writings Relating to the Apostles; Apocalypses and Related Subjects*. Louisville: Westminster John Knox, 1991.

Schoedel, William R. "Theophilus of Antioch: Jewish Christian?" *Illinois Classical Studies* 18 (1993) 279–97.

Schultze, Victor. *Altchristliche Städte und Landschaften. III. Antiocheia.* Gütersloh: Bertelsmann, 1930.

Shorey, Paul, ed. and trans. *Plato. The Republic.* Loeb Classical Library. Cambridge, MA: Harvard University Press, 1935.

Shotwell, Willis Allen. *The Biblical Exegesis of Justin Martyr.* London: SPCK, 1965.

Simon, Marcel. "The Bible in the Earliest Controversies between Jews and Christians." In *The Bible in Greek Christian Antiquity*, edited and translated by Paul M. Blowers, 49–68. Notre Dame, IN: University of Notre Dame Press, 1997.

Simonetti, M. "La sacra scrittura in Teofilo d'Antiochia." In *Epektasis: mélanges patristiques offerts au Cardinal Jean Daniélou*, edited by Jacques Fontaine and Charles Kannengiesser, 197–207. Paris: Beauchesne, 1972.

Simonetti, Manlio. *Biblical Interpretation in the Early Church: An Historical Introduction to Patristic Exegesis.* Edited by Anders Bergquist, Markus Bockmuehl, and William Horbury. Translated by John A. Hughes. Edinburgh: T. & T. Clark, 1994.

Skarsaune, Oskar. "The Development of Scriptural Interpretation in the Second and Third Centuries—except Clement and Origen." In *Hebrew Bible / Old Testament: The History of Interpretation*, edited by Magne Sæbø, 1:373–442. Göttingen: Vandenhoeck & Ruprecht, 1996.

———. "From Books to Testimonies: Remarks on the Transmission of the Old Testament in the Early Church." *Immanuel* 24–25 (1990) 207–19.

———. *The Proof from Prophecy. A Study in Justin Martyr's Proof-Text Tradition: Text-Type, Provenance, Theological Profile.* Supplements to Novum Testamentum 56. Leiden: Brill, 1987.

Stanley, Christopher. Review of "*And Scripture Cannot Be Broken*," by Martin C. Albl. *Journal of Theological Studies* NS 52 (2001) 293–96.

Stead, Christopher. *Philosophy in Christian Antiquity.* Cambridge: Cambridge University Press, 1994.

Steinmetz, David C. "The Superiority of Pre-Critical Exegesis." In *The Theological Interpretation of Scripture: Classic and Contemporary Readings*, edited by Stephen E. Fowl, 26–38. Oxford: Blackwell, 1997.

Stemberger, Günter. "Exegetical Contacts between Christians and Jews in the Roman Empire." In *Hebrew Bible / Old Testament: The History of Interpretation*, edited by Magne Sæbø, 1:569–86. Göttingen: Vandenhoeck & Ruprecht, 1996.

Steyn, G. J. "Luke's Use of ΜΙΜΗΣΙΣ ?: Re-Opening the Debate." In *The Scriptures in the Gospels*, edited by C. M. Tuckett, 551–57. Leuven: Leuven University Press, 1997.

Strecker, George. "Ebioniten." In *Reallexikon für Antike und Christentum*, edited by T. Klauser, 4:487–500. Stuttgart: Hiersemann, 1959.

———. "On the Problem of Jewish Christianity." In *Early Christianity and Judaism*, edited by Everett Ferguson, 31–75. New York: Garland, 1993.

Tabbernee, William. "The Montanist Oracles: A New Classification." Paper presented at the Southwest Seminar on the Development of Early Catholic Christianity, February 19, 2004, Baylor University, Waco, TX.

Tabor, James D. "The Theology of Redemption in Theophilus of Antioch." *Restoration Quarterly* 18, no. 3 (1975) 159–71.

Taylor, Joan E. "The Phenomenon of Early Jewish-Christianity: Reality or Scholarly Invention?" *Vigiliae christianae* 44 (1990) 313–34.
Thom, Johan C. "The Journey Up and Down: Pythagoras in Two Greek Apologists." *Church History* 58, no. 3 (1989) 299–308.
Torrance, T. F. "Early Patristic Interpretation of the Holy Scriptures." In *Divine Meaning: Studies in Patristic Hermeneutics*, 93–129. Edinburgh: T. & T. Clark, 1995.
Turner, H. E. W. *The Pattern of Christian Truth: A Study in the Relations Between Orthodoxy and Heresy in the Early Church*. London: Mowbray, 1954.
Usher, Stephen, ed. and trans. *Dionysius of Halicarnassus The Critical Essays in Two Volumes*. Cambridge, MA: Harvard University Press, 1974.
Vermander, J. M. "Théophile d'Antioche contra Celse: A Autolycos III." *Revue des études augustiniennes* 17 (1971) 203–25.
Vogt, Hermann Josef. "Die Geltung des Alten Testaments bei Irenäus von Lyon." *Theologische Quartalschrift* 160 (1980) 17–28.
Vouaux, Leon, ed. *Les Actses de Paul et ses Lettres Apocryphes*. Les apocryphes du Nouveau Testament. Paris: Letouzey et Ané, 1913.
Waldstein, Michael, and Frederik Wisse, eds. *The Apocryphon of John. Synopsis of Nag Hammadi Codices II, 1; III, 1; and IV, 1 with BG 8502,2*. Nag Hammadi and Manichaean Studies. Leiden: Brill, 1995.
Weinrich, William C. Review of *Theophilus of Antioch: The Life and Thought of a Second-Century Bishop*, by Rick Rogers. *Journal of Early Christian Studies* 9, no. 4 (2001) 601–3.
Wilken, Robert L. "'In novissimus diebus': Biblical Promises, Jewish Hopes, and Early Christian Exegesis." *Journal of Early Christian Studies* 1 (1993) 1–19.
Wilken, Robert Louis. *The Christians as the Romans Saw Them*. New Haven: Yale University Press, 1984.
———. *The Spirit of Early Christian Thought*. New Haven: Yale University Press, 2003.
Wilson, Stephen G. *Related Strangers: Jews and Christians 70–170 C.E.* Minneapolis: Fortress, 1995.
Winden, J. C. M. van. "Frühchristliche Bibelexegese. 'Der Anfang.'" In *Arche: A Collection of Patristic Studies*, edited by J. den Boeft and D. T. Runia, 3–48. Leiden: Brill, 1997.
Winter, Bruce W. "Official Proceedings and the Forensic Speeches in Acts 24–26." In *The Book of Acts in Its Ancient Literary Setting*, edited by Bruce W. Winter and Andrew D. Clarke, 305–36. Grand Rapids; Carlisle: Eerdmans, 1993.
Yamauchi, Edwin M. "Gnosticism and Early Christianity." In *Hellenization Revisited: Shaping a Christian Response within the Greco-Roman World*, edited by Wendy E. Helleman, 29–62. Lanham, MD: University Press of America, 1994.
Young, Frances M. *Biblical Exegesis and the Formation of Christian Culture*. Cambridge: Cambridge University Press, 1997.
———. "The Rhetorical Schools and their Influence on Patristic Exegesis." In *The Making of Orthodoxy: Essays in Honour of Henry Chadwick*, edited by R. Williams, 182–99. Cambridge: Cambridge University Press, 1989.
———. "Tradition and Interpretation." In *Virtuoso Theology*, 45–65. Cleveland: Pilgrim, 1990.
Zeegers, Nicole. "Les trois cultures de Théophile d'Antioch." In *Les apologistes chrétiens et la culture grecque*, edited by Bernard Pouderon and Joseph Doré, 135–76. Paris: Beauchesne, 1997.

Zeegers-Vander Vorst, Nicole. *Les citations des poètes grecs chez les apologistes chrétiens du IIe siècles.* Leuven: Publications universitaires, 1972.

———. "Les citations du Nouveau Testament dans les Livres Autolycus de Théophile d'Antioche." In *Papers presented to the Sixth International Conference on Patristic Studies*, edited by Elizabeth A. Livingstone, 371–82. Studia Patristica 12/1 [=TU 115]. Berlin: Akademie, 1975.

———. "La création de l'homme (Gn 1, 26) chez Théophile d'Antioche." *Vigiliae christianae* 30 (1976) 258–67.

———. "Notes sur quelques aspects judaïsants du Logos chez Théophilile d'Antioche." In *Actes de la XIIe Conférence internationale d'Etudes classiques "Eirene,"* 69–87. Bucharest: Editura Academiei Republici, 1975.

———. "Satan, Eve et le serpent chez Théophile d'Antioche." *Vigiliae christianae* 35 (1981) 152–69.

Ziegler, Adolf W. "Die Erklärung des Gottesnamens bei Theophilus von Antiochen." In *Einsicht und Glaube: Festgabe Gottlieb Söhngen*, edited by Joseph Ratzinger and Heinrich Fries, 332–36. Freiburg: Herder, 1962.

Ancient Document Index

OLD TESTAMENT/ SEPTUAGINT

Genesis

1–10	41
1–3	7n23
1–2	95
1	41, 145
1:1–2	143–44
1:1	140–41, 143–45, 190
1:2–3	145
1:2	145–46, 190
1:3–2:3	190
1:3	190
1:4	190
1:5	144–45, 191
1:6–9	146
1:6	144–45, 191
1:9	144–45, 191
1:11–12	145, 191
1:11	192
1:12	191
1:14–19	145
1:14	188
1:16	29n56
1:22	191
1:26	11, 42n26, 188, 191
1:27	153
1:28–29	191
1:28	191
1:31	191
2	27
2:1–2	191
2:4–5	191
2:6–7	191
2:8—3:19	191
2:8–15	192
2:8–9	192
2:9	26n46, 191, 192
2:10	192
2:11	192
2:13	192
2:14	192
2:15–17	192
2:17	192
2:21–24	98n88
2:21–23	98n88
2:21–22	192
2:21	98n88
2:23–24	98
2:23	98n88, 192
2:24	192
3	100n100
3:5	192
3:9	192
3:10	191
3:14	191
3:23	192
4	5n15
4:1–10	101n103
4:1–2	192
4:1	192
4:4–5	192
4:8	192
4:9–11	192
4:12	5, 192
4:17	192
4:18–22	192
4:25	192

Genesis (continued)

5	43
5:2	153
5:3	195
5:6	195
5:9	195
5:12	195
5:15	195
5:18	195
5:21	195
5:25	195
5:28	196
5:32	196
7:6	196
7:20	195
8	41
10:9–14	192
11	43
11:1–9	101
11:1	192
11:4	192
11:7–8	192
11:10	196
11:12–13	196
11:14	196
11:16	196
11:18	196
11:20	196
11:22	196
11:24	196
11:26	196
14:1	193
14:2	193
14:4	193
14:5–6	193
20:2	193
21:5	196
25:26	196
26:1	193

Exodus

1:11	195
3:5	101n105
4:11	40, 189
12:40	194, 196
14:28	195
14:31	194
16:35	196
20	17
20:3–5	101n105, 194
20:5	101n105
20:12	194
20:13–17	101, 193–94
20:13–15	147
23:6–8	112, 194
23:9	114n154, 194
31:18	111n140

Deuteronomy

4:19	193
4:28	81n45
5	111
5:17–20	194
5:17–19	147
18:18	194
28:36	81n45
28:64	81n45
32:43	54

Judges

3:8	196
3:11	196
3:14	196
3:30	196
3:31	197
4:3	196
5:31	196
6:1	196
8:28	196
9:22	196
10:2	196
10:3	196
10:8	196
12:7	196
12:9	196
12:11	196
12:14	196
13:1	196
16:31	196

1 Samuel

4:18	197
28	75

1 Kings

2:11	197
11:42	197
14:21	197
15:2	197
15:10	197

2 Kings

8:17	197
8:26	197
12:1	197
14:2	197
15:2	197
15:33	197
16:2	197
18:2	197
21:1	197
21:19	197
22:1	197
23:31	197
23:36	198
24:8	197
24:18	198
25:2	198
25:9	198

2 Chronicles

2:13	81n45
12:13	197
13:2	197
20:31	197
21:5	197
22:2	197
22:12	197
24:1	197
25:1	197
26:3	197
28:1	197
29:1	197
33:1	197
33:21	197
34:1	198
36:2	197
36:9	198
36:11	198
36:17	198
36:19	198
36:21	198

Job

9	60
9:7–8	60
9:8	59–60, 188
9:9	59, 188
9:11	60, 61n74, 62
23:9	61n75
34:14–15	188
34:29	61n76
38	60
38:1–7	60
38:8–11	60
38:12	60
38:15	60
38:18	59, 188

Psalms

13	147
13:1–3	147n63
13:1	147, 193
13:3	101, 147, 193
17:49	54
18:4	188
23:2	188
32:6	188
32:7	188
50:10	103, 193
88:10	188
93:9	40, 189
95	84
95:5	138, 188
113	84, 138
113:10–11	138
113:10	81, 139
113:11	159
113:12–16	138
113:12–14	81, 159
113:12	138, 188
113:13–15	81n45
113:13–14	188
113:16	138, 188
116:1	54
134:18	139n25
146:4	188

Proverbs

3:8	103, 193
3:19–20	188
4:25–26	55, 114, 153, 195
4:25	101, 193
5:2–23	153
5:5	153
5:6	153
5:8	153
5:21	153
6:26	55
6:27–29	55, 114, 195
6:28	55
8	142
8:22–23	143, 190
8:22	140–43, 190
8:23	143
8:25	143
8:27	190
8:29–30	190
8:30	190
24:21–22	8–9, 17, 49, 189

Isaiah

1	149
1:11–16	149n67
1:11–15	151
1:11–13	151
1:15	151
1:16–17	115, 149–50, 151
1:16	151, 194
1:17	151, 194
2	52
11:10	54
30:28	103, 193
30:30	103, 193
31:6	55, 114, 194
40:22	100n101, 144–45, 190
40:28	101, 193
42:5–6	101
42:5	193
42:12	101
45:12	193
45:22	55, 114, 194
55:6–7	55, 114, 148, 194
58:1–11	151
58:4–5	151
58:6–10	151
58:6–8	115, 149n67, 151–52, 194
58:6–7	151
58:7	151
58:13–14	151
64:3	140
66:5–11	154
66:5	116, 154, 195

Jeremiah

6:9	55, 114, 194
6:16	115, 194
6:22	198
6:29	101
10:12–15	101
10:12–13	188, 193
25:12	198

Ezekiel

18:21–23	55, 114, 148, 194
20:32	81n45

Hosea

13:4	115, 194
14:10	103, 193

Joel

1:14	115, 195
2:16	115, 194

Micah

4	52

Habakkuk

2:18–19	101, 193

Zechariah

1:1	195
7:9–10	115, 149n67, 151, 195

Malachi

3:19	103, 193

OLD TESTAMENT APOCRYPHA

1 Esdras

2:1–7	198
2:10–11	198

4 Maccabees

12:12	40, 189

Sirach

Prologue	141n34
24.22ff	141n34

Wisdom

7.23–24	146n59
7.23	146n59
7.25–26	141n34
8.1	146n59
14:21	81n45

OLD TESTAMENT PSEUDEPIGRAPHA

2 Enoch

9	151
42	151

Apocalypse of Abraham

1.1–3	81n45
7.1–2	81n45

Life of Adam and Eve

40.4–5	5n15

Odes of Solomon

7	143n45
41	143n45

Psalms of Solomon

17	147
17.15	147

Sibylline Oracles

3–5	101n104
3.97–103	101n103
3.105	101n103
3.669–701	103n115
8.1	101n103
8.5	101n103
frg.1	101n106

Testament of Simeon

5.2	153

NEW TESTAMENT

Matthew

3:15	115
5	114
5:18	6n20
5:23	153
5:28	114, 152–54, 195
5:30	114
5:32	114, 152–54, 195
5:44	116, 153–54, 195
5:46	43, 116, 153–54, 195
6:3	116, 153, 195
6:19–20	28n51
7:12	6n20
18:3	27
19	21, 25n45
19:4	153
19:16–30	21
19:16–26	157n3
19:17	21
19:25	21, 21n30
23:9	53

Mark

10:6	153

Luke

1:35	140n31, 191
16:31	85
18:27	190
27:47	191

Ancient Document Index

John

1	43n26
1:1–3	42, 42n26
1:1	42, 44, 100n100, 143, 191
1:2	143
1:3	42, 44, 100n100, 143, 190–91
12:24	85n54, 189
16:21	191
20:27	189

Acts

14	54
17	157n2
17:17–34	22n31
24	157n2
24:24–25	25n44

Romans

2:6	40, 139–40, 163, 189
2:7–9	140
2:7	40, 140, 189
2:8–9	40, 140, 189
2:8	40
3:10–12	147n63
5:17	192
13	8
13:1	9, 189
13:7–8	116, 195
15:9–12	54

1 Corinthians

1:18	40n22, 43, 43n26, 88, 190, 194
1:24	42n26
2:9	40, 139–40, 163, 189
3:1–3	27n50
7:1	83
12:11	102n108
15	138
15:35–38	85n54
15:37	85n54, 189
15:50	192
15:53–54	138
15:53	137–38, 188

2 Corinthians

1:21	189
6:15–18	34n6, 57, 84n52
7:1	34, 57, 188
11:6	88
11:19	34, 43, 43n26

Ephesians

1:18	140n28
3:10	188, 191
4:18	6n20

Colossians

1:15	42n26, 191

1 Thessalonians

1:9–10	22n32

1 Timothy

2:1–2	116, 195
2:2	189
6:19	28n51

Titus

2:12	6n20
3:5	191

Hebrews

5–6	22, 31
5	27
5:12—6:2	27, 27n50, 158
5:12–13	27
5:12	22n33, 23, 27, 27n47, 27n50, 31, 192
6:1–2	22, 25–26, 31
6:1	24–25, 24n41
6:2	24–25, 27
6:4–12	22
12:9	22n33, 192
12:17	28n52, 28n54
13:4	101

1 Peter

1:18	193

2	8
2:1–2	27n50
2:13	189
2:15	189
2:17	189
3:20	43, 195

2 Peter

1:21	190
3:5	146

Revelation

9:20	81n45, 138

NEW TESTAMENT APOCRYPHA AND PSEUDEPIGRAPHA

3 Corinthians

40	85n54

Hellenistic Jewish Writings

Josephus, *Against Apion*

2	8n28

Philo, *Allegorical Laws*

1.45–46	6n18

Philo, *On the Change of Names*

2	23n37

Philo, *On the Confusion of Tongues*

146	142n40

Philo, *On the Creation*

131	145n56

Philo, *On the Decalogue*

52	99n92, 112n147–48
106–10	113n153
119	99n92, 112n147
154–75	111n141
154	111n139

Philo, *On Dreams*

1.164	23n37

Philo, *On Mating with the Preliminary Studies*

120	111n141, 112n148

Philo, *On Rewards and Punishments*

2	111n141
53	99n92, 112n146

Philo, *On the Special Laws*

4.134–35	112n149

Philo, *Who is the Heir of Divine Things?*

172	113n153

Pseudo-Philo, *Book of Biblical Antiquities*

16.2	6n15

GRECO-ROMAN WRITINGS

Aristophanes, *The Birds*

695	93n69

Aristotle, *Art of Rhetoric*

1.15.13–19	71n19
1.15.13–15	76n28
1.15.17	76n28
3.13–19	66n2

Aristotle, *Art of Rhetoric* (continued)

3.13	77n30, 77n32, 89n63, 118n165
3.13.4	80n43
3.17.14	122

Cicero, *On Invention*

1.8.10	79n39, 104n120
1.13.8	79n39
1.13.18	104n120
1.21.30—22.31	80n40, 88n59, 104n121

Dionysius of Halicarnassus, *Isaeus*

3	104n118
15	104n119

Dionysius of Halicarnassus, *Isocrates*

6	105n124
7	99n92, 113n150
9	105n124

Dionysius of Halicarnassus, *Letter to Pompelus*

6	99n92, 113n151

Dionysius of Halicarnassus, *Lysias*

17	79n37, 87n58

Dionysius of Halicarnassus, *On Literary Composition*

5	83n50
7	55n55
9	55n55

Hesiod, *Theogony*

73–74	92n67
104–33	92n67
116–23	92n67
126–33	92n67

Homer, *Iliad*

23.71	103

Homer, *Odyssey*

11.222	103
16.856	103
22.362	103

Isocrates, *Letters*

8	77

Plato, *Apology*

24d–28a	73–75

Plato, *Laws*

677c-d	110n136
683c	105n127

Plato, *Letters*

3	72–73, 78

Plato, *Meno*

99e	117n160

Plato, *Republic*

596a-c	93n70

Pliny the Younger, *Letters*

10.97	82n47

Plutarch, *On Superstition*

167b	83n51

Pseudo-Aristotle, *To Alexander*

13	80n42

Ancient Document Index   233

Pseudo-Cicero, *To Herennius*

1.2.3	66n2
1.10.18	80n41
2.1.2	80n41
2.6.9	70n19
2.30.47	93n71, 111n143
3.8—10.18	66n2

Pseudo-Hermogenes, *Concerning Invention*

3.3	82n49, 107n130, 117n159

Quintilian, *Institutes of Oratory*

4.Pr.6	77n30, 89n63, 118n165
4.1.9ff	77n30
4.4	77n30

Seneca, *Letters*

84	62n80

Sophocles, *Fragments*

876	94n73

Thucydides, *History*

6.54.1.2	88n60, 124n171
19	79n37

EARLY CHRISTIAN WRITINGS

1 Clement

7:4–5	28n52
8.2	ixn1
24–26	85n54

2 Clement

11.6–7	139

Ambrose, *On Paradise*

7.35	26n46

Apostolic Constitutions

7.34.1–8	144n53, 145

Athenagoras, *Plea on Behalf of the Christians*

10	42n26, 143n45
11–12	154
11	154
12	154
18	92n67
32	152n71
34	154n74

Clement of Alexandria, *Miscellanies*

2.18	19n25
4.5.39ff	143n47
5.6.38	10n36
6.5.43	86n57

Didache

2.3	147

Epiphanius, *Against Heresies*

46.1	42n26, 118n164

Eusebius, *Ecclesiastical History*

4.24.1	15n10
5.1	2
24.1	81n45

Irenaeus, *Against Heresies*

1.10.1	ixn1
2.28.1	ixn1
2.28.3	9n33
3.12.6–7	ixn1
4.1.1–2	53

Irenaeus, *Demonstration of the Apostolic Preaching*

12	26n46

Jerome, *Letters*

121	137

Jerome, *On Outstanding Men*

25	15n8

Justin, *Apologies*

1.14–15	154
1.15	153
1.36	143n44
1.37	151
1.38–39	143n43
1.41	138n23
1.44	103n114, 149–50
1.61	20n26, 149–50
1.65	20n26
2.6	42n26

Justin, *Dialogue with Trypho*

8–9	4n9
12	150
14–15	151
14	151
15	151
18	2, 150
27	151
55	138n23
61	142n42
73	138n23
79	138n23
83	138n23
85	154
110	99n93

Letter of the Apostles

21	137

Letter to Diognetus

12.2	26n46

Martyrdom of Polycarp

2.3	139

Melito, *Paschal Homily*

104	144n50

Pseudo-Barnabas

2–3	149n67, 151–52

Pseudo-Justin, *Exhortation Against the Gentiles*

16	9n33

Tatian, *Oration Against the Greeks*

4	145n57
5	42n26
31	94n75, 118n162
36–39	118n162
41	118n164

Tertullian, *Apology*

47	ixn1

Theophilus, *To Autolycus*

1	19, 39–40, 43, 79–80, 86–87, 89, 103, 121–23, 138–39
1.1–10	138
1.1–2	84, 120, 159, 161n8
1.1	26, 57, 79, 81, 84n52, 107n130, 117n159, 123, 138
1.2–5	124
1.2–3	138
1.2	6n20, 23n38, 24, 34n5, 57, 62n77, 80, 83–84, 120, 123, 140n29, 161n10
1.5	54, 84, 120, 161n10
1.6–8	54, 54n54, 58n64, 124, 160
1.6	54, 58n64, 60n70–71
1.7–8	24
1.7	6n20, 24n39, 55, 84, 112, 120, 137–38, 140n30, 161n8, 161n10, 163
1.8	24n40, 84
1.8–10	120, 161n9
1.9–10	120, 124, 161n8
1.9	84, 138

Ancient Document Index   235

1.10	84, 138, 144n49, 163	2.18	42n26
1.11–13	49, 124	2.20–33	124
1.11	5n11, 17	2.20	98n86, 117n161
1.12	25n43	2.21	98n87
1.13	39, 85, 120, 123, 161n9	2.22	9, 42n26, 44, 98, 100n99, 120, 143n43, 161n7
1.14	1, 39, 43n26, 46n35, 62n77, 80n44, 82n46, 86n56–57, 108n134, 120, 123–24, 139–40, 144n49, 161n5–7, 163	2.24–27	26
		2.24	6n16, 26, 29–30
		2.25	24, 27, 27n47–48, 157n1
1.17	29n56	2.26	28n53, 29–30, 29n56
2	40–44, 87, 89, 94–95, 97, 99–100, 103, 105n125, 121–23, 144, 146	2.27	21, 25n45, 28, 28n51, 29n55
		2.28	98, 120, 161n5
		2.29–31	120, 161n7
2.1–37	124	2.29	5n15, 6n17, 28n53, 29–30, 101n103
2.1–8	40n22, 93		
2.1–7	93	2.30	84n53, 97–99, 101n102, 120, 161n5
2.1	40n22, 87–89, 123–24, 144n52		
		2.31	99n90, 101n103
2.2–31	50	2.32–33	84n53, 120, 161n5, 161n10
2.2–8	89, 124	2.32	96n80, 99
2.2	90, 120, 144n49	2.33	5n11, 97n81, 108n134, 161n7
2.3	94, 120, 161n11–12		
2.4–8	94, 120, 161n9	2.34–37	124
2.4	90, 92	2.34	6n20, 9
2.5–7	92n67	2.35–38	120, 161n7
2.5	84n53, 91–92, 96, 161n10	2.35	6n20, 97–98, 101, 102n108, 112, 120, 146–47, 161n5, 163
2.6	92		
2.7	93	2.36	100n98, 101n106, 102n110
2.8	5n11, 93, 108n134	2.37	102n109, 103n113, 120, 148, 161n9
2.9–33	49		
2.9–19	124, 147	2.38	89, 124, 148
2.9–10	86, 120, 161n7	3	2, 19, 40n22, 43–44, 104–6, 114, 121–23
2.9	9, 90, 97n82, 99, 100n96, 120, 161n5–6		
		3.1–8	44, 109, 115
2.10	100n97, 102n108, 140, 141n38, 142n40, 143, 144n49, 144n50, 163	3.1	103–4, 108, 123–24
		3.2–37	124
		3.2–8	124
2.12–14	163	3.2	84n53, 105n124, 120, 161n10
2.12	84n53, 95–96, 120, 161n5, 161n10, 161n12		
		3.3	106, 120, 161n8
2.13	120, 144–46, 161n7, 163	3.4–6	107
2.14–16	99, 120, 161n6	3.4	34n4, 43n26
2.14	100n94	3.5	107
2.15	29n56, 100n95	3.6–8	120, 161n8
2.16	100	3.6	107
2.17	29n56	3.7–8	161n9
2.18–22	97, 120, 161n5	3.7	107–8, 110
2.18–19	97n84	3.8	108–9

Theophilus, *To Autolycus* (continued)

3.9–15	18, 43–44, 115–17, 124
3.9–14	110
3.9–10	114, 120, 161n6
3.9	6n20, 108n134, 109–11, 114–15
3.10	114
3.11–14	120, 161n7
3.11	55, 115, 148
3.12–14	9, 155
3.12–13	120, 154, 161n6
3.12	8, 9n33, 114–16, 116n158, 148, 149n67, 150–51, 154–55, 160n4, 161n8
3.13–14	44, 152–53
3.13	55, 114, 116, 152–55
3.14	9, 154–55
3.15	18, 54n54, 109–10, 120, 161n8
3.16–30	43–44, 117
3.16–27	124
3.16	84n53, 105n126, 109–10, 120, 161n9–10
3.17	116–17, 120, 160n4, 161n5, 161n7
3.18–19	119n166
3.20–23	117, 120, 161n5
3.21–23	118
3.21–22	118
3.21	117
3:22	118
3.23	118
3.24–25	118–19
3.24	39, 43
3.25	119
3.26–27	120, 161n5
3.26	110, 118–19, 161n9
3.27	3n6, 119
3.28–30	104n123, 124
3.28–29	108n134
3.30	84n53, 106, 110, 120, 161n8–10

NAG HAMMADI CODICES

Apocryphon of John

21.34	26n46
44.14	101n105
59.17—60.8	98n88
59.17–18	98n88

Hypostasis of the Archons

90.9	26n46

Modern Authors Index

Albl, Martin C., 128–29
Alexander, Loveday, 76
Allenbach, J., 8n29
Aune, David E., 20, 49n41, 122

Bacq, Philippe, 53–54, 62
Bauer, Walter, 15, 65
Bentivegna, J., 18, 30
Betz, Hans Dieter, 72
Bingham, D. Jeffrey, 8n29, 38n16
Bousset, W., 125, 128

Carroll, Marie, 36, 46–48, 50, 63, 159
Clark, Elizabeth A., 51
Conte, Gianbiagio, 49
Credner, C., 126
Crouzel, Henri, 51

Daniélou, Jean, 51, 127
Dawson, David, 163
Desjardins, Michel, 15n10
Diels, H., 102
Dodd, C. H., 126, 130, 135, 145, 164
Droge, Arthur J., 123n170
Dulles, Avery Robert, 5
Dunn, James D. G., ix

Erbes, C., 3n6
Ernest, James David, 38, 47–48, 167, 208, 209n5

Finkelpearl, Ellen, 62
Fontenrose, Joseph, 97n83

Geffcken, Johannes, 69–70, 118n163

Good, Deirdre, 79
Grant, Robert M., 7, 9–11, 15, 33, 42n26, 43, 55, 65, 90n64, 92n67, 111–12, 115–16, 116n157, 128, 137, 146n59, 153

Hanson, R. P. C., 51
Harnack, Adolf von, 3n6, 6, 7–10, 115, 116n157
Harris, J. Rendel, 126, 128
Hays, Richard B., 56–57
Hitchcock, F. R. Montgomery, 43n26
Hollander, John, 56–57, 60
Horner, Timothy J., 168

Kannengiesser, Charles, 41, 61
Kennedy, George A., 67n6, 70n17, 71n19
Kinzig, Wolfram, 4n11
Kraft, Robert A., 125–26, 128, 149n67

Lampe, G. W. H., 51
Lindars, Barnabas, 126
Litfin, Duane A., xiin3
Long, Frederick J., xiin3
Loofs, Friedrich, 22, 27n47, 61, 65
Louth, Andrew, 51
Lubac, Henri de, 51

Mack, Burton L., 67–68
Marcovich, Miroslav, 6, 37, 58, 89, 208
Martin, J. P., 23n36
Massaux, Edouard, 10
McIver, Robert K., 36, 46–48, 50, 63, 159

Mitchell, Margaret M., 66–67, 68n11, 72, 75, 78, 163
Muilenburg, James, 68

Nautin, Pierre, 141, 144
Neymeyr, Ulrich, 3

Olbrechts-Tyteca, Lucie, 67–68
Otto, Karl, 6

Paulsen, Henning, 86n57
Pépin, Jean, 51
Perelman, Chaïm, 67–68
Perendy, László, 14, 18–20
Prigent, Pierre, 126–28
Puech, Aimé, 14

Rogers, Rick, 14–19, 141
Rousseau, Adelin, 53
Runia, David T., 23nn36–37, 65
Ruzer, Serge, 5

Sailhamer, John, 59n67
Schoedel, William R., 11
Schneemelcher, Wilhelm, 144n48
Schultze, Victor, 15, 33
Selwyn, E. G., 19
Simonetti, Manlio, 10
Skarsaune, Oskar, 11, 37, 45–47, 49–50, 63, 125, 127–28, 136, 139n25, 144n48, 159, 163, 169
Stanley, Christopher, 129
Stemberber, Günter, 11

Tabor, James, 14, 17–18
Turner, H. E. W., 16n10

Weinrich, William C., 18
Wilken, Robert Louis, ix, 51–52, 165

Young, Francis M., 76n29, 75, 76n29, 78, 163

Zahn, Theodor, 9
Zeegers, Nicole, 6n17, 10, 35n12, 43, 69–70, 92n67, 93n72, 102, 103n116, 107–8, 116, 142n39
Ziegler, Adolf W., 82n50

www.ingramcontent.com/pod-product-compliance
Lightning Source LLC
Chambersburg PA
CBHW050439240426

43661CB00055B/2445